MAN IN THE MOON

MAN IN THE MOON

ESSAYS ON FATHERS & FATHERHOOD

Edited by
Stephanie G'Schwind

THE CENTER FOR LITERARY PUBLISHING
COLORADO STATE UNIVERSITY

Printed in the United States of America
First edition

The Center for Literary Publishing
9105 Campus Delivery
Department of English
Colorado State University
Fort Collins, Colorado 80523-9105
coloradoreview.colostate.edu

Typeset in Apollo MT by the Center for Literary Publishing
Manufacturing by Courier Westford
Printed in the United States
Cover design by Drew Nolte

Library of Congress Cataloging-in-Publication Data

Man in the moon : essays on fathers and fatherhood / Stephanie G'Schwind.
pages cm
ISBN 978-1-885635-35-8 (paperback) -- ISBN 978-1-885635-36-5 (electronic)
1. Fathers--Literary collections. 2. Fatherhood--Literary collections.
3. Fathers and sons--Literary collections. 4. Fathers and daughters--Literary collections. I. G'Schwind, Stephanie, editor of compilation. II. Title: Essays on fathers and fatherhood.
PS509.F34M36 2014
810.8'035251--dc23 2014010860

1 2 3 4 5 18 17 16 15 14

For my father and yours

CONTENTS

INTRODUCTION

Stephanie G'Schwind

IN THE EARLY STAGES of putting this anthology together, I was catching up with a colleague I hadn't seen in a while, telling him about the book, the essays I already had in mind, what a great collection it would be. He was nodding with interest, and then asked me, "So where did this come from?"

"Well," I said, "I've published a number of essays in *Colorado Review* about fathers, and I thought it would be interesting to gather them together with some others, you know, in a collection."

Bruce was quiet for a moment, and then he tried again. "No, I mean where did the interest in *fathers* come from?"

Oh that.

It is something you live with for so long that you really do, eventually, become so used to it—the grief, such a familiar companion—you hardly notice it anymore. Until someone points it out. Yes, there it is, still, no longer raw, not nearly as tender, but there nonetheless. Your loss. Your lost father. My lost father.

No real surprise, that tender spot stirs a curiosity in me for stories of other people's relationships with their fathers. Do they—did they—really *know* each other? What did they talk about? Were they close? It seems for many of us that a father can be at times so unknowable, the distance between him and his children so great, he might as well be the man in the moon.

My father and I were almost there, having just crested the long uphill climb of my adolescence and about to be two adults who might have, over so many more years, come to know each other not as adult and child, but as father and daughter. And surely we'd have figured out how to say all those things we hadn't yet been able say to each other—anything, everything, nothing in particular—closing an awkward gap.

He died when I was twenty-two, that distance between us forever fixed.

Since then, I've spent a great deal of time trying to understand why it was so difficult for us to be closer. I've come to believe it probably had a lot to do with his struggles with his own father. Assigned in various parts of the world with the Army Corps of Engineers during World War Two, Grandpa was gone for the first three years of my father's life, and they did not have an easy time becoming acquainted with each other upon his return, never settling into a comfortable affection, never able to find a common language. They had a rather miserable go of it through my father's childhood and adolescence—sparring and feuding when they weren't entrenched in prolonged silences—before moving into a tacit détente for the rest of their lives, the space between them vast and unoccupied.

That space—in its nearly infinite dimensions, textures, and configurations—is what intrigues me. If we are to make sense of this terrain, this relationship, we must venture out into it, because that is where we will find our fathers, where they will find us. Bill Capossere studies the night sky, attempting to preserve his waning memories of his father through their shared passion for astronomy. Though her father lives just one floor below her, Gina Frangello watches him moving away from her "on a journey across the white barren land" of dementia. Brendan Wolfe, Robin Black, Richard McCann, and Jerald Walker search for theirs in stories, in fiction, in writing. Neil Mathison looks to helixes of DNA and recollections of family road trips. Joan Marcus imagines her merchant marine father "on deck, alone in that pocket of fog . . . All around him, silent markers of ruin." And Dinty W. Moore scans the television airwaves for a surrogate father.

And when we find them, what will we say? For some of us, to even talk with our fathers, to have a simple exchange, is fraught. "A conversation with him," Brendan Wolfe writes, "is like playing tennis with someone who, instead of volleying the ball back to you, catches it, turns it around in his hand, and then stuffs it in his pocket." The silence between Thomas White and his father "continued until a deep rut of miscommunication formed from which neither of us could willfully emerge, and the rut, so toxic, became the relationship." Debra Gwartney holds vigil by her father's bed in the intensive care unit, awaiting the three words that he's never spoken to her.

How, then, can we ever connect with our fathers, understand them, be understood by them? Carole Firstman sifts through her elderly father's arachnology research and specimens, considering "what the scorpion reveals—what it might tell me about my father's life work, about my father himself. About the connection between my father and myself." Reflecting on not following her father's path to a career in chemistry, Deborah Thompson asks, "Did my father feel betrayed when I rejected his world?" Matthew Ferrence, though, rejecting his father's love of hunting, suggests that perhaps "closeness resides when differences mount." Richard McCann recalls his attempt to complete his father's unfinished novel and wonders, "Was I hoping that by entering his words, I might somehow come to know him?" Donna George Storey watches a man and his daughter shopping at a bookstore—"the rhythm of his voice, the way he bends close to the girl" recalling the ritual she and her own father shared.

But then, perhaps, the most luminous point of connection: the child becomes the parent, the son becomes the father. "Parenthood, for me," Dan Beachy-Quick writes, "is inextricably caught in the paradox of being a father and a child at once—a child with a child, a father with a father." Thomas White channels his father's forgiveness as he lifts his own son from the muck of a muddy hike. Jim Kennedy remembers a split second of magnificent, three-generational grace as his young son was falling down the stairs: "Just as I grabbed Thomas upside down in my arms . . . my father and I looked into each other's eyes and experienced the moment as one."

Many of these essays are painful. Fathers are dying or have died, and in one, a boy slips forever from his father's hands; some fathers are angry and neglectful, though some gentle and loving; and some are just not there at all. But you will find, too, beauty and sometimes humor and, of course, compassion, forgiveness, and love—the real occasions for many of these pieces. And perhaps in them, or just beyond them, you will find your own father, find yourself.

MAN IN THE MOON

Bill Capossere

MAN IN THE MOON

There be of them, that have left a name behind them, that their praises might be reported. And some there be, which have no memorial; who are perished, as though they had never been; and are become as though they had never been born; and their children after them.

—Sirach 44 v. 8–9

IN OUR HOUSE there are, at last count, fourteen clocks. Crossing from one room to the next, one level to another, it is almost impossible not to mark time's steady martial pace. Or it would be if the clocks on the mantle, the bookshelf, the dining room hutch, the headboard in the spare bedroom, and the small three-legged piece of unnamed furniture in the stairwell were actually running. Given to us as gifts for our wedding a dozen years ago, they have not yet lowered themselves to actual utilitarianism, and so time, in their case, does not march so much as preen, in modest yet decorative fashion.

Our living room clock too has begun to blur the line between form and function. Its battery has been running low for weeks, and neither I nor my wife is ever quite sure if the other has corrected the hands, and if so, how long ago. It is good enough therefore to use as a general measure of time—early afternoon, late evening—but we have learned not to trust to it our more rigid needs—when to leave for work or what time to turn on the VCR. For those occasions we will step into the kitchen, where both the clock on the stove and the one above the sink mark correct time. Or we will check one of the components in our entertainment center since the television, the cable box, the VCR and DVD, all have their own clocks, their sleek black exteriors and glowing digital displays promising a technological precision our wall clocks can only pretend to with their seriffed numbers and thin, sweeping hands.

Upstairs, that same promise of precision made by our alarm clock—also digital and glowing—is belied by the fact that it is set fifteen minutes fast in the misguided belief that somehow we will forget this overnight and so spring out of bed in the morning believing ourselves to have overslept. Instead, we end up performing arcane calculations, juggling such variables as the number of minutes the clock is ahead, the period of time engendered by the snooze button, and how long it takes to shower, eat, and drive to work. All of which, in the winter, is made more comfortable by an already warm house, heated by a programmable thermostat that quietly keeps pace with the temperate rhythms of our home, its tiny clock the smallest of all, smaller even than the one that moment by moment drives the cadence of my own blood as I lay my ear against the pillow to fall asleep in the drift of its ever-thrumming measure.

It is easy to miss, this tiny date—7/62—printed neatly in the top right corner of each yellow envelope. So small that even though it appears on envelope after envelope, the same four slight marks in the same place, even the lettering always the same, I do not notice it for the longest time, not until the fifteenth or sixteenth envelope has slipped through my hands to be opened, emptied, and tossed aside.

The envelopes themselves are small, the size of narrow playing cards—the kind you buy for cramped travel—each containing somewhere between one and a dozen old coins. Both the coins and the envelopes were my father's, his coin collection, which twenty-five years after his death, sixteen years after claiming it from my childhood home when it was sold, seven years after I moved it from my last apartment to the basement of our new home, I am finally going through to sort and classify and eventually, ideally, pragmatically, supposedly, sell. That, at least, is what I tell myself.

I have been working on this all night, will not in fact finish until the sun comes up, although I don't know that now, and because it is past two a.m., because the writing is so small, it isn't until now that I notice the date. And because I am tired and doing what I do not want to be doing, it takes another minute or two before the date sinks in. 7/62. July 1962. Which just happens to be one month shy of August 1962, whose last day was also my first—August 31, 1962—the day I was born.

It is a strange feeling, this sudden recognition. It is something new added to the mix of emotion that has shadowed this whole endeavor, that same pale wash of emotion that falls over me at any reminder of my father's passing. Sadness. Regret. Grief, of course. But grief shorn of its rough edges. Grief worn comfortably around the shoulders like a faded jacket, thin but serviceable, a familiar weight that softly settles with a thin, dry rustle. Or, more apropos of tonight's task, grief worn smooth like an old coin passed through many hands.

I have felt that slight weight all through tonight's task, but now a part of me can't help but smile, holding the envelope in my hand and staring at the date. Here was my father in his early twenties with one ten-month-old child in hand and another barreling down on him from just over the horizon. And there he is, sitting at a Formica table amid a smorgasbord of coins, taking them one at a time and placing them carefully in their respective blue books, coin rolls, or yellow envelopes, carefully noting the number, date, and condition of each. How good it must have felt for him to, if only for a short while, enter a world where everything was so strictly delineated as to kind and value.

In the top right corner of each envelope, he neatly notes the month and year in tiny precise writing. "I will never again," he might have thought, "have the time I have had to do this small thing that I have enjoyed doing." He would have been right of course, though he surely must have thought that he would have more time than he did, a dozen short years until his death at the age of thirty-four.

In fact, he didn't even have the time to finish the job he began whatever night it was in that July of 1962. The books were done, each Mercury dime, Liberty-head nickel, and so on, placed in its particular slot above the correct year and mint stamp. And the older, more valuable coins as well were all cataloged, each envelope's contents carefully labeled: 1854 quarter XF (extra-fine), 1873 Shield nickel G (good), 1857 half-dime AG (almost good).

What was left undone, and for me to painstakingly do tonight and into this morning, were pennies. Lots of pennies. Or cents, as I would learn tonight they are called by those who collect them. He had finished some of them, placing them in rolls and labeling each roll. But many more were simply loose in the heavy cloth bag his collection came in. As well, some of his hard work had come undone—several of the paper rolls and envelopes had worn away and broken so that their coins had spilled out to mix with all the others, or at the very least, the letters on the rolls had faded away so the coins had to be reidentified, recounted, relabeled.

So one by one, I separated the coins. First by color: brown in this pile, silver over here. Then by size: large silver here, small silver here. And finally by date, putting them at last into my own envelopes and labeling each according to type and date, though not condition, having no clear idea of the technical differences between fine and extra-fine, good and almost good.

As I worked, I couldn't help but imagine my father's hands doing the same tasks. Moving a penny with my index finger over to a pile of like-yeared coins, I pictured the same small motion across our old kitchen table, my mother watching, or perhaps even helping, reaching awkwardly over her heavy belly to shift the coins from pile to pile. My sister would have been too young to walk at the time, probably still in her crib or playpen, so perhaps this would have been something my parents did together, hoarding their quiet moments against the noise to come, the only sound the scratch of copper across new Formica.

Or maybe instead it was a hot summer night, my sister was asleep upstairs, the stereo was blasting Elvis, and the two of them drank beer and sorted coins, growing more and more tipsy as the night wore on until my father, realizing he had just thrown a pair of Indian-head cents into the pile of Lincoln-heads, decided to call it a night, his large hand bulldozing the remaining coins over the edge of the table so they could cascade into the bag, which my mother held just below the table's rim. Dimes falling like tiny moons, pennies like a swarm of shooting stars. Small coins all, and none of them particularly valuable—a dollar here, three dollars there—but what a sound of wealth and liberty that waterfall must have made as the coins spilled one over the other into a clinking pile of silver and copper. The sound a child imagines a pirate's hands make as they eddy one last time through an about-to-be-buried treasure chest. The sound an adult imagines when he pictures himself standing before the just-paid-off slot machine in the lobby of Caesar's Palace in Las Vegas. The sound of glitz and richness. The sound, I imagine the two of them thinking to themselves, of one kind of freedom, though not the one either would wish for, or each would eventually have.

It is difficult to see the stars where we live, a fault in our housing situation I've always mourned. For the most part we are a location surrounded by convenience; there is little essential to body or soul that is not within a fifteen-minute walk: the town library, with its playground and community pool; five bookstores—both new and used; two parks; four bagel shops; Indian, Thai, and Middle Eastern restaurants; a small market; several drinking establishments; two delis, a bakery, and two ice cream shops; a tailor; a store that sells only nuts; a hardware store; our bank; and even my doctor (assuming the visit is merely routine and doesn't involve major loss of blood). But we cannot see the stars.

Oh, on clear nights of course, we can see some. The sky, though seldom clear here in Rochester, is never merely void. But living as we do just three miles from the city center, we see only as many as we might paint ourselves on our ceiling in a day's whim, a smattering of faint white specks, the countless, unseen others drowned out in ambient light of storefronts and office buildings, streetlights and houses. Even the sky's special effects lose, somewhat, that which makes them special.

To see the annual Perseid meteor showers we are forced to take folding chairs and blankets to the lake, miles from the city and its obscuring luminosity. While the grand viewing event of the past decade, Comet Hale-Bopp, was a barely noticeable presence just above the treetops—a slightly brighter star with little discernible tail or corona, more curiosity than spectacle—it was only while camping in the Smoky Mountains, far from the interfering lights of civilization, that we were able to see the phenomenon in all its stellar glory. *Ahh,* we thought, gazing at it against a backdrop of a million lit matches, *this is what all the fuss is about.* And then we fell asleep under its dazzle.

It was my father who first interested me in the stars. He taught me their names, how they formed patterns in the sky we could trace and name while standing on our lawn or sitting on the low roof over our porch, taught me their beckoning lure that fueled the astronauts' desire and fired the minds of the science fiction writers whose books he stacked on the fireplace mantel: Isaac Asimov, Robert Heinlein, E. E. "Doc" Smith, and others.

In one of his stories, Asimov imagined a planet whose solar system was structured such that the inhabitants of the planet lived always in the light of day due to the presence of at least one of their six suns in the sky at all times. It was only every thousand years, when the suns and planets aligned so to form a solar eclipse (several actually), that darkness fell and the stars became visible. Had he only waited a few decades, Asimov need not have looked to so far-flung a setting to conceive such a scenario. As the bright-nighted cities expand daily beyond their former borders, creeping across the country like so much phosphorescent lichen, the stars, pressed by the light of millions of artificial suns, recede more and more into the background, their appearance more remembered than experienced, more sung about than seen.

Astronomers, no longer able to finely distinguish the fainter stars amid the visual cacophony of modern, industrialized civilization, have begun to flee the planet altogether, centering their hopes on orbiting telescopes such as the Hubble, which circle the earth above the interference of atmosphere and artificial light.

Earlier humans would have been dismayed to look up at such empty skies as we nightly observe. People read in the stars the entire story of their lives, mapping out celestial motions in an attempt to order their own random experiences, measuring their lives both figuratively and literally by the stars. Our year comes to us from Egyptian stargazers, who observed that the "Dog Star" (Sirius) rose next to the sun every 365 days, corresponding roughly to the annual flooding of the Nile.

We need the sight of the stars above, need their gentle, nightly reminder of our own small place in this greater home of ours. It is no ill thing to be so humbled. Otherwise we might become as the characters in Asimov's story who, knowing no stars but their own until the thousandth year, were stunned by the appearance of so many millions. They found it a crushing blow. Faced with sudden insignificance, driven mad by the swift inconsequence of their lives, their civilization crumbled. The universe was not what they thought it was. It seldom is.

Recently I stood in our driveway and in a moment's time counted the stars—the Little Dipper, the North Star, and a few I could not name. Eleven in all. Tycho Brahe, from his island stronghold of Uraniborg, counted a thousand. Hipparchus of Nicaea even more, taking a break now and then to invent trigonometry. Granted, it was heavily overcast, a poor night for stargazing made worse by the damping light of a gibbous moon reflecting off the clouds. And certainly had I crossed behind our house I would have seen several more. But a handful more would have made the total no less meager, and there is something in me that sighs at such an empty sky. The stars of my childhood have, like the moments of my life, like the memories of my father—his voice, his hands, his eyes—winked out one by one, leaving the night diminished, and me outside wondering what greater world I now will show to my own small and wondering son.

Among the various pictures in our living room is the only one I have of my parents together, a black-and-white wedding picture of the two of them dancing cheek to cheek and smiling into the camera. They are festooned in ribbons, my mother's face partially obscured by several strands that flutter just above her chin. Neither, of course, could have guessed that in another fifteen years my father would be dead, and in another two my mother as well. Instead they stand and smile, seeing the world through the capricious glimmer wound round their heads and hands, a constantly shifting band of imagined color that must have seemed to stretch out forever before them. If I could, I would reel them back by just such a ribbon, one thin enough to slip through time and grief, and color again these swift-dimming memories grown old and monochrome.

For years growing up I wanted to be a paleontologist, devouring books on the subject as fast as I could take them out of the library or convince my parents to purchase them. Dinosaurs crowded my bookshelves, my bedroom walls, even my body as I slept—marching across sheets, pillows, pajamas, slipping from cool fabric between the membranes of my skin to run rampant through my dreams, abjuring, for the evening, extinction.

On weekend afternoons, John Guereno and I would take our plastic dinosaurs to the backyard and wage massive wars—laying waste to grass and soil and leaving a wake of trampled Matchbox cars behind. Or we'd bury them deep in the earth so as to dig them up again later, scraping away layers of mud and clay to reveal sudden small flashes of color—duckbill crests or ankylsaurus tails—some no doubt buried there still, waiting like their real-life cousins for the sudden upheaval of dirt and detritus that augurs the wonder of discovery.

Those early toys are long gone, but I have others, better behaved, more structurally accurate than those previous ones. They perch on top of my computer monitor or on the table beside my desk—two triceratops, two stegosauruses, an apatosaurus, and a tyrannosaurus—their postures less lumbering, their expressions less drowsy, befitting recent theories that dinosaurs were more akin to birds than to slow-moving, cold-blooded reptiles. John Guereno and I never had put much stock in the old view; our dinosaurs had always been fluid, agile animals that could run down a fleeing protoceratops or 1968 Corvette with similar ease. Today's fleet creatures would not have shocked us in the least.

What would, however, is the absence of brontosaurus from the modern inventory of dinosaur species. The placid, swamp-dwelling creature, it turns out, never existed, the whole thing a case of mistaken identity begun when someone incorrectly placed the wrong head atop a misconstructed pile of apatosaurus bones. Reconstituting history, I've learned, is always a dangerous job; we trace the skeletal fragments of our past, following like a map the marrow of our memories, thinking to ourselves, as the song says, that the hip bone is connected to the thigh bone and so on down the list, fabricating the whole time a thin stretch of tissue to lay across the gaps in our ersatz structure. If I can't link together the scattered segments of my own forty-two years, I hold out no blame whatsoever to whatever confused curator it was who, reaching back a hundred million years ago, over- or under-reached ten thousand or so. Still, "Thunder Lizard" seems to me a fine name for a dinosaur and I confess to feeling a sense of sorrow that the name, like the creature it was meant to describe, will soon sink of its own weight beneath the sediment of memory.

It was that image of extinction, I think, that most drew me to the dinosaurs. Even their small brains, I thought, must have sensed in the cooling air and poisonous plants their inevitable end, and I wondered if they finally grew weary of a mercurial world that seemed always to reshape itself in ways ever more hostile; under an ash-draped sky still shimmering with the afterglow of the comet we now suspect killed them off, might not the opening earth or suffocating tar pit appear as welcome release rather than dangers to be avoided? That the dinosaurs were here and then, simply, were not lent them a sense of pathos I could not have enunciated back then but colored my world in shades that I had not known existed at age eight or nine.

The night I finally grasped the concept of extinction I lay in my top bunk crying while my brother below slumbered on blissfully unaware at four or five of what I had just figured out—that we, that all of us, like the dinosaurs were faced with an ever-changing climate and that eventually we would be left alone in a world turned cold with absence.

I tried explaining this first to my father, who came upstairs when he heard me crying, and then to my mother after he had carried me back down to sit between them on the couch while they tried to tell me that I had misjudged the amount of time involved, that it would be many, many years before they weren't around, as if those transitory promises of years to come were somehow consolation. None of their protestations could pierce the shadow I felt enveloping me, and it was only from pure exhaustion that I finally fell asleep in their arms, none of us aware that already underway was the slow corrosion of body and blood that would make of their words nothing but twice-told lies.

One of the mainstays of our family gatherings was my uncle's movie camera, a 16-millimeter instrument that he would pull out during badminton games in my grandparents' backyard or during the contests of endurance we called meals. Outside one barely noticed him, but inside, his camera was augmented by a hand-held spotlight whose candlepower must have rivaled that of the lantern in our local lighthouse. On film, our family always looks like a group of criminals being brought forth from the station house, our heads constantly turned away from the camera while one upraised hand shaded our faces. For hours afterward, it seemed, the world presented itself to you in a watery haze of dancing black dots. Much of that world still seems to.

For example, I remember that on July 20, 1969, my family was grouped around the console television in my grandparents' family room, waiting to watch Neil Armstrong exit the *Eagle* and step foot on the lunar surface. That scene has been replayed so many times on television and in the movies that I cannot tell where memory leaves off and viewing begins. I remember it was a small room, crowded with adults and heavy furniture. I was seven. Someone—my father, my uncle—was trying to maneuver around the bodies to take pictures of the TV screen. Someone else was asking us all to be quiet so they could hear the crackling voices.

It is a moment I'd like to recapture if I could. Where was my uncle with his movie camera then? What ever happened to those pictures of the image on the screen? In another ten years both my mother and father would be dead, ten more and my uncle and both grandparents as well. And I am left with memories too often viewed as from one side or the other of my uncle's camera. Shadowed faces or blinded eyes, too little clear, too little concrete. Too little to hold to.

In 1969 Neil Armstrong stepped out onto the Sea of Tranquility. And I, and my mother and father, and uncles and grandparents, and sister and brother, stepped out there with him, leaving our prints on what turned out to be a dusty and windless world.

I was eleven when the two men in suits pulled up to the front of our house and went inside to tell my mother that my father had died earlier that day of a sudden massive heart attack. He was thirty-four, seven years younger than I am now. For most of us, our parents' age is ever-receding, a moving target growing constantly more remote and strange. But I have spent so much of my life catching up to my father, and now, somehow, he lies behind me.

I wonder a lot lately about what was going through his mind during those years. He himself was only fourteen when his own father died, also of a heart attack, also before fifty, and as I orbit around that frozen spot of time, I wonder if he too felt, as I do, the quickening arc of the sun and moon across the sky and the impatient way they seem to pull at the shared waters of our blood.

Forty had always seemed incredibly remote when I was young, and now that I am here, I find that hasn't changed much. I don't feel like forty was supposed to feel and I can't help but question if my father, even younger, found the same to be true. Married for over a decade, already raising four children, could he possibly have felt as still-young as I do?

Perhaps this explains the time he and my mother separated, a full year of scattered visits, awkward phone calls, and several false starts at reconciliation before the decision was made to return home to his family. A year I barely recall—the Triumph Spitfire and then the silver Jaguar, the different matchbook covers in the pockets of his new sport coats, his new apartment smelling of smoke and ringing at times with the too-loud laughter of women who spoke to us kids as if we were deaf, as if by dint of sheer volume they could suppress our other senses so we wouldn't notice the nervous gestures, the sidelong glances. Maybe he found his life at thirty-three as unimaginable as I do, unimaginable and perhaps, looking ahead, unlivable as well.

Chased by the echoes of a father's faint heart creeping ever closer and facing a wife who had already been diagnosed with terminal cancer, death must have seemed to have him surrounded; who could blame him for pretending that if he changed his address, his clothes and car, his family, it might not recognize him?

My mother, for one. She certainly had her reasons, left to take care of four kids while enduring the debilitating futility of radiation and chemotherapy. My aunt blamed him as well, one time spitting in his face when she picked us up, crossing all the way back from the driveway across the lawn to the porch to do so. I don't remember her reason, or if she even had one beyond defending her little sister. It didn't matter. My father figured wrong and death found him anyway, five hundred miles away in Washington, D.C., packing up his desk to return home to his wife and family.

Somewhere during that separation my father had taken up jogging. He must have been doing it regularly—people don't "jog" just once—but the only recollection I have of him running is the time I joined him during one of his weekend visits home.

The memory begins with me on the bottom landing of the stairs leading up to the bedrooms. The blue carpet is leaving an itchy impression in the back of my thighs, but I'm too lazy to stand and too afraid of falling asleep to lie on my back. So I sit and watch my father as he stretches in the middle of the small foyer where our front door opens onto the intersection of our living room and hallway.

When he finishes and moves to the door, I open my eyes only at the sudden breeze that blows in across my skin. It is early summer, still cool enough in the mornings to be a shock to the system, and the two of us shiver for a moment on the porch steps, then begin a small-stepped trot down the driveway to the road, taking more steps than necessary and windmilling our arms to warm our bodies. When we reach the end of the driveway, marked by the pine tree he and I had planted together three or four years earlier, we move off to the right with him on the outside, between me and the center of the road.

At the cross-point of our street, which formed a large capital A, we agree that he will continue around the block while I take the cross street and wait for him on the other side. The crossing is only four houses long, but I take my time walking to the other end. No use running now, especially since the grass is still too wet to sit on. When I reach the corner I stand leaning against the street sign and wait. I have, I think, all the time in the world.

I have taken lately to spending a lot of time on NASA's website, viewing photographs taken by the Hubble Space Telescope. The digitized images, despite their pragmatically indifferent titles—M6, quadrant A11—are beautiful: swirls of light amid billowing clouds of interstellar gas, nebulas shaped like golden hourglasses with stars like cat's-eyes in the centers—science found swimming in the maelstrom of art.

My father would have loved this area. An amateur astronomer at heart, he would every now and then rent or borrow a small telescope that we would set up in my bedroom for a few days. There, for several nights running, we would take turns peering into the nighttime sky, examining the moon's face or trying to find Saturn's rings. I don't remember what we talked about at those times, or even if we spoke at all. What returns are sights and feelings—the slender slickness of the white tube under my fingers, the ease with which it swiveled from one point to another, and my father bent across its length, an eye pressed to its side, his rounded head with its growing spot in the middle held perfectly still so as not to disturb the universe within his reach. One August I remember we watched the opening nights of the Perseids, when shooting stars fell like flaming rain, each coruscating flash a potential wish, and I wonder now if he even tried keeping up, or just watched each one drop across the horizon, burning up in the rarified atmosphere.

To look through a telescope is to peer backward in time; the light that guided the Egyptians in their calendar-making was already nine years old by the time they named it the Dog Star. A being currently standing in the Vega system could watch as my father and I jog down our street, while one in the more remote Pollux system would even now be viewing my birth. How far out, I wonder, could we see with that small scope? How far would we have chosen to see if we could? How far would we have traveled before stopping to turn back and simply watch? To what moments would we have turned again and again?

The images we are receiving today from the Hubble Telescope are the closest we have ever been to the center of our universe. It was there that we believe our universe began, a nanosecond of seething hot creation followed by a sharply violent hurling outward. We ride the expanding rim gazing ever behind us, each more distant galaxy we view another step backward toward creation, another billion-year stare into the past, trying to ignore the feeling that ahead of us lies nothing but galactic dark matter, black holes, and an inevitable cooling down. The Greeks have had their say in the stars; the names of the constellations belong to them. But the man in the moon is no stranger to me; I have seen his face before and it is my father's, and his father's, and my own.

Carole Firstman

LIMINAL SCORPIONS

I RECENTLY FOUND a scorpion on my father's desk, which I have since stolen. Not a live creature, but a specimen, long pickled in formaldehyde. The handwritten label inside the jar reads: *Paruroctonus silvestrii: Las Estacas, Mexico—1971*. The scorpion floats in suspended animation, trapped in the jar I now balance on the flat of my palm, its body preserved for display. Appearing neither dead nor alive, it hovers near the bottom, leaving an almost imperceptible gap between its abdomen and the glass that rests on my hand.

I discovered it a few days after my father telephoned from Mexico to say he had decided to stay there until he dies. "I'm not long for this world," he said. "I need you to ship me some things." I reached for the notepad next to my computer and took down his list, an itemized request that would trigger my weeklong scavenger hunt inside his unoccupied central California home, my discovery of this particular scorpion specimen bottled on the shelf above his desk, and my subsequent thievery. Although my father built a career, a life, around his research on the evolution of arachnids—spiders, mites, and scorpions—he made no mention of his specimen collection the day he rattled his list into the receiver.

"The Great Lectures DVD collection and the most recent catalogue from the Teaching Company," he said. His voice cracked with urgency. "My *Encyclopedia Britannica* set, including the annual almanacs. Posters of *The Blue Boy* and *Pinkie*—the reproductions I got last year at the Huntington Museum, not the photocopies in my bedroom, but the original posters—you'll have to remove them from the frames."

With the phone clamped between my shoulder and jaw, I repeated the list back to him.

He added a few more items, then proceeded to describe in detail where each object lay inside his house.

"I know where it all is," I said several times. And "Yes, of course I know that, too." His house stands just five doors down from mine, so I know the layout of his home quite well. But he didn't stop with the directions no matter how many "I-knows" I uttered, because once he gets going on a train of thought it's impossible for him to stop. Impossible.

After a while I doodled on the notepad, saying "uh-huh" every few seconds.

My father had gone to Mexico at my urging. A few months ago my brother and I bought him a one-way ticket with the vague promise of a return flight at his convenience. We hoped that without a specific return date in mind, he might be more inclined to stay longer than three weeks—perhaps forever. This isn't quite as harsh as it seems. For decades he'd dreamed of moving there permanently, surrounded by the language and landscape he loves, the deserts and beaches and mountains where he'd gathered arachnid specimens for half a century. Best of all, he would be near relatives who could look after him. Relatives other than me. Far away.

Among the list of things he requested were his *Great Books of the Western World,* a hardbound series originally published in 1952, fifty-four volumes covering classic literature, including works of fiction, history, natural science, philosophy, mathematics, and religion. I didn't tell him that the information contained in these books is readily available on the Internet, or that it would be cheaper to mail-order new books online and have them sent directly to his new apartment in Mexico rather than have me ship the old books. But he doesn't use computers. Anyway, once he sets his mind to something, he automatically disregards all other options.

"On the bookcase next to my bed," he said, as always, hyper-enunciating.

"Yes, I know."

"I must have them with me. They are monumental works by and about great authors. The most influential thinkers of our time."

I know, I know, I fucking know. But I did not say this either, because I've long understood that once he gets started he cannot stop. Cannot.

"Be sure to include the supplemental texts on Aristotle. Aristotle lived from 384 BC until 322 BC. He was a student of Plato and he taught Alexander the Great."

My father's speech patterns—his vocabulary and syntax—while noticeably formal in comparison to the average person's, are characteristic of him. Classic Asperger's from what I understand, albeit undiagnosed. His mannerisms balance on the edge of the autism spectrum. Strained social interaction, repetitive patterns of behavior, obsessive focus on specific interests—these traits manifest themselves as tiny droplets of personality toxins, not fatal, but unpleasant.

I doodled through his monologue on Plato and the dates of Chaucer and Sir Francis Bacon.

Also on his list: five pairs of leather shoes, four new suits, a case of unopened vitamin supplements, odor-free garlic tablets, a carton of bottles labeled All Natural Male Enhancement, a small leather-bound address book, back issues of *Scientific American,* and several file folders of correspondence—each labeled by name, including one marked "Stephen Jay Gould."

"I'll be so grateful to you for sending me these things, Carole."

"Uh-huh."

"I'm on the line between life and death. These things will keep me alive longer, do you understand?"

I suppose I said the things one is expected to say to a father. I suppose I said, *Don't be silly. You're not dying anytime soon,* or *Stop talking such nonsense,* or *But I thought you'd live to be one hundred and five—remember your plan? You're only eighty-two, so you have twenty-three years to go.* Or maybe I didn't say those things but thought them instead. Our conversations are so cyclical, our topics recurring so frequently—including his ever-immediately impending death, which he's been predicting for some forty years now—that I often lose track of what I've specifically said on which day.

I cradled the phone against my lower jaw and bulleted each item with little curly-cues. In that moment I wasn't sure if I was a good daughter or a bad one; I said the things a daughter should say, carried out actions expected of me, took dictation, wrote the list; but part of me considered throwing the list away, folding it in half and letting it go in the breeze outside. While my father prepared for his final respite by gathering earthly items of comfort and interest, things to make his remaining life enjoyable, I wasn't sure I wanted to deliver. Perhaps if I withheld his treasures he would postpone his passage from this world—stave off death—in which case my inclination to tear up the list was morally just. On the other hand, my withholding would cause him some degree of discomfort. I could let him squirm down there in Mexico—waiting and waiting for his things that would never arrive—pinch him with passive-aggressive retaliation for his past transgressions, a fuzzy litany I haven't fully articulated even to myself. Good daughter or bad? Perhaps I was both in that moment, a morally liminal creature with one foot on each side.

"Are you getting all this down?" he asked.

Hoards of specimen jars once filled both my father's offices, one office at the university where he taught in Southern California and a second study at home. Years after my parents split, he lived for a while in a double-wide mobile home in Chino where the hollow floor shook if you stepped too heavily, sending vibrations up the walls and rattling rows of specimen jars on their plywood shelves. When I was a teenager visiting during the summer, I once slammed the door on purpose just to watch my friend Lana's reaction as the scorpions fluttered momentarily awake, their legs and pincers gently rising in rippling isopropyl tides sloshing rim to rim. I laughed when her shoulders twitched with a get-them-off-me reflex. Clenching her teeth, she involuntarily bent forward to slap her bare shins, as if the reptilian, survival part of her brain were unable to differentiate between real or imagined threats. While I now know that her reactive behavior is a result of our genetic predisposition to fear noxious animals, in that moment I reveled in her uncertainty as hypothetical scenarios played out in her head, as her hypothalamus and sensory cortex conversed, assessing the repercussion of her every decision should these scorpions have been alive and loose.

Suppose you were bitten by a scorpion. Let's say the Death Stalker, *Apistobuthus pterygocercus.* The initial sting feels like several bee stings at once. You cry out in pain, then kick your foot into the air to jolt the scorpion from your ankle. Your heart soon races, banging furiously against your sternum. Has the scorpion's venom caused your heart to pound, or is this merely a psychological reaction? You linger for a few minutes, suspended in inaction, indecision—should you seek medical attention or just let the pain in your ankle subside? Let's say you wait it out. No need for drama. Scorpion stings are overrated, overplayed—the stories of agonizing deaths are neither false nor true, you say. Urban legends grown to monstrosities, you reason. So you apply an ice pack to ease the pain on your ankle, the red circle radiating from the puncture. Your heart pounds harder. Blood thrums against your eardrums. You feel hot. You start to sweat. You close your eyes, lean back on the couch, and elevate your ankle with a pile of throw pillows. As neurotoxins surge through your brain, they clamp onto sodium channels, alternately blocking and activating signals to your nervous system. The first convulsions take you by surprise—your arms tremble, your feet tingle, your lower abdomen contracts several times, like a shiver but stronger.

You're neither moving your body nor are you still; you quake on the threshold of voluntary physical action and involuntary reaction. It's time to seek help, so you look at the phone a few feet away; but within this sliver of time, the time you took to contemplate your situation, paralysis has crept in. Your eyelids slam back in their utmost open position, your eyeballs halt, now trapped in a frozen gaze, and your limbs, now trembling, flop up and down with the rhythm of your heaving torso as it folds and unfolds like a piece of paper trapped in the wind. Finally, your blood pressure drops and muscles release. Your limbs are loose again. The last thing you see is the telephone nestled uselessly in its cradle, and as fluids seep into your lungs and painkilling endorphins flood your brain, you welcome the coma, the sleep, the flood of deep relaxation that feels so, so good.

The day after my father's phone call I began packing his books. I opened all the blinds and doors to allow as much light in the house as possible. February's winter chill wafted in from the front and back yards, and although I intended to work quickly to stave off the cold, I found myself lingering, occasionally pausing to open certain books. At first my curiosity was random: pull a book, crack it open, notice a word or two, slide it into the open banker's box on the floor. I lifted Arnold van Gennep's *Rites of Passage,* originally published in 1908, reprinted in 1960. The pages smelled of dust, of moisture. I read. Pondered. Reached for the dictionary to look something up, then the encyclopedia, then back to *Rites of Passage,* then reached for something else, losing myself in a linked meandering of then-and-then, piling open books on the carpet around me rather than filling the cardboard box.

My digressive thread—liminality: *The condition of being on a threshold or at the beginning of a process.* To be *in "limbo,"* says the resurrected anthropologist Gennep, *is to inhabit an intermediate, ambivalent zone.* In liminal phase an individual experiences a blurring of social environment and reality, occupies the in-between stage. The term derives from the Latin *limen,* which means *boundary, transitional mark, passage between two different places. Liminal space represents a threshold of a physiological or psychological response,* the place where you teeter between action and inaction, the moment you consider calling for help; the instant your eyes dart between the phone and the red spot spreading from your ankle; the window of time between your last inhalation and your first convulsion—and there it is, the sliver of time that precedes paralysis, a sliver so fine, so sharp, it defies balance. You must step off, onto one side or the other. Go or stay; float or sink; here or there. Which way will you lean?

And what can I say to ease your fear, dear father, alleviate your angst: *one hundred and five, remember the plan?* Or maybe I should give you a push instead, tell you to count backward from eighty-two and let your abdomen sink, rest on the smooth glass bottom. When the lid turns to seal the portal, the flood will feel so, so good. Liminality: *The psychological point beyond which a sensation becomes too faint to be experienced.*

By noon, the liminal hour between morning's lingering chill and afternoon's oncoming warmth, the neighborhood outside my father's silent front door chirped with sounds of life. I looked up from whichever book I held and walked to the window. Two young mothers from around the block pushed strollers side by side in the street as a preschooler rode his bicycle alongside them on the sidewalk, his rear tire wobbling safely between training wheels. I imagine now that if that little boy were to fall, if the training wheels failed to keep him upright, he would not hesitate to cry out for help, and his mother would rush to his aid, either tilting the bike upright with an outstretched arm to get him back on track, or scooping him up off the ground should he topple and fall to the concrete.

I remember the first time I rode a two-wheeler, a secondhand blue and white Schwinn my parents had picked up at Leroy's Thrift Store in Pomona the winter of my first-grade year. I don't recall my father being present for that particular rite of passage, the day I learned to ride a bike. He wasn't the type to ride bikes, play ball, or attend Open House at my elementary school, but preferred instead to hole up in his study alone, or engage a few of his students in deep intellectual debate while smoking pot under the fig tree in our backyard. Lana was there the day of my inaugural lesson, though, along with a gaggle of neighborhood kids. One of the tall boys from the apartments across the street instructed me before I got on the bike while the other kids huddled around. We stood at the interior end of my parents' driveway next to the house, a long concrete corridor shaded by thick mulberry trees and the slatted-wood carport covering, a structure my father had built the preceding fall. The tall boy braced the bike upright as I climbed into place and rested my feet on the pedals. The other kids shouted instructions at me as I sat on the wide leather seat, still unmoving, still braced, aimed toward sunny Ninth Street far ahead at the other end of the dark driveway.

"Ready?" the tall boy asked.

I didn't answer right away. I paused. A moment of indecision.

The kids' voices swirled past my ears, making little sense to me at that moment—advice on which way to lean, how to grip the handlebars, how pressing backward on the pedals would engage the coaster brake. One voice I did hear, though: "We'll catch you if you fall," someone said.

"All set?" the boy asked again.

I nodded.

On the count of three, the boy gave me a push. At first I teetered, overcorrecting the handlebars several times, wrenching them side-to-side. But as I gained forward momentum, I finally straightened out the front wheel. I found the sweet spot, the arrow-like glide. Balance. Exactly in between left and right. *Lean. Let up. Lean.* My friends ran alongside as I rolled toward the light, still solely propelled by the force of the tall boy's initial push, through the darkened corridor toward the bright open space where the sidewalk divided our place from everyplace else, a concrete boundary separating Insulated-In-Here from Risk-Laden-Out-There.

I think it was Lana who finally screamed for me to pedal.

I pumped my right foot down, then my left. The bike burst forward, powered past the voices and scampering feet, and sailed into the open, wide street hot with asphalt and sunlight and possibility.

My father's absence that afternoon is representative of so many absences, a single line-item in my catalogue of his inattentive moments and self-sequestered years. Even when he was around, he wasn't *really* around. The day of my birth, for example (which, coincidentally, fell on his thirty-sixth birthday), marked the beginning of our shared lives. He tells the story of racing my mother to the hospital before dawn the morning of his birthday, the second of June, and when my mother started to crown right there in the elevator, the nurses ushered her directly into the delivery room. He paced the waiting room with bated breath, he says, his mind wild with the possibilities ahead, good and bad. On one hand he was eager for the baby, the skin and bone manifestation of his DNA, his contribution to humankind's evolution. On the other hand he wrestled with worry and guilt about how the baby might turn out. When they had first learned my mother was pregnant with me, my father wasn't at all happy. Something had to be done. "There are doctors that handle this," he'd said. On the day of her scheduled pregnancy-termination procedure, my mother had returned home that afternoon without having gone to the clinic. She lied to my father, though, claiming that while she'd received a hypertonic saline injection (which, in fact, she had not), for some reason the six-week embryo didn't abort. "I guess we're stuck," she told him. Now, seven-and-a-half months later, he paced the delivery waiting room and wondered how that super-salt shot might have mangled the gestating fetus. Would this baby be physically deformed or mentally affected? A hell of a price to pay, he thought.

Finally the doctor emerged from the delivery room, smiley-faced, at twenty-two minutes past six to announce the news: "It's a girl," he said. "Congratulations, Bruce."

At my mother's bedside my father carefully balanced my head in the fleshy crook of his folded arm, and when he had counted all ten fingers and all ten toes for the third time, his eyes watered and he told my mother how perfect we both were, she and I.

My father usually omits from his recounting that, within days of their return to the house, my baby noises were too much of a distraction for him inside the house where he studied, so he erected a tent for my mother in the backyard, the large army-green canvas shelter they used on my father's scorpion-gathering expeditions in the Mexican desert. I know this may be hard to believe, but I shit you not, dear reader. There on the dry Bermuda grass, with a lawn chair inched to the edge of a Woolworth's plastic wading pool, behind her a pair of camping cots and a floor fan powered by an extension cord stretching from the house to the tent, she tended me during the day, the nineteen-year-old mother and her red-faced newborn, cooing, crying, nursing, and sleeping through the summer heat.

In contrast to the underlying dynamics between my parents that must have been quite complex, the photos from that time, at least as I remember them, paint a deceptively simple picture. I've seen only a few snapshots from those days, and it's been so many years since I've seen them that the image in my mind is a bit fuzzy. All appears relatively serene through the camera lens—a hippie-ish scene with my mother smiling from behind the frames of her cat-eye glasses; my father bare-chested and barefoot in dress slacks cut off above the knee. I imagine them taking turns holding their new infant in the yard, snapping a camera loaded with a fresh roll of Kodak slide film and sipping sun tea with fresh lemon wedges picked from the side yard. He probably took several little breaks like this over the course of the day, walking back and forth from the living room to the yard. Then in the evening, when the sun sank beneath the neighborhood's drooping power lines, my mother joined my father in the house for spaghetti and sliced cantaloupe. My mother slept with me inside the house at night and returned to the backyard campsite each morning.

No, he wasn't exactly cruel, at least not intentionally. He just wasn't all that interested in fatherhood. Many people don't really want to be parents; rather, parenthood sort of happens to them. We all deal with it in our unique ways. Some of us learn to balance personal need with responsibility and end up enjoying it. Others meet their responsibilities and mask their disdain, sometimes successfully, other times not. Perhaps it's a manifestation of the Asperger's (which is the label *I've* assigned to him, anyway), but my father rarely camouflages his intentions. If he doesn't want children he simply says so, then tells his pregnant wife to make an appointment at the appropriate clinic. If the crying baby bothers his reading, again he simply says so, then rummages through the garage until he finds the tent poles. Does this prove him one or the other, good father or bad? One incident, taken in isolation—no, I don't think so. But when does the cumulative effect enter the algorithm? On one side of the equation, he missed pretty much all my rites of passage growing up. Never did he attend (or even know about, in most cases) a single parent conference, open house, graduation, swim meet, driving lesson, birthday party, marching parade, or music recital.

On the other side of the equation, I remember the morning he rushed to my rescue during the San Fernando earthquake of 1971—which rumbled from its epicenter fifty miles northwest of Pomona—just weeks after I'd learned to ride my bike, the same year he would later capture the scorpion I have recently stolen. Asleep in the top bunk of my bedroom, I was awakened by the clank-clank-clank of the head- and footboards rattling erratically against the wall. At first I sank my head deeper into the pillow and drifted back to sleep for maybe a second or two, incorporating the side-to-side rocking motion of the bunk bed into the dream I'd been having, until the noise in my dream thumped louder, then took on weight, cannoning past the pit of my stomach. My eyes flew open with instantaneous focus. The whole bunk bed teetered away from the wall. The force threw me against the outer guardrail, which stopped me from rolling off the edge. Then abruptly the bed swung back the other way again, ramming against the wall so hard it popped the guardrail up and out of its shallow niche, hurling it across the room like a giant scorpion tail in full attack. The top bunk arched away from the wall again, farther out this time. I sat straight up, turned away from the wall and leaned back, against the bed's outward momentum. If the bed had been the front tire of a wobbly bike, my body was the handlebar: *Lean. Let up. Lean.* Back and forth the bunk frame shuddered while tiny bits of plaster rained from the ceiling. Just as the window next to my headboard pinged, then cracked, my father burst through the door in his underwear. He pushed the bed up against the wall with all his weight. He wedged himself at an angle, a human plank, with arms outstretched, palms pushing upward against my mattress, his bare toes curled into the rug for traction.

"I gotcha," he said.

We rode out the earthquake like that, him leaning into the bunk frame, me leaning backward, away from him and into the wall. I had no idea at the time, and wouldn't fully understand until years later, that during those moments the world outside our house crumbled. I didn't know what Richter 6.6 meant or that sixty-five people would die that day. While twelve bridges fell onto highway lanes, two hospitals collapsed, an entire medical center heaved off its foundation, and the lower section of the Van Norman Dam crumbled—my father and I found the sweet spot, the upright balance, if only for a few slow-motion seconds. We managed to leverage our bodies against the shifting continent below us. While the earth's crust transitioned—buckled and split and sank—my father and I inhabited a fleeting moment of limbo. We countered the vibrations pulsing through the wooden floor on its raised, hollow foundation.

While my shoulder blades thumped against the wall, I watched over my father's bare shoulder as the crack in the window grew longer and more complex, ascending at a slight diagonal and splintering off like a windblown bush, or a tree permanently etched on the horizon.

Forty years later, I looked through the screened window of my father's vacant home, some three hundred miles north of my childhood Pomona house, going through his things. Outside, the little boy continued riding his bike down the sidewalk, his plastic training wheels pinging with grit and gravel fragments. He pumped the pedals hard several times, then turned to look at his mother as he glided past her. She didn't seem to notice his daring feat because she was deep in conversation with her friend, so he hooted, "Look at me!"

She turned and raised her fist in way-to-go encouragement.

I moved to my father's desk in the office, a converted room at the back of the house. There I found seven old specimen jars with spiders, mites, crabs, and scorpions. One jar had long ago shattered in place; the spider, no longer preserved in liquid, lay dried and crumbled amid shards of glass. It occurred to me then, not for the first time, how little I understand of my father, yet how quickly time narrows the boundaries of our shared earthly existence: soon he'll be gone. It's not the chronology of his life that evades me. I know much of what he did and when, despite the fact he was intermittently absent from my life until he moved to my town, my neighborhood, a few years ago. Although I've read much about the high-functioning edge of the autism spectrum—the lack of empathy, intense preoccupation with a particular subject, one-sided verbosity, impaired emotional reciprocity—part of me still can't understand why his work was so important to him, why his intellectual life took precedence over our family. Wait. I take that back. Truth be told, I actually do understand *why* he is the way he is. What I wonder is why *I* ended up with such a parent.

Over Thanksgiving dinner in my living room last November, he said again—in the exact same words, with the same intonation and cadence as the hundred times before—how lucky we are to exist at all. How fortunate we humans are to be alive, let alone sentient. While the rest of us at the table talked about mundane things—about road construction blocking the downtown freeway exit and which alternative route might be best over the next few weeks—he interrupted with his own train of thought.

"The probability of the existence of your individual, unique genome is about one over a googolplex," he blurted to no one in particular, but looked at my mother-in-law.

"Oh," she said, not knowing how else to respond.

"Do you know what a googolplex is?" he said to everyone, but looked at me.

"No," I said on cue.

"Do you want to know?"

"Sure." Still on cue.

"It can be represented in a mathematical equation."

The table thus quieted, he lifted a pen and three-by-five-inch notepad from his breast pocket. He wrote: $10^{(10^{100})}$. "Or it can be written out as a number. A googolplex is the second largest number with a name. It's a one, followed by a googol of zeros."

He paused.

"Do you know how much a googol is?" he finally asked.

My cue again. "How much?"

"A googol is a one followed by a hundred zeros."

My mother-in-law said nothing, just nodded politely and pushed the mashed potatoes with her fork.

"You had a one-in-a-googolplex chance of being here today," he said.

Very long pause. We all teetered on the threshold of awkward silence. I wondered if I should let the moment settle, or if I should say something to alleviate the social pain I imagined my guests felt. Let it die, or rescue it?

And then, before I could decide what to say, he mended the moment himself. "Carole, would you please be kind enough to pass the salt?"

The likelihood of our existence, of everything around us, in fact—all life on earth—has been the subject of much scholarly discourse. In his book *Wonderful Life,* Harvard paleontologist Stephen Jay Gould describes bio-evolution as a copiously branching bush that originated by an improbable accumulation of accidental contingencies. Gould posits that if the evolutionary tape were played again, there is no way to predict what would happen—and no reason to expect that humans would have existed at all. He later explains in an interview with *Time* magazine, "It is like *Back to the Future.* In the movie Doc Brown goes to a blackboard and draws a chart. The top line is history as it actually occurred. But if you make this teeny little change, which is Biff Tannen getting that sports almanac, then history veers off. It isn't that it is random that it happened the second way. . . . It's just that what actually happened is one of a billion possible alternatives, and you'd never get it to run exactly the same way again."

There in my father's office, next to the crumbled spider and shards of broken glass on his desk, the tail of the *Paruroctonus silvestrii* leaned against the inner wall of its cylindrical tomb. *Las Estacas, Mexico—1971,* the label said. The jar, two-and-a-half inches tall and one inch in diameter, stood upright like a coffin set on end. The scorpion inside was positioned head-down and tail-up, with its abdomen and front claws slouched unnaturally in the bottom's corner. I wondered that afternoon as I went through his things, and I still wonder now, what the scorpion reveals—what it might tell me about my father's life work, about my father himself. About the connection between my father and myself.

I tipped the jar on its side so the scorpion rested more naturally—flat rather than upright.

For the scorpion, its last day alive might have gone like this: With its two fighting claws thrust forward in guardian stance, the *Paruroctonus silvestrii* emerged with a dry rustle from a finger-sized hole under the rock. In the center of a patch of packed earth, it balanced on the tips of its four pairs of legs, nerves and muscles braced for action. Hairlike protrusions on its legs queried for vibrations, minute air movements that would determine its next move—attack or retreat.

Normally the scorpion would not come out of its burrow during the day, but an overcast sky pushed inland from the Pacific and toggled between light and dark, creating a twilight effect the scorpion mistook for dusk. In a dome of shade cast by the rock, its two-inch yellow body glinted where the moist, brown stinger protruded from the last segment of the tail, now arched over, parallel with the scorpion's flat back. Slowly the stinger slid from its sheath. The nerves in the poison sac relaxed.

A few feet away, at the base of a yucca, a small, oblivious beetle trudged nearer. The scorpion's downslope rush gave him no time to spread his wings. The beetle's legs quivered in protest as the sharp claw snapped round his body. The stinger lanced into him from over the scorpion's head. The beetle teetered between life and death for an instant, then stilled.

The scorpion stood motionless for several minutes, pausing to identify its dead prey and retest the ground and air for hostile vibrations. Confident, its claw retracted from the half-severed beetle and its two small feeding pincers stretched forward to pierce the beetle's exoskeleton.

Deliberately and methodically the scorpion ate its victim.

An hour later, as it slowly sucked the last morsels of beetle-flesh off its pincers, the signal for the scorpion's own death went undetected from behind the yucca—faint sounds audible to a human, but vibrations just outside the range of the scorpion's sensory system.

A few feet away, a freckled hand with uneven, dirty fingernails raised an overturned glass jar.

The scorpion felt a tiny ripple in the air. At once its fighting claws hoisted and groped. Its stinger was erect in the rigid tail, its nearsighted eyes staring up for a sight of the enemy.

The jar came down. From underneath, a heavy index card slid between the scorpion and the sand, and with one swift move the man flipped the jar and the card upright, then upside down again, dropping the scorpion into a second jar, filled with formaldehyde. The scorpion clawed at the glass walls, writhed and reached sideways and up. Submerged, it strained for the surface, snapped again at the walls, again down, again up, until finally its convulsions slowed.

Still squatting, the man slipped the index card into his breast pocket. When the scorpion's stinger finally limped and its pincers floated peacefully to either side, the man stood, rubbed his hands down the sides of his pants, and stepped past the yucca toward the road.

In the echoing silence a cicada clickity-zinged from inside the thorny bush, and from below, an anxious lizard scuttled between leaves as dry and thin as molted snakeskin.

Over the next several days I sorted my father's personal belongings. I burrowed through drawers, cupboards, shelves, boxes, organizer trays, envelopes, cabinets, files, magazine stacks, grade books, checkbook registers, ornamental covered dishes, pockets, hampers, bills, memos, letters, receipts, journals, jars, bowls, plastic containers. At some point my mission to collect the items he'd requested had morphed into something else.

How would I feel if he died today? We had shared homes, off and on, for the first ten years of my life. Then we lived three hundred miles apart, visiting once a year at most, until a few years back, when he moved to my town. In some respects, I hardly know this man. In other ways, I can anticipate his every move. What label describes our relationship? And would I regret not knowing him better—or could I at least appreciate him more if I understood him from a different perspective?

Alone in his house, I committed personal invasion. I pinched and clawed through his things. I wanted to know what my father sought in scorpions—if I could make meaning of his work, perhaps that would balance the equation for me; perhaps it could justify the uneven weight of family man versus scholar, intellectual versus emotional connection. Snooping through his personal things was a way of getting closer to the man I consciously held at arm's length—rooting out his unsavory secrets would help me justify my ongoing participation in our father-daughter dance of disconnection. Intimacy from a safe distance. My eyes and fingers queried for insights that would determine my stance as a daughter—poised to deliver the itemized goods or reconciled to withhold his treasures? Let him squirm, perhaps. I am not proud of my actions, in retrospect, but, in my defense, I was driven. Even if I had wanted to cease my search, it would have been impossible to stop. Impossible.

As an adult I recognize many qualities in myself that I also see in my father, some good, some bad. I think most of us can say that about our parents. So how do we distinguish between good parenting and bad? Good daughters and bad? If our life experiences contribute to determining the adults we become, and if some seemingly negative experiences germinate some sort of timely lesson, then how are we to judge the actions of our parents—of ourselves, of anyone—with black and white clarity? Each action, each event, each nuance of life introduces new variables, new risks, new possibilities. Perhaps the tall boy from the apartments across the street pushed my Schwinn bike with a slightly different velocity or angle than my father would have, or maybe Lana would not have been as shy around my father as she had been in the presence of the handsome, tall boy. Had it been my father giving the lesson, perhaps Lana wouldn't have waited so long to shout her instructions for me to pedal—in which case my bike-riding experience might have evolved into a different lesson than the particular one I came away with that day, something other than how to compensate for a series of over-corrections, which weeks later translated to my intuitive strategy for counterbalancing the teetering bunk bed. Or perhaps I would have eventually learned the exact over-compensation-counterbalance lesson under my father's instruction at a later date, but too late to help me during the earthquake on February 9, 1971. Who knows?

I wonder about the scorpion in the jar: If the evolutionary tape were played again in Las Estacas, Mexico, that hot July day of 1971, which variables would remain constant and which contingencies, if altered, would have prompted the scorpion to act differently? And what repercussions might that have had for the scorpion? For the beetle? My father? One changed variable might have set in motion another chain of reactions, a chain that may have altered the scorpion's fate. Or my father's. Or mine. Suppose the scorpion had stung my father. Suppose he had died in the Mexican desert that day. Or suppose he'd lived, but was so shaken that he decided to change his career path. What if he had stayed in Pomona to read children's books aloud to me on the sofa instead of driving twenty-five hundred miles cross-country to present his research to Harvard medical students?

Gould, of course, is right—there is no way to predict what would happen. Even if we could change a particular variable in the past, the chain reaction of possible outcomes alters the very structure of the branching bush. I wonder how far each leaf reaches, how wide the circle of our apparent spheres of influence.

During one of my scavenger-hunt days inside my father's home, around dusk, a neighbor called to his dogs in the front yard, clinked tools on the driveway. He seemed to be looking my way, looking toward the window where I stood, where I scoured and pilfered. I stepped aside and reached for the plastic wand. Twist, twist, and the blinds tilted in unison, fluttered closed like the gills of a giant, hungry fish.

During the years I taught third grade, my students often picked scorpions as the topic for their independent research projects. A socially defiant but exceptionally bright boy named Tyler hunkered behind a barricade of several large hardbound books propped upright on his desk during sustained-silent-reading time one afternoon. He loved the close-up photographs depicting spine-like tail segments, nearly transparent abdominal cuticles, and elongated pincers. Earlier in the year I'd figured out that if I wanted Tyler to keep reading something, I had to feign disapproval—otherwise he instantly lost interest in the topic and redirected his attention to something else, like flinging straight-pin-spiked spit wads across the room with a makeshift slingshot fashioned from a stolen pencil and his deskmate's hair scrunchie.

"Whatcha reading?" I asked.

Tyler lowered one of the books. He smiled at me through squinted eyes and pointed to an enlarged image of one scorpion cannibalizing another.

"Gross," I said. "Why do they do that?"

"The females eat the males after they mate."

"Yuck."

"So cool."

"I think you should put this away. And if there's a chapter on giant sea scorpions from the dinosaur days, don't read that, either. Have you heard about ancient scorpion monsters? I wonder if it's true. Never mind. You'll have nightmares."

As I walked away Tyler flipped to the index at the back of the book, then spent the rest of the afternoon, including the time he should have been participating in a social studies lesson, scribbling in a notebook resting covertly on his lap. To the horror and gleeful fascination of his classmates, a week or so later, Tyler delivered his oral report, explaining that four hundred million years ago, ten-foot giant sea scorpions violently reigned at the top of the food chain. "They grew so big because there was a lot of oxygen in the air," he said, and then he went on to describe how large fish, more fierce than the giant sea scorpions, forced the scorpions onto land, where they evolved back to a smaller size again. "They went from small to huge to tiny," he said, holding up a picture he'd drawn himself, a comic-book type of scene with one scorpion biting off another scorpion's head while nearby a fang-jawed, shark-looking creature dripped anticipatory globs of saliva from its tongue.

"Any questions?" Tyler asked.

Hands shot up.

When I was a kid, my father led graduate students through the sand dunes of Baja to collect all manner of arachnids during university-sponsored field trips. I imagine they hiked among the yuccas, and when my father paused to speak in his undulating rhythm of hyper-enunciated words, long-haired twenty-somethings scribbled furiously in their notebooks.

I recall one particular drive through the Mexican desert in our Volkswagen camper van with the music blaring, the windows down. I was around seven years old, small enough to stand upright on the floorboard between the driver and passenger seats. My father loosely fingered the steering wheel with one hand while his other hand rested on the gearshift knob. I swayed left-right-left in the growing gap between my parents as the van shimmied side to side from the vibrations of the tires. My mother mouthed the words to Biff Rose's "Buzz the Fuzz" while I balanced barefoot beside her. I could have easily toppled over, but I kept my center of gravity low, like an arachnid braced for action, my legs slightly bent. With my bare thighs safely cradled against the armrests of the two seats, I danced. *Lean. Let up. Lean.* I danced with knees limber, danced to keep myself upright, danced in the hot Mexican wind like a folded piece of blank paper, flapping, free.

Years after my parents divorced, when I had grown into the door-slamming teenager who laughed at my friend's leg-slapping heebie-jeebies in a room full of dead bugs, my father often tried to explain the nature of his work to me—some of which I understood, but mostly did not. The problem was that he spoke to me in the only language he seemed capable of, which was the same language he used in his university lectures and scholarly publications. In 1973 he published a paper in the *Journal of Arachnology* on the evolution of the arachnid internal skeleton and its relationship to the evolution of the circulatory system. In this paper, he suggests "the neoteny as the major mechanism to explain the origin of the non-scorpion arachnids from scorpion ancestors." Among other things, he details his discovery of what he calls "a perineural vascular membrane of certain lungless, rare arachnids."

In bits and pieces, I am slowly coming to comprehend some of the theoretical significance of his discoveries regarding the anatomy of the scorpions he collected during those trips. To paraphrase (and oversimplify) his words: Tracing the changes of arachnid anatomy (specifically the circulatory system) through both fossil records and modern-day specimens provides evidence to support the evolution of ancient sea scorpions into many various modern-day spiders and scorpions. I glean from his research that the sea scorpions that evolved from gill-breathing swimmers to lung-breathing land walkers to vascular-membrane-breathers (with nonfunctional lungs) were indeed liminal creatures.

Among the items my father asked me to send him was a file folder containing his correspondence with Stephen Jay Gould. While fishing for Gould's file among several four-drawer filing cabinets that line the walls of my father's study, I discovered that the drawers hold hundreds of manila folders, each labeled and alphabetized by last name. Apparently my father was quite the letter writer. Not only did he write hundreds, perhaps thousands, of letters over his lifetime, but he kept copies of many of the letters he wrote as well as those he received. I don't know why he did this. It could have been part of his compulsion to collect, inventory, and categorize things. After days of rifling through his files, it began to appear to me that he has been documenting his life. Perhaps he anticipated that his future value to the academic world would merit the preservation of his every printed word, both personal and professional. Poised for fame. Or posthumous recognition. Or maybe this archive is a manifestation of his narrow yet multi-branched intensity. His groping on the edge of a neurological spectrum.

It had been several days since my father called with his list. Technically I had everything he'd requested, but still I holed up in his office. I explored the files for hours, reading under a dim lamp while the sky outside turned black. I randomly pulled letters, one after another. When I look back on those hours now, I see myself as if through the wide-angle lens of an old camera mounted near the ceiling, a grainy image I have contrived in my mind: In the photo's frame, I straddle the open sliding-glass door that separates the house from the backyard; I stand, papers in hand, with one foot on each side of the threshold. In the light, I will deliver—fulfill the request made of me by gathering items on a list; in the dark, I scavenge—search for meaning. I traverse the line between intimacy and emotional distance, empathy and resentment, self-serving voyeurism and objective observation. Good daughter or bad? More to the point, does the motivation justify the behavior?

As I kneeled before an open drawer, my eyes rested on a file name: *Rolf Lyon*. I remember Rolf from my childhood—a pre-med biology student who became good friends with my father. He often camped with us in Las Estacas, patiently threading marshmallows on a wire for me, then blowing out the flames when they caught fire. The letters in the folder span from 1964 to 1999.

> *April 4, 1977*
>
> *Dear Rolf,*
> *. . . I've been sort of depressed lately because it seems to me that I haven't accomplished anything important in my career as a professor. When I was your age I thought that by the time I was my age I would either be dead or else a world-famous zoologist. Well, I'm 48 and still alive and nobody.*

So my father, too, struggled to find meaning and purpose in his work. And to think, all these years I'd assumed him to be so self-certain. At the time he wrote this letter, he was close to my age now. I understand his angst. The question gnaws at me, too. I've often wondered if and when I'll make it, and if the value of my life's work will appreciate or depreciate over time. For those of us who don't have children, how do we contribute to mankind's evolution if not through the passage of our genetic material? It seems so obvious to me that my father's academic accomplishments were indeed worthy, that asking about the natural world may not result in definitive answers, much less fame—but the value is in the asking, the search that leads from one question to the next, like a ripple on the ocean's surface that swells toward the continental shelf, then crashes on the sand before pulling into itself again. All intellectual thought, all humanistic notions of education, are based on the act of questioning. Socrates asked questions. His form of inquiry rippled debate between individuals with opposing viewpoints; it was the asking and responding that stimulated critical thinking, illuminated ideas. Plato asked. Aristotle asked. Ideas swelled, evolved into sub-ideas of related origin, answered or not. Modern scholars, giants in their fields of expertise, joined the collective discourse as it stretched upward, arched and curled with too many voices to distinguish one from another—scientists and spiritual leaders and laypersons and your next-door neighbor. My father. Me. My third-grade students. My current students at the university. Our ideas and our wonderings rush toward the shore and crash in on one another. Temporary chaos ensues. A beautiful cacophony of seaweed and salt that splays, then draws back to rejoin the huge body of water that pulls into itself again and again.

In a 1989 letter to Dr. Gould, my father says of his own research and discovery:

> *This supports the macro-evolutionary aspects of punctuated equilibrium theory. It is my current belief that all macro-evolutionary novelties arise from the mutations of regulatory genes that cause changes in developmental timing. These allometric changes in body proportions can either be localized or else generalized. The mutations occur randomly, of course, but they do not need to be immediately advantageous; they only need to be viable. They can be carried in the gene pool until such time as they are favored fortuitously by environmental selection pressures, at which time their frequencies will be increased in the gene pool because of differential reproduction rates.*

In other words, the reason certain anatomical features of modern scorpions matter is that this evidence supports the theory of evolution—especially aspects of Darwin's theory that have been the focus of dispute by evolution-oppositionists. So by providing evidence of scorpion evolution, my father aims to fill in one small blank spot in Darwin's argument.

Today's discourse on evolution teeters between the known and the unknown; consideration of either side of the debate, either creationist or evolutionist, invites you to temporarily occupy an intermediate position—a liminal space—and to figuratively linger on the damp Mexican shore that connects land and sea. This gives me pause: If research yields no immediate answer to humankind's inquiry into nature (or God, for that matter), does that mean a person's life work is for naught? Perhaps, then, his or her work has no value; or maybe the point, if not to solve an equation, is to take inventory of possibilities. Or better yet, to speculate on how today's actions might influence an as-yet unviewed documentary. What if we could anticipate the fast-forward? You're still on the couch with your red, swollen ankle elevated on a tower of throw pillows; if you knew the convulsions would lead to paralysis, would you still hesitate to reach for the phone?

I imagine myself in this situation, pondering, hesitating. Who would I call? My father, perhaps. The expert.

When we returned from each desert trip, my father meticulously labeled each jar, either by placing a handwritten note inside or by taping a typewritten note on the outside:

> *Paruroctonus silvestrii: Las Estacas, Mexico—1971*
> *Family Vaejovidae—it stings but is not fatal.*
> *B. Firstman*

At the height of his career he'd amassed at least a thousand jars, each containing from one to a dozen arachnid specimens. Inside their glassy tombs, each creature drifted in a sort of limbo—neither alive, nor allowed to begin the process of decomposition that would normally happen in nature. By decomposing, they would have become part of the soil, thus contributing to the next cycle of life. But preserved, they inhabited a space somewhere between life and death. Upon retirement he gave most of them to colleagues. Today only a few jars remain.

When he calls again to add more things to his list, I do not tell him I've taken his scorpion—the one, for reasons still unknown to me, he deemed worthy of saving. I have covertly excavated it for myself. It floats in suspended animation just an arm's reach from my desk now.

"And my electric typewriter," he says. "And ribbon cartridges. All of them."

"Yes, I already packed those."

"You'll find them in my bottom desk drawer."

"Already got 'em."

"Pull the drawer fully open and look behind the metal divider."

"Uh-huh," I say, because I know he cannot stop. I reach for the scorpion and hold it at eye level. Much of the formaldehyde has either leaked or evaporated.

"Are you writing all this down?"

"Yes, of course," I say, and I wonder if the amount of liquid affects the preservation of the dead animal, and if I should remove the cap and add more liquid. It would be a shame, after all these years, to let this particular scorpion dry up and crumble.

Deborah Thompson

WHEN THE FUTURE WAS PLASTIC

WHILE THE ENVIRONMENTAL activist talks on the radio, I watch an "urban tumbleweed" out the window. It scuttles across the street and attaches to a tree branch, where this synthetic, unnaturally white ghost flaps and sways. The polymeric chains composing this shopping bag entrap my father's legacy, their memory stronger than mortality. Human life is short, but plastic is forever.

The environmental activist on the air dares us to go a day without plastic—no touching it, no using it, no benefiting from it. At the risk of betraying my father, I decide to take the dare, as I push the plastic "off" button on the plastic radio.

I choose a day I can sleep late, partly so I won't have to turn off the alarm clock (plastic knob), and partly to make the day shorter. When I rise, I pause at the light switch, and consider cheating by covering my fingers with a towel so I won't technically touch it, but then remember that the towel is probably a cotton-polyester blend. So I fumble in the dark for my glasses. But they're plastic, too. Then there's the toilet seat to deal with, the PVC flooring, the acrylic fibers in the bathmat, my comb, shampoo and conditioner bottles (and the phthalates in their contents), my contact lenses, lens solution bottle, synthetic blends in clothes fabric, the buttons on my shirt, the teeth of my pants' zipper, the aglet of my shoelaces. And what about all the hidden plastic, such as the synthetic micro-beads in exfoliants? Three minutes after I begin my day without plastic, I give up.

Meanwhile, the Great Pacific Garbage Patch, an amorphous island of whirling plastic waste, possibly as large as the continent of Africa, expands. Some researchers say there are six additional major plastic-packed gyres in the world. Lethal to the sea creatures, and practically indestructible, these continents of churning plastic keep growing, even as my micro-beads swirl down the drain.

What would this world of synthetic polymers have looked like to their early inventors? Or even to my father upon receiving his doctorate in chemistry in 1962, at the precipice of a brave re-moldable world?

Ronald Earl Thompson, a golden-haired, blue-eyed baby, was born in December 1931 to a household largely without plastic. There may have been a few synthetic polymer products around his St. Augustine, Florida, home—perhaps a Bakelite telephone and a few vinyl record albums—but there were no plastic baby bottles, no plastic-lined disposable diapers, no plastic teething rings, and no sippy cups. Ronnie's crib was made of solid wood and nails, and the fibers of yarn with which his mother, Lotta, crocheted his baby blanket were wool or cotton, not the poly-blend we've accepted as natural today.

It's not that plastics weren't invented yet. In fact, the first plastics were nineteenth-century creations. From the Greek word for "malleable," the term "plastic" was applied to the emerging polymer compounds that were moldable when hot but rigid once cooled. The invention of the original synthetically produced polymer—or extremely long chain of repeating carbon-based molecular units—is generally attributed to Alexander Parkes in 1862. His creation, Parkesine, used nitric acid to modify cellulose. In 1868, John Wesley Hyatt improved on it by combining cellulose and alcoholized camphor to create celluloid, originally intended to replace ivory for billiard balls. Celluloid was soon developed as the substance for film, allowing us by the turn of the century to begin dreaming en masse. (Some of the late Victorian corsets used celluloid. Unfortunately for their wearers, they proved to be highly flammable.) Another cellulose-based polymer was the "artificial silk," rayon, which, rolled into thin sheets, makes cellophane. Polystyrene and polyvinyl chloride were also discovered in Victorian laboratories, though their future applications were still unimagined. Their commercial breakthrough came in 1907, when, attempting to come up with an alternative for shellac to line bowling alleys (the new fad), Belgian chemist Leo Hendrik Baekeland patented phenol-formaldehyde reaction techniques, which produced a resin sold under the trademark Bakelite. (If you rub a Bakelite item today—such as my Scottish Terrier napkin ring—you can still sometimes smell formaldehyde.) Until Bakelite, Victorian plastics were primarily laboratory curiosities, their future shapes as yet undreamed of.

I see these chemists as my father's intellectual ancestors. What elation they must have felt at the emergence of whole new compounds with properties the world had never before seen. What a rush felt from creating substances unknown in nature, substances that could take limitless shapes. Now anything was possible. For those first polymer chemists, stringing monomers into mega-chains must have been like discovering the alchemical secret to turn copper into gold.

By my father's birth, an array of plastics already permeated American culture: vulcanized rubber, the celluloid of film, the vinyl of records, the Bakelite of silverware handles, radios, and telephones. But these items were still minor luxuries in the Depression era, and, as a young boy, my father's interactions with plastic would have been limited. He might well have gone whole days without touching a single polymer resin.

By the time my father was tinkering with his first chemistry set—I imagine a clunky metal box chock-full of corker-stopped glass vials—the Second World War was underway. With it came the U.S. government's push to develop synthetic rubber and other substances in short supply and necessary for modern warfare, including insulators for electrical wires and lighter resins for aircraft. Chemistry was heroic, and plastics were patriotic.

During WWII, my father's family, poor but resourceful, raised rabbits and chickens, and kept a Victory garden as an expression of their patriotism. My grandfather, Raymond Earl, had fought in Europe during WWI, where he was exposed to the mustard gas that gave him severe emphysema and ultimately killed him. Though no immediate family members fought in the Second World War—my grandfather was too ill and Ronnie too young—they tried to serve in their own ways.

The garden was also an extension of my father's love for nature. To him, it was not inconsistent to be both a nature lover and a chemist. After all, organic chemistry was the chemistry of life, and of the carbon-based molecules that enabled it. It was his fundamental curiosity into the nature of things that underlay both his experiments with planting techniques in the garden and his explorations with chemicals in his makeshift lab in the garage. And when he accidentally blew a hole in the garage roof by mixing a strong acid with a strong base, he called the resulting explosion—he would tell me years later—"an act of nature."

His was a family of railroad people, barely high school graduates. But Ronnie, growing up at the polymeric frontier, dreamed of being a chemist, and that meant college. Through his high school years, as his blond hair reddened, he worked as an assistant to a pharmacist at a drugstore, and got to take home expired chemicals for his garage lab. (My grandparents resigned themselves to parking in the driveway for the entirety of Ronnie's senior year.) In those days, he later told me, pharmacists themselves mixed chemicals right at the bench. My father was in charge of keeping the raw chemicals in order and handing them to the pharmacist as needed. I imagine that the pharmacist recognized in my father the traits that stayed with Ronald Thompson his whole life: the extreme shyness and social awkwardness, but also that surety of mind and movement. By the time I knew him, my father never spilled anything, ever. He was slow and deliberate, and always moved as if constantly aware of his center of gravity; if he ever lost track of it, he paused to relocate it. (I would come to lose mine often, and, as an impatient teenager, sarcastically rolled my hands at my father to get a move on. Only later did I learn to value his steadiness.) I imagine, too, that it was from this pharmacist that Ronnie developed his life-long habit of sticking his tongue out the side of his lips when concentrating. (Sometimes, thinking hard, it pulsed and throbbed in a way that embarrassed me as a prudish teenager. "Tongue in mouth," I'd hiss-whisper when he did it in public.)

Ronnie graduated from high school in 1949. With the post-war boom came the first wave of post-war plastics, many of them discovered for their military potential and now domesticated. But Ronnie's boom was yet to come. He enlisted in the air force during the Korean War so he could attend college on the GI bill. On special evenings when I was a child, my father set up the slide projector and showed us image after image of the vibrant flowers he'd photographed during his time in the Philippines. Most of the pictures were extreme close-ups, so detailed they were almost analytical, as if the best way to appreciate beauty was to study it.

In 1957, when Ron Thompson was a junior at the University of Florida, Monsanto opened its House of the Future exhibit at the newly opened Disneyland. Often referred to as the House of Plastic, this spaceship-looking building seemed to float over a manicured landscape. It was made almost entirely of synthetic polymers: floors, walls, ceilings, windows, cabinets, countertops, furniture, even curtains. It was as if they pressed into maximum literalization Dupont's motto "Better Things for Better Living . . . Through Chemistry" (more commonly remembered as "Better Living Through Chemistry"). This exhibit in the Magic Kingdom embodied Americans' modern dream to surpass nature—or to think of nature itself as pliant. Though my father never saw this exhibit, he saw the future that it represented, aligned himself with its narrative of progress, and dreamed along with it of plastic possibilities. Our environment would be malleable and reliable, flexible and enduring. We could mold future homes to our visions, and they would last, floating germ-free above nature, washable and wipe-able, sterile as a hospital but multi-colored as a toy store. There was, as a character in the 1967 movie *The Graduate* would later say, "a great future in plastics."

Ron believed in this synthetic future. When he received his doctorate in 1962 (having researched "Electronic Interactions in Certain Vinylethers"), plastics were entrenched in American culture as mass consumer items. The young son he and his new wife doted on—my brother David—played with resins originally developed for combat, as plastics research gave way to postwar junk. A typical example: during the war, James Wright, attempting to make synthetic rubber, created a silicone-enhanced polymer, but when it failed to harden properly it was shelved. In 1949, the polydimthylsiloxane mixture was encased in synthetic eggs and launched just before Easter as Silly Putty.

An array of mass-marketed childhood toys followed in quick succession. In 1955 the first PEZ dispensers (offering such options as Santa and Mickey Mouse) hit the market. The next year, the plastic hula hoop, made by Wham-O, appeared in stores. Mattel launched that now iconic polymer, the Barbie doll, in 1959. By 1962 the Danish Lego company brought its primary-colored plastic bricks to U.S. stores.

This was the heyday of plastics' domestication. In 1946, Tupperware, with its burp of airtight contentment, began its long residence in American kitchens. Saran Wrap, which Dow Chemical marketed commercially in 1949 (after originally developing it as a spray to treat fighter planes), increased food longevity and helped the suburbs to sprawl farther from their food sources. Throughout the fifties, Americans learned to wrap, seal, and package their food against the germs that, like communists, lurked everywhere.

Medicine, too, recognized plastics' potential. Latex gloves (starting in 1964) greatly reduced infections in surgical settings, as did the disposable hypodermic syringe (1974). Oxygen pumps, infusion bags, inhalers—the impact of plastics on everyday medicine was phenomenal. It even became possible to imagine an artificial heart.

Legend has it that when the House of the Future was dismantled in 1966, it proved resilient against the wrecking ball, which merely bounced off its walls, and stubbornly resisted the hacks and handsaws to which the workers had to resort. But that was still in the future in 1963, when Ronald—with a wife, a son, a newborn daughter (me), and a promising job as a research chemist at a major chemical corporation—seemed to have achieved the American dream. With his hair now deepened to a chestnut brown, he looked so much like the newly elected JFK that he drew double-takes.

My childhood was very different from my father's: more comfortably middle-class, more suburban, and far more synthetic. Like that of many baby boomers in America, my world was Saran-Wrapped. As a baby, I sucked on a polymer pacifier and wore water-resistant diapers. I was well insulated.

As a child, I assembled Mr. Potato Heads and wobbled Weebles, while my brother marshaled his plastic green soldiers into formation. I wore press-free polyesters, including—in my purple phase—a stretchable plum pantsuit dotted with shiny yellow smiley faces. My father's work as a chemist sometimes came into our house. Dad brought home bubble-wrap to jump on and barrels of plastic popcorn to dive into. Just out of our reach above his garage workbench gleamed an array of mysterious brown glass bottles labeled with unpronounceable syllables. At one of my birthday parties, we played "guess the scent" by sniffing at glass bottles he'd brought home from the synthetic flavors division: butter, butterscotch, licorice, rum, banana, spearmint, peppermint, and cherry, all more mouth-watering than anything in nature.

My father's easy access to chloroform came in handy when we

went butterflying at the Forest Preserves. After Dad sprayed us with DEET, my brother and I set out with nets and jars stuffed with chloroform-soaked paper towels. We'd transfer the still-flapping insects into a jar, while trying not to inhale the powerful vapors. (Well, I, the obedient one, tried not to. My brother inhaled.) We watched as the slowing wings—which we learned to classify as monarch or admiral or swallowtail—came to rest. Later, my father, tongue pointing out the side of his mouth and quivering with concentration, pried open the butterflies' wings and mounted them on fiberglass-backed frames that hung on the wood-paneled family room walls next to the shelves lined with *National Geographics*.

Because of my brother's allergies, we couldn't get a family dog or cat, so David and I kept a series of reptiles (mostly his) and rodents (mostly mine). I especially loved the hamsters—Frisky, Fluffy, Teddy, Hamlet, and Piglet—with their squirmy noses and feeling whiskers, their relentless hoarding and burrowing and busyness, their delicate alienness. None of them seemed to last very long. The Habitrail hamster cage in my room expanded with each new hamster. A modular design of interlocking, translucent yellow plastic tubes connecting square rooms, some of which sprouted cylindrical towers, the Habitrail system approximated the "imagineered" House of the Future, scaled down to hamster size. In the sunlight, it glowed. Though it was nothing compared to today's rainbow of futuristic, space-ship-like modules, the 1970s Habitrail house modeled the dream of a perfect future. We could have nature without the dirt, the mess, and the microbes.

I couldn't figure out why the hamsters would want to escape, but they often found a way, usually at night. I woke my father to shine his flashlight into basement crevices until the rescue mission succeeded. Returning the captive to the safety of its plastic habitat, he regularly assured me that the hamster wouldn't last long in the wild and was far better off in the life of luxury we provided. But mostly the hamsters couldn't escape. Instead, they spun in circles. By day they rolled up and down the hallway in their translucent yellow acrylic ball. By night they reeled. I fell asleep nearly every evening of my childhood to the smell of cedar chips that permeated even my bedsheets and to the rhythms of one nocturnal hamster after another treading his red wheel. I'd dream of living in a golden plastic castle.

The first chink in my plastic world appeared when I was nine. It was the early seventies. Because I was cripplingly shy, my parents enrolled me in 4-H, where I could practice speaking before friendly audiences. I found that I loved making speeches and demonstrations, which turned out to have nothing to do with my social anxiety. For the speech competition I talked about blindness. I wrote it myself. "Good morning," my speech began. "Each of us has five senses. They are sight, sound, touch, smell, and taste." I had notecards and a poster of the Braille alphabet. I'd practiced for weeks. My audience smiled encouragingly, waiting for the thesis that never came to tie together my list of Braille trivia, then clapped politely at the end. My father winked at me.

The girl after me talked about environmentalist Rachel Carson and her nemesis, DDT, a powerful pesticide whose evils she was trying to alert the public to. "I *urge* you to take action," the girl said, with such impressive emphasis on the word *urge* that I stored this line away for use in future speeches. I knew she would win. She had a cause with a clear enemy: chemicals. "We *must* keep nature free of chemicals," she said, and I stored away that *must* with the *urge*.

"Everything's a chemical," my father mumbled next to me. "All of nature is made up of chemicals. Even water is a chemical."

When the speech was over, my mother whispered to me, "There's no way she wrote that speech herself. She should be disqualified."

In the car on the way home, I asked my parents, "Is it true about the bad chemicals?"

"People like to demonize chemicals," my mother said. "It's easy."

"Even the oxygen molecule is a chemical," my father said into the steering wheel.

But for the most part my own plastic bubble rolled along. I learned to be skeptical when people criticized the "chemicals" being put in food. "But food *is* chemicals," I learned to say. "Glucose, sucrose, citric acid, amino acids; they're all chemicals."

In high school, when I decided my college major would be chemistry, my father ordered me a T-shirt from the back of *Chemical & Engineering News*. Over a large flask containing a non-descript cloudy liquid were the words, in proud red and blue letters, CHEMISTS HAVE SOLUTIONS.

I did major in chemistry, following in my father's footsteps at the University of Florida in the early eighties. But (as with so much else in my life) I was better in the classroom than in the lab. On paper, molecular structures were neat maps into invisible worlds. I loved the reliability of valences and the cleanness of balanced equations. I loved working mechanisms, more fun than crossword puzzles. I loved having answers. But in lab I was a disaster. I either got 13% yields or, disproving the law of conservation of mass, 113% yields. Nothing about the system of flasks, tubes, and Bunsen burners, or the filtration and titration columns, was intuitive, at least not *in situ*. I was always the last to leave organic chem lab, which the poor grad student monitors must have resented, though they were always polite, with their soft rural-Southern accents, usually nerdy lab rats like my father.

One particularly wild-haired John Lennon look-alike mentioned casually one day that, statistically, organic chemists die young. I hadn't heard that before.

"Why?" I protested.

He shrugged. "We're around some pretty toxic stuff. Known carcinogens, for starters. Even if we're scrupulous about using the hood . . ." He shrugged again. Although he planned to be a career organic chemist, he had only a couple of years on my nineteen, and was therefore still immortal.

But I thought of my father, now in his fifties, and realized for the first time that he was going to die someday. In a wave of nausea, I remembered the slowing wings of the butterfly in a jar of chloroform-soaked paper towel. I needed air.

Not for the last time. With no air conditioning to counteract the Florida heat augmented by Bunsen burner flames in closed windows, the labs became stifling. I grew to dread them, and to develop headaches and nausea in their cage-like structures. In retrospect, I was probably affected by the acetone. Years later, when I had an office above a printmaking shop, I got the same waves of nausea, and the same urges to run for air.

But I suspect I was also somaticizing. By the mid-1980s, there was no denying that the dream of "better living through chemistry" came with costs, which were being documented and publicized despite the counter-campaigns of the chemical industries. The environmental movement alerted us to acid rain, the depleting ozone layer, air and water pollution, species extinction and the erosion of ecosystems and biodiversity. A range of artificially produced chemical compounds were proving to be toxic or carcinogenic, from food additives to petrochemicals to pesticides. (DDT was banned for residential uses soon after that 4-H talk, but other chemicals potentially as dangerous quickly replaced it.) Even when these products didn't seem toxic, their by-products might be.

To make matters worse, plasticizers—compounds added to plastics to make them more pliable (including phthalates, dioxins, and Bisphenol A)—were suspected of leaching out of the plastics and causing endocrine disruption in organisms. We would soon reach a point where nearly all Americans would have detectable levels of plastics or plasticizers in our urine. Ultimately, we were eating oil. Our plastic-eating, plastic-peeing bodies were getting heavier, more asthmatic, more cancerous, more prone to auto-immune diseases, and rife with symptoms of endocrine disruptor toxicity, such as lower sperm count and earlier onset puberty. We were beginning to doubt the promise of better living through chemistry.

Meanwhile, I endured long hours in the lab by bribing myself with a novel at the other end. I started taking English classes for balance. Then one day I came home from chem lab heaving and sobbing. I knew it was over. I ran for air by changing my major to English, enabling me to click away on my plastic keyboard all day long without ever having to set foot in lab or field.

My father, meanwhile, carried on in his cage-like lab, mixing toxins under the sterile hood day in and day out, as the daughters and sons of the plastics boom, whose comfortable lives he'd helped to enable, began—to his dismay—to vilify him.

Did my father feel betrayed when I rejected his world? It felt so, though he never said anything. In fact, as I turned to writing and teaching, he became my biggest fan, read everything I wrote, and became my guinea pig in trial runs for lesson plans. Unlike most people in the world, I never had to wonder if my father was proud of me. Instead, he once wished aloud that I could be proud of him. I reassured him that I was, but I suspect his doubts lingered.

There was never a big showdown in which our diverging ideologies had it out. Instead, as I forked to the left and he to the right, we developed an unstated mutual agreement. I wouldn't preach my new-found lefty ideologies, and he wouldn't press his conservatism, including a devout faith that chemistry brings progress, and that chemists have solutions. That way we could keep loving each other.

By the time I finished grad school and started my career, my father's was winding down. He was exhausted. His weekend naps, my mother told me, were getting longer and longer, until all his days consisted of work and recovery. My mother budgeted and re-budgeted until she found a way that Ron could take early retirement at sixty-two. He planned to spend mornings planting a garden and afternoons crafting model airplanes at his basement workbench. I was teaching in Canada then, so I didn't go to his retirement party. When the packet of reception photos arrived a few weeks later, I was surprised by how sunken my dad had gotten, how hunched and puffy. He'd gone from JFK to the late Ted Kennedy. My father's celluloid smiles, none of them what my mother called "the Ronnie smile," registered pained laughter rather than joy, as various co-workers in the background roasted and toasted him. The final photo showed my father, at the podium, wearing the horn-rimmed reading glasses that doubled as safety glasses. He held out a piece of paper, on which was surely written one of his "poims" (as he called them in his residual southern accent). He was legendary among colleagues for these occasional Ogden Nash–style riffs with inventively strained rhymes and offbeat punch lines. Preparing to read this final poem, his tongue pointed in anticipation out the side of his mouth. By now I no longer winced at this inveterate gesture, so much a part of his face. I might even have smiled—a smile he would never see now that the physical distance between us was even greater than the ideological one.

In the packet with the photos was a list of the patents and projects of Ronald E. Thompson. They included titles like "Polymetic Hindered Amine Light Stabilizers" and "Unsaturated Ester Group Terminated Polydienes as Unsaturated Polyester Modifiers." His final project, as best I could decipher, involved making plastics with shelf lives. I wish I'd asked him if, after spending most of his career making plastics more durable and stable against light and heat, it felt like a reversal to turn in his last years to developing plastics that were biodegradable. Did he hold fast to his faith in plastics to the end, or did he bend with the growing critique of his profession? By then, as perceived by the culture all around him, organic chemistry had moved so far from the chemistry of life that it had become almost the opposite: the chemistry of carbon-based polymers, whose monstrously long chains were increasingly cast as the stranglers of life.

My father did die relatively young, less than a year after taking early retirement. Leaving a pet store in the mall, he slumped over. My mother saw his frozen face and knew it was a stroke. He was rushed to the hospital and was given all the plastic-infused benefits of modern medicine. But they didn't save him. I got to his hospital bed just in time to say goodbye and thank him for being the great father that I'd never told him he was—and to apologize for my teenage years. I believe—I have to—that he heard and understood me, though he couldn't reply. He was sucking for life on a huge plastic apparatus, more elaborate than the array of flasks and tubes of the organic chemistry lab. I knew, of course, that all this elaborate tubing was keeping him alive. But to a nineteenth-century person plopped into the scene, even one of the early organic chemists—Leo Baekeland, perhaps, or Alexander Parkes—it might have looked like the opposite: that all that plastic—the rubber hoses, the infusion bags, the hypodermic syringes, the tapes and bandages—had risen up and engulfed him, that the tubular tentacles, like some surreal alien in a futuristic movie, were strangling him. When, long after he stopped breathing, they removed the oxygen tube and its paraphernalia, my father's lips were oddly contorted to mold themselves around the plastic mouthpiece. Frozen in death, they kept this shape. The tubing, spent, lay all around him, waiting for disposal.

Brendan Wolfe

STORIES FROM THE LOST NATION

MY FATHER GREW up fatherless in nearby Delmar. But his father's grandfather—who landed in Lost Nation, Iowa, after leaving Kerry in 1847 and who became, according to his esteemed son the judge, "one of the largest landholders and most successful farmers" in the area—*his* spirit seemed to whistle through these fields. The Wolfes of Lost Nation. For a hundred years they spread like quackgrass across the township, raising farms, crowding the rolls of the Democratic Party, and marrying McGinn girls, and McAndrews. And in the summer, their boys would tumble down the hill to play ball, including my dad's cousin Dave.

"He and Rich always seemed to find a game," Dad said, pointing toward St. Patrick's, which sat squat against a cornfield, looking bored. The diamond hid just behind.

We sat there in my rental car, and I imagined Dad trudging dusty miles into town, an infielder's glove tucked under his arm.

"It was easier for them," he said, "Rich and Dave. There were already two of them, and if nobody was around, why, they could climb right back up the hill. I, on the other hand—"

And the precision of his English hung there in the car for a second, searching for something to cut. He flipped the shades down over his glasses.

His father died of colon cancer when my dad was nine months old. There's a snapshot of the two of them, just weeks before the end—

Ray, in a dirty white button-down and farmer's suspenders, lying uncomfortably on his back, cradling tubby little Tommy against his knees, the baby sporting large, round sunglasses and a single shock of thin hair tufting up from his crown. Sixty-seven years later and Dad looks exactly the same, right down to the pinch of his lips. He was ironic even then.

Ray's death was appalling and slow, and when it was done, Gladys brought Pete Lassen in to work the farm, with occasional help from Dad's three older sisters. And when there wasn't work, there was ball.

"Swing the car around," he said. "Dave's farm isn't far from here. He still owns it, you know."

When the car left the paved road and hit gravel for the first time, it felt, a little unpleasantly, like we were floating.

"Did we pass it?" he said. I slowed down, but it's hard looking for something no longer there. The house was gone. The outbuildings were gone. The dumb cows and pissed-off roosters and the foggy chunk of dry ice I remembered fearing as a kid—they were gone, too. There was a brown cornfield, and it covered everything.

"That's the front gate there," he said. "Now pull over, will you? I need to whizz."

So I did, and he did. And I sat in the running car staring at my dad's backside and his too-baggy blue jeans, a sadness coming off his slumping frame like the fog that came off that dry ice. How, I wondered, could I have once been so terrified of this man?

The welt from a belt buckle, I guess. He apologized and never did it again, and when I think of being terrified of my dad, this is not what I think of. I think of Uncle Dave.

At the beginning of each summer, Dad insisted I get a job, something on top of the paper route, something to insulate me from the appearance of being lazy. So I would dutifully collect applications from nearby restaurants and grocery stores and then refuse to fill them out or return them.

"By the end of the week," he'd say, "or so help me."

And that was my cue to call Uncle Dave. He was always happy to subcontract a cornfield or two for detasseling. I hated detasseling—a task that involves tromping down mile-long rows in hundred-degree heat while reaching up and removing the plant's soft, pollen-producing tassel, one stalk at a time. Still, I returned year after year.

On one particular afternoon, I dried up and fainted. Uncle Dave was a half-mile away at least, oblivious between his Walkman speakers while I sprawled face down in the dirt. I remember the dirt up my nostrils, and the crickets, and the rash-like cuts on my arms from the cornstalks' sharpened leaves. And the sun. I remember the way it sucked the juice right out of me. What I remember most, though, is the smell: it was a dry, crackling smell I associate with bug-eaten leaves and clumps of sod in my hair. It's a smell that dries out as the day wears on and the sun climbs higher. It dries out the way that the fields dry out, the way that my morale dried up, and then my body. I remember thinking: *What the fuck am I doing?*

The answer was Uncle Dave. I would have followed him into the desert. Although he no longer worked his Lost Nation farm—instead, he taught algebra at the Catholic high school in Davenport—Uncle Dave still carted the farm around with him, its dirt lightly crusted over his entire personality. He was a big man, with blue eyes, lots of body hair, a competitive, tough-guy grip, and a bullhorn voice that always called me *honcho*. He wore Converse sneakers and denim cutoff shorts with loose white threads dangling in an uneven orbit around his legs. Like the beat-up, deep-throated Honda he drove, he gave the impression he might backfire and break down at any moment. He was tan, dirty, and constantly applying lip balm with the tip of his pinky finger. He was always sweating.

Where Dad was removed and opaque, Uncle Dave was aggressive. Uncle Dave was brutally sincere. Uncle Dave was an hour late to pick you up for your tenth straight day in the fields, and he was calling you *guy* and explaining between slurps of coffee that he had been stuck on the crapper. He was telling you what he had for breakfast.

And then he turns to your dad, towers over your dad, who's still wiping the sleep from his eyes, and only half jokes, "Tom, I've got a couple good acres for you. All you have to do is say the word."

And your dad—who's a few pounds overweight, who suffers from headaches and epilepsy and a bad back, who's in terrible shape—is forced to say, "No thanks."

Then one summer Uncle Dave was not around—busy with something else. So instead I boarded a rusted blue school bus each morning with high school boys who spit chew into Pepsi bottles. We worked the fields in teams of two, manning baskets attached to lumbering, diesel-powered tractors. We followed the same mile-long rows, only this time we didn't have to walk. Still, I hated it. I missed Uncle Dave. And while I zoned out to early R.E.M. on my headphones, the kid who shared my basket passed the time chucking freshly picked tassels at some other kid hanging from a tractor a few rows over. The sun rose. The sun sucked. And then our tractor abruptly stopped.

Our driver, a twenty-something dude who, inexplicably, wore an Italian bike racer's cap, marched down the row and commenced yelling at the kid in my basket.

"You're fired!" he screamed, citing some rule about not throwing tassels.

"You're a douchebag!" the kid screamed back, citing the bike racer's cap.

And the day ended with us talking tough in the parking lot.

First thing next morning, out of loyalty to the kid who had shared my basket but also out of disgust at the bike racer's cap, I picked a ripe, wet tassel and threw it, perfectly on target, at the driver's head.

I was fired on the spot.

No one was more surprised at this behavior than I. Generally speaking, I was terrified of authority, of belt buckles and accusations of laziness. I did what I was told, if only mostly. The principal of my elementary school, who happened to be supervising a crew in the next field over, must have sensed this, because he offered me a job with his boys, effective immediately. I imagined myself deliberately, almost thoughtfully spitting chew into a Pepsi bottle, after which I told him I could start day after tomorrow.

The next morning, then, there was no rusted blue school bus. There was just me in my PJS sitting in front of the TV when Dad finally came down the stairs and wondered what, exactly, I was doing.

Mom was at work. My sisters Bridget and Sara were off and occupied with lives of their own. It was just me and him, and you could hear the clock on the wall tick.

I nervously mentioned the first tassel, and the angry bike racer's cap, and then I mentioned the second tassel, which, in my telling, was something like a mighty blow struck for justice. I also mentioned the principal of my elementary school, who just happened to need someone to fill a spot on his crew—starting tomorrow.

Dad sighed. Dad swore. And Dad demanded I find a job until then.

"By the end of the day," he said, "or so help me."

"You're a douchebag!" I screamed, and burst out the front door in my pajamas and bare feet. I landed a few blocks away in Duck Creek Park, in a grove of black oak trees, seething with fear and anger and something else that had to do with the whole unseemly spectacle of it all: humiliation. The trees seemed friendly, though, and I hid out among them for the rest of the day. Eventually the sun started to droop, and what I remember most about that day is not my dad, but the absence of my dad.

When I finally came home, I made sure not to let the screen door slam.

We crunched the gravel of Route 136 east and I noticed, as I always do, the rolling, Grant Wood-ness of Clinton County. "Saying a place is flat," writes Patricia Hampl, "is another way of pretending it's simpler than it is." People who say that Iowa is flat are people just driving through or just visiting, people whose attention is focused on spotting I-80 speed traps or maybe getting a writing degree. For them, it is flat in the way that maps are flat—static and one-dimensional, outside of history. With only a map, they aren't in a position to see the hills like I do. They aren't in a position to notice the exaggerated way in which they bubble up from the earth like the Indian mounds I visited as a kid on the Mississippi, or like the ancient tumuli that pimple the Irish countryside: "The mound like a round / of earth pregnant / with fragments, bones," writes the Welsh poet Mike Jenkins.

"There," Dad said, pointing in the direction of a tidy, white farmhouse. We had just crossed Highway 61. "Pat fell off that silo there."

"Jesus."

Pat Farrell was Dad's best friend growing up. The image of his body diving helplessly toward the earth—that's been terrorizing me since I was little.

"Wasn't his father—"

"Eaten by sows. That's right," Dad said. "He was walking through the pen and he slipped." Then, employing that skeptical, history-teacher tone he spent thirty-five years in the classroom perfecting, he added: "Impossible to say if that's how he died. Who knows, he might have had a heart attack. Might have been dead before he hit the mud."

"Jesus."

Dad had clippers on his keychain and, as is his habit when he is nervous, he began snipping away at his nails. I slowed down in front of the Farrell place.

"Mom and I were once chased by a tornado down this road," he said. "It wasn't too big, really, but boy it was scary, and she was taking that old Ford about as fast as she could go."

Snip snip.

"Anyhow, we sped by the Farrells' here, and I remember catching a glimpse of Pat standing in the front door. His face—the look on his face was confused."

Chuckle, then *snip.*

"So?" I said.

"Oh," he said, "we made it home just fine. And after it passed, I went looking for damage. Couldn't find any, except for one narrow section of fence. It was like the twister had just tiptoed through."

Snip snip.

"Unbelievable," he said, with a hint of fear in his voice.

I grew up in Davenport, Iowa—a city, not a town, an honest-to-god city where cars honk and police sirens wail, where houses are robbed (although Mom says only Republicans lock their doors), and where, when I was a kid, a local chiropractor murdered his wife with a billiard ball, chainsawed her body into pieces, and threw the lot into the Mississippi River. I read about it in the papers I delivered, and yet Dr. James Klindt never struck me as unbelievable. What was unbelievable was the clammy outside twister-fueled emptiness of Clinton County.

My dad's Clinton County.

When I was six or seven, Dad moved out of his and Mom's bedroom and down the hall into mine. I, in turn, moved downstairs into the cold, wood-paneled, only partially finished basement, sleeping for months on the spiny fold-out couch next to the grumbling dehumidifier. I was scared of everything down there. I was especially scared of thunderstorms, which sounded to me like Soviet tanks rolling into Gomorrah. (Combine in a kid's head the Confraternity of Christian Doctrine, the Cold War, and frequent television images of nuclear annihilation, and I suppose that these are the sorts of metaphors you'll get.) On one particularly cloud-crossed night, Dad unhappily slipped on a pair of shorts and marched me back downstairs, out the back door, and into the back yard. We were both instantly bone-soaked, and the sky flared up like we were being bombed.

"See?" he said. "Nothing to be afraid of."

I might have started to cry.

Once inside again, he sat me down at the kitchen table to drip-dry. He grabbed a beer out of the fridge and started some hot chocolate. This had been what he referred to as "the Navy Way" of teaching, a term he insisted on using despite never having been in the navy. His father had joined, only to end up scrubbing decks Stateside during the Great War. Dad, on the other hand, because of his epilepsy, had been 4-F during Vietnam. Regardless, he knowingly termed any total-immersion, sink-or-swim method as the Navy Way, and more than once he threatened to use it in order to teach me how to swim. On this night, though, the Navy Way had accomplished little more than guaranteeing me a cold and a nervous tic. Dad, meanwhile, punched a hole in his can of Pabst and began telling stories about the farm. His stories were, to me, slightly menacing, like the bleating sheep at Uncle Dave's. They were full of chores and being outside. He once told about how, on an evening when the rest of the family was out, his older sister Mary K threw open the front door, spread some fake blood around, and pretended she had been hacked to death.

"You shouldn't have left the door unlocked," she protested to her trembling mother.

This is the sort of Capote-like vision I carried around of life on the farm.

On this night he told me another story, this one about a thunderstorm. He described the wind and the way it swept over the county like the back of God's hand. "Nothing to stop it," he said.

Because his own father had died, it was Dad's job, come morning, to check on the downed power lines. "I picked up just the one," he said.

And here—after a meaningful silence punctuated by a long slurp of his beer—Dad delivered up the first piece of advice I can ever recall receiving. He said: "Never test a wire with your palm."

And that was it.

He had picked up that wire and been savagely electrocuted. He had picked it up palm down, so that the surging current forced his fingers into a tight fist he couldn't for the life of him release. He was forced to wait until Mary K noticed him missing, shut down the power, and called for a doctor.

I sat there wet and wild-eyed, Dad's fist glowing in my brain like a mushroom cloud. The doctors speculated that this incident might have been the cause of his epilepsy, and for the first time I began to understand why he carried a pill case in his shirt pocket. I remember the familiar noise it made when he walked and the expert way his thick hands pried it open—the way he regularly popped several tablets at a time into his puckered mouth, sans water.

These, of course, are just stories. There's a whole subset of stories about Uncle Dave—not surprisingly, they're known in the family as "Uncle Dave stories"—my favorite of which has him visiting his in-laws in Pasadena, California. A combination of boredom and alarm over his wife's credit card use drives Uncle Dave through the doors of a local temp agency and he ends up working a factory job for the balance of his trip. That's Uncle Dave. My dad, on the other hand, is more difficult to pin down. This is how he prefers it, I think. One of his favorite phrases is "none of your business," although there's more to it than that. To have a conversation with him is like playing tennis with someone who, instead of volleying the ball back to you, catches it, turns it around in his hand, and then stuffs it in his pocket.

You stand there flummoxed.

"I just finished a book you'd like," you might say. "It's about Sherman's March."

A short silence. Then: "I've been leafleting for a friend of mine who's running for state senate. She's a nice enough lady, but over the weekend she attacked her opponent, which is bad enough. I *detest* negative advertising. But this attack was personal. Really beyond the pale. So I rounded up all the literature she had given me to distribute, even took my yard sign down, and I drove it all straight down to her headquarters. Then I wrote a letter to the paper telling her that her strategy stinks and may very well backfire, and if it does, she would richly deserve it."

To which you might respond: "Wow."

"I haven't heard anything from her since."

"Are you still going to vote for her?"

"None of your business."

I never know quite where I stand in stories such as these. There is always something missing. In an earlier draft of this essay, I wrote that "I imagined the ghost of my dad trudging dusty miles" into Lost Nation, but for obvious reasons, that didn't make sense. I wasn't imagining a ghost; I was imagining my dad. Maybe, though, there has always been something of the ghost about him, the way he eludes me.

Which is why I turn to stories in the first place.

Stories are like maps. They are the opposite of flat. They are like the hills of Clinton County, to be climbed in your shiny blue rental car on a rare trip home, so that you can see for miles, across a brownish-yellow quilt of corn and the silhouettes of silos. These people who say that Iowa is flat—*How could you have lived in a place without any hills?*—they must be thinking of Nebraska. Iowa isn't flat, it's open. What makes it seem flat, though, is the way you can drive and feel the openness surround you, wrap around you, almost crowd you. I always feel more comfortable once we climb the hill. From above I can see where things go.

Up here, I know where I stand.

Take that story about detasseling. Not until I started writing did I realize that it was a story about courage and cowardice. When I was a kid, my parents sometimes babysat my cousins Kate and John. They were hellions, those two. They ran around grass-stained and barefoot and paid zero attention to my dad's rules. My dad yelled and yelled and they just laughed and laughed. Not until many years later, as my mom dragged on a Marlboro and remembered those days like a dirty joke, did it occur to me how such behavior placed in stark relief my own absolute compliance. Put another way: I hit that dude with a ripe wet tassel. I did it on purpose, and in my world that was an act of courage. Of course, the story ends in cowardice, with me—fifteen years old, for crying out loud—hiding in the woods. I may have been barefoot, but I was no Kate or John.

And how did my dad spend that day? He could have come looking, I suppose, or he could have turned on the Cubs. Rick Sutcliffe might have been starting that afternoon, with Jody Davis behind the plate. Sutcliffe was so deliberate on the mound, you honestly could get up and grab another beer from the fridge between his pitches. Is that what Dad did? I don't know. The story doesn't say.

Like a good map, though, it does begin to connect the dots: Fear is everywhere, but it doesn't just separate us. It binds us, like in the biblical story.

Fist, wire. Father, son.

Not all of it's true, obviously. Or at least it's obvious to me. No story can be all true, and few stories, for that matter, are all lies.

I never called my dad a douchebag. No doubt I *wanted* to call him a douchebag, but I'm not sure that I've ever actually sworn around him, let alone at him. The reverse, I'm pretty sure, is also true. When annoyed, he might go so far as to say "fiddlesticks."

But maybe this kind of lie serves a different kind of truth—a story-truth where courage and cowardice strike together and cast a spark. It seemed true for a moment, and it helped to feed the ghost.

So what *did* I say to him?

None of your business.

In his 1998 collection of essays, *The Lie of the Land,* the Irish journalist Fintan O'Toole directs his readers to *The Fractal Geometry of Nature* (1982), a complex and theoretical work in which the Polish-French-American mathematician Benoit Mandelbrot asks a seemingly simple question: "How long is the coast of Britain?" The closer one investigates this question, however, the less simple it becomes.

"The coast is obviously not smooth and regular," O'Toole writes.

> It goes in and out in bays and estuaries and promontories and capes. If you measure it at one hundred miles to an inch, all of these irregularities appear. But if you measure it at twenty miles to an inch, new bays open up on the coastlines of promontories and new promontories jut out from the sides of bays.

> When you measure these as well, the coastline gets longer. At a mile to an inch it is even longer . . . and so on, until you crawl around on your hands and knees measuring the bumps on the side of each rock that makes up the coast. The more accurately you measure it, the more uncertain it becomes.

The truth of my family is different when I coast down off the hill. The bumps begin to add up. This is country where it is easy to get lost, even for my dad and my aunts, for people who grew up here and whose people once settled here. I once rode in the car with Dad and Mary K on a trip back—this was just a couple years before Mary K died, and her hair was white and Einstein-ish and her grin typically elvish; nobody could ever giggle with more high-pitched ambiguity than Mary K—and they spent the entire fifty-minute ride debating the efficacy of various routes to and fro, although "debate" is the wrong word. They weren't arguing; this was more a ritual, a mapping out of Clinton County in conversation the way that Joyce is said to have mapped out Dublin in *Ulysses.*

"You always took the Such-and-Such Road, didn't you?"

"Oh no"—and that voice of hers would dance up two or three octaves—"goodness no. Now, Tom, the only way to get to So-and-So's was to take That Other Road."

"But didn't That Other Road go west?"

"Did it?"

And so on, with rhetorical stops in DeWitt, Delmar, and Maquoketa. In Toronto and Lost Nation, Petersville, and Charlotte—pronounced shar-LOT. When Dad turned off 61 to find the "old homestead," as he likes to put it, there was the obligatory mention of Mr. McClimon, that cigar-chomping Irish farmer who, back in 1926 or thereabouts, refused to sell his land to the government, which was trying to extend the highway. The line on the map was forced to loop around him.

And the conversation also began to loop, confusing even Dad and Mary K. It was as if the geography of Clinton County refused to sit still for them. On another trip back, a few years earlier, we actually did get lost, hopelessly lost. We were headed for a McGinn family reunion at the home of Father Ed Botkin, another of Dad's cousins, and we ended up stopping at a Casey's for gas and advice. My aunt and uncle and two cars full of cousins happened to pull in at the same time, retreating from the opposite direction. We hadn't planned it, but we became a caravan and were all lost together.

Stories are like maps. They are the opposite of simple. As Mandelbrot suggested, the more carefully you study them—zooming in on perfectly straight lines until they begin to waver and then finally to squiggle—the less they're able to perform their original function.

They don't answer questions; they only ask them.

Here, for instance, is a story from thirty thousand feet: Ray Wolfe, a Lost Nation farmer, finds himself smitten with young, black-haired Gladys McGinn. He is so smitten, in fact, that in his hurry to ride over to see her, he's willing, literally, to cut through his neighbors' wire fences.

Now here's the same story, only how my dad the history teacher tells it:

> My parents first met, I believe, at a dance in DeWitt. According to my Uncle Dan McGinn, one of Mom's older brothers and a man who loved to talk but was not above embellishing a story if it pleased him, Dad would ride his horse to Petersville to see Mom, sometimes taking shortcuts through fields by cutting the fence wires (a detail I really find hard to accept). In those days, it wasn't all that easy to get around. Henry Ford's Model T was popular, but the roads were terrible, a family would have only one car, and the car would often be jacked up with the tires removed during the long winter months. That's why Dad probably did ride his horse to see her, but I don't know about that wire cutting story.

That was from a letter Dad wrote to my cousin Mary Katherine sometime after her mother, Mary K, died. She had asked him for some stories, and he e-mailed his response to all fourteen of us first cousins. "I've been meaning to respond to your note for a long time now," he began, "but I've found it hard to do—largely, I think, because it's hard to write about Mom, and I never knew Dad. I'll give it a try though." And he does, and it's poignant in a way that is poignant for someone who has of his dad only stories—not even stories, but skeletons of stories—to then interrogate them until they crumble at his feet.

What has he now?

Anyway, it's not clear what about the wire-cutting story Dad doesn't accept. He explains why it's plausible for Ray to have visited Gladys on horseback, and in the process he gives us mud-slogged winter roads and jacked-up Model Ts. (Those cars are so much more vivid here than Ray.) But as for what makes the wire cutting implausible, he doesn't say. Perhaps he has heard other stories that contradict the notion of his father as a petty vandal or an overly enthusiastic suitor. Or, as he seems to suggest, perhaps he's reacting not to his father but to Uncle Dan, an Irish-born bullshitter and well-to-do farmer who paid for my dad's college education. I imagine Uncle Dan was something of a father figure to Dad, and he may have been disappointed when Dad didn't return from St. Ambrose to take over the farm. (I know that some of Dad's other uncles felt that way and perhaps Uncle Dan did, too.) And now maybe Dad is disappointed—or even angry; I don't think I'm crazy to sense anger here—that Uncle Dan is playing the bullshitter again.

Quit telling stories, I imagine my dad saying.

Fiddlesticks.

Snip snip.

So it is with my family. In 1911, my great-great uncle Patrick B. Wolfe, a politician and district court judge and the first Wolfe born in America, published two thick, solemn-looking volumes titled *Wolfe's History of Clinton County*. In 1975, my dad carefully typed up and photocopied his own twelve-page treatise, "Origin of the Species, or Whatever Happened to Old What's-His-Name?" Both documents, as far as I can tell, are heavily larded with lies, half-truths, and humorous untruths. In introducing his older brother, for instance, Judge Wolfe goes on about the "Emerald Isle, far-famed in song and story," while my dad quips that one ought to "picture a choir of angels with trumpets blaring" when reading such prose. Dad then goes on to suggest that Judge Wolfe's father was a horse thief and that Dad's own grandfather was a Marxist who "attended his agrarian pursuits in spurts which he called 'five year plans.' His favorite tools were the hammer and sickle."

About Ray he writes:

> He joined the Navy in World War I. He caught no Germans, but he did catch the flu. In 1925 he caught Gladys McGinn of Petersville. (She was only twenty-two at the time, but that didn't stop her from continually telling her own children that no one with a grain of sense marries under thirty. To gently remind her of her own age in 1925 only brought about a foot stomping and the response, "That was different.")

On a recent Saturday, I spent about an hour digging through cardboard boxes to find a copy of this piece, which I've always loved and about which my dad, who typed it up for a family reunion, now feels embarrassed. "It was too flip," he says. "I was reading a lot of Richard Armour back then. I don't think everyone got the joke." What I found instead was an old black-and-white family portrait of Gladys and Ray with her parents, John and Kathrine, and her innumerable siblings, in-laws, nieces, and nephews, all assembled on the front porch of the McGinn family home in Petersville. Snot-nosed Mary K is right up front, picking her teeth, while Gladys stands just to the right of her mother—mischievous-looking and pencil-shaped, with a V-neck dress and a severe part in her hair. Ray, meanwhile, is mostly hidden. He's behind and to the right, his face round, his head mostly bald. I can see just enough of him to see my father. Any more, I think, and the resemblance would be lost.

—

Scratch that. Dad wasn't angry at Uncle Dan for playing the bullshitter again. After all, he could have accepted that story prima facie. He could have accepted it as a gift in the way he accepted, for instance, his college tuition. But he didn't. (Just as he didn't—and I don't think it's crazy to sense a parallel here—accept his uncles' invitation to return to the farm.) I think that perhaps there was something too frightening about the opportunity to know his dad, even a little bit. Perhaps he just couldn't bear to imagine Ray elbowing his way out of the back of that black-and-white crowd of in-laws and down the porch steps, past Mary K in her Sunday best—his wire clippers firmly in hand.

Tommy! he might say, and look his son square in the eye.

But here's another problem: this isn't really my dirt and it's not my land.

I wrote that line during graduate school, as part of an essay titled "Lost in Clinton County." It was well received—the essay, I mean—in County Cork of all places, but the reaction back home was more ambiguous. At a very writerly soirée she was hosting, a classmate of mine put her hand on my shoulder and, with an exaggerated smile, told me she loved it.

Just *loved* it.

As this was the sort of gathering where we nibbled on Bûche de Chèvre and spoke admiringly of Barthes, I assumed she was making fun of me. What I had meant to say in the essay was that my father and the landscape had conflated: I knew them both, and I absolutely didn't know them. It's possible, I suppose, that she understood this, even appreciated it. But my advisor had just e-mailed to say that my ambitious, book-length expansion of "Lost" was dead on arrival. "You don't have a thesis here, in my view," she wrote. "There's no development of thought or feeling that I can perceive." In the meantime, someone also had accused me (briefly) of lifting the bit about detasseling.

I was insecure, in other words.

Can I claim the land? *I can't even claim my own stories!*

It had been four years since my dad left a note on the kitchen table for Mom to find the next morning. It contained his new address and phone number and that was all.

Earlier that summer, Mom had driven to Iowa City. It was the summer of the Great Flood, of storms that seemed to have no beginning and no end.

"He's been drinking again," she whispered. "Really going at it this time." She pulled another cigarette from her purse.

"You're going to have to talk to him."

"Oh, I got him good just a couple of days ago." She took a full drag, and I could hear the soft burn of the tobacco. "He didn't come home until past one-thirty. And when he tried to stumble through the dining room, he broke one of my antique lamps. Can you believe that man? I just screamed at him."

Inhale.

"Oh, I got him good. I took all of his liquor from the cabinet and put it on the counter next to a note that said, 'Here, really go to it this time.'"

Exhale.

For weeks after he left, his friends—colleagues he saw every day at school—continued to call the house and ask for him.

"He's not here," she would say. But it was in vain. It was as if he *were* still there, lounging in his favorite living-room chair. Grading papers. Watching the Cubs.

When they kept calling, she just hung up on them.

Then, four years later, just before Christmas and a few months after that writerly soirée, Dad suffered a massive heart attack while running to make a connection in the St. Louis airport. It was perfect in a way: he was neither here nor there. Instead, he was entubed and oxygenated and surrounded by various blinking, bleeping machines, deep inside the awful nowhereness of some local hospital. When my sister Bridget and I first arrived, he was white and his eyes were closed. Bridget was an army officer and a nurse not far removed from duty in Bosnia; her default was alpha. She immediately began ordering people around and consulting with the ICU doctors about the possibility of delirium tremens. They talked about another surgery. And I stood in the corner watching.

So much came rushing into my mind right then, all of it beginning to take order. The tassel and the trees. So help me. The belt buckle. And I remembered how a year earlier, Aunt Sara, my dad's oldest sister, had invited us to Christmas dinner. She was always willing to take him in when no one else would, and we spent that evening drinking whiskey and beer and wine and carving through her famous prime rib.

"Tell me about your dad," I said, and my cousin Kate, this time wearing shoes, kicked me under the table. But Sara, who by now was drunk, began to talk. She was fourteen when he began to die, and eventually they put him up in the attic.

"He smelled like rotting fish," she said.

One day they came and pulled her out of school. It must have been a highly dramatic moment, leaving the building like that in the middle of the day, all of her friends watching. Fifty-six years later and there were still tears.

Now, here was *my* dramatic moment. As I stood in the corner watching, as no-nonsense Bridget walked through the survival percentages with men in blue scrubs, I was tempted to mourn. I was tempted—but I didn't. Instead, I began to read this scene as though it were in the pages of my writing. It was a habit I had cultivated over the years—living my life through the filter of my words.

Here is my dad, I thought. And here are the tubes.

This was the development my thesis required.

I imagined two equally plausible storylines unfolding. Dad lives, and we bundle him into the car and drive him home to his one-bedroom with its library books, pizza boxes, and laminated "Poblacht Na hÉireann" poster taped to the wall. Uncle Dave calls regularly and I run to the store on weekends. Or, alternatively, Dad dies, and we bundle him into the car and drive him to Clinton County, where

Father Ed Botkin intones "the Lamb of God" so that his breath hangs in the air, frozen. Kate pours me another glass of Jameson's and Uncle Dave, in a dark suit, grips my hand.

Of course, something's always missing in stories like these. You don't know where you stand. You hear only the faint bleeps of machines coming from far out of nowhere. But here's another problem: this isn't really my life and it's not my story. What's missing is me.

And my dad.

Now here's a true story:

After passing the Farrells', we continued on to Delmar, population 520. We passed the tiny jail of rough-hewn stone and bars on the door, and we passed the infamous front-lawn tree stump that must be four to five feet in diameter. Then, after doubling back on 136, we arrived at St. Patrick's, the town's Catholic cemetery. Dad takes me here every time I'm home; it's part of what Bridget calls the Cemetery Tour.

As in, "Oh Christ. The cemeteries again. Brendan, our family is obsessed with death."

Which is true. When Dad and Mary K weren't mapping out the roads of Clinton County, they were discussing who had died, or who was about to. They were either going to a funeral or coming from one. They were planning the next tour. At my wedding reception, the cousins huddled around a cell phone and called Mary K, who was too sick to attend. Kate, dressed in black, took a gulp of her beer and shouted, "Mary K, I'm wearing the dress I bought for your funeral!"

Mary K giggled.

A few weeks later, she was lying in bed reading the obituary page when she called out to Uncle John. She had found a photo of a woman whose hair was also Einstein-ish, whose grin was also elvish.

"I'm already dead!" she said, and days later it was true.

I turned left and onto the dirt path that wended through St. Patrick's. Dad grabbed his jacket from the backseat and set off at an amble, into a field of names.

Foley Flatley Dolan Shea Costello Quinlan Lassen Schrader Hanrahan Strutzel O'Meara McMullen Goodall Grandick McMeel Reilly McMahan Norton McAuley Fitzpatrick Rotzpatrick McClimon Donahue Burke Callahan Farrell—

"Over here," Dad said.

—*McGinn Wolfe.*

In an elegant row stood the headstones of his people: grandparents John and Kathrine, parents Ray and Gladys, sister Sara. And there, just in front of the stones, was an additional, rectangular marker, low to the ground; it read "Thomas A. Wolfe."

Dad knelt down to brush some leaves off of it and struggled to regain his feet.

"Help me back up, will you?" he said, and I grabbed his arm.

For a moment he felt real.

Debra Gwartney

WHEN HE FALLS OFF A HORSE

IN THE MIDDLE of a night long ago, my sister Cindy called me at my home in Arizona to tell me that our father had been crushed by a horse. She meant what she said: most of his vertebral column had turned to rubble. A lung was punctured; his spleen burst. Then Cindy told me doctors had informed her and other family members gathered at the Boise hospital that he probably wouldn't survive the surgery, ongoing as I pressed the phone to my hot ear.

After I hung up I stood on the tile floor of our living room. I didn't switch on a lamp, as light might have made the news more fact than rumor. I leaned against an armchair and let myself feel alone, abandoned even. In some ways, that's where I stayed and for a long time—in the dark, too scared to consider what it would mean to lose a father with whom I exchange maybe three or four sentences a year. It seems it would be easier to lose a parent you don't know well, and who doesn't know you, but in fact the prospect of his passing sent a terror through me—I'd believed that someday he would soften, he would turn nice. He would undergo one of those fairy-tale transformations that would bring to my doorstep the father I thought I deserved.

I stayed up the rest of the night, packing quietly so I didn't wake my four children, my then-husband groaning at me from the bed, telling me I should get some sleep. I didn't seek comfort from this man I'd been married to for twelve years. We were ground to nubs by then, tolerating each other's presence for the sake of our kids, or maybe lulled into the torpor that comes from waiting for the other one to say: it's over. That night, I stuffed a bag with clothes and books; I paced our kitchen and pinged the caps off bottles of beer, drinking in long swigs. I sent mind messages to my father, as if he could pick up my thoughts from hundreds of miles away, as if he ever had. I asked him to stay alive until I got there and could sort things out with him. What there was to sort out, I wasn't quite sure, but it seemed like certain words should be said between us.

At least he could give me that.

At dawn, I started phoning airlines—this was 1990, there was no Internet—to get my ticket to Boise, although when I spoke to her later in the morning, my father's wife encouraged me not to come. He'd survived the twelve-hour surgery, but he was unconscious and in terrible shape. What good could I do in Idaho? There was nothing now but the waiting. I told her that I certainly did not plan to wait in Tucson, where we had moved a year earlier for my graduate program and so my husband could live closer to his family. If I had to wait for my father to resurface, if he was to resurface, I'd be in the ICU ward, along with my two sisters and two brothers. Hovering.

Though I hadn't taken a poll on such matters, I believe I can say that none of us knew whether he liked being our father or if he'd spent his adulthood regretting the backseat tryst with our mother when he was a sophomore in high school, fifteen years old, that led to my birth and to three quick subsequent births, leaving him with four children by his twenty-first birthday. Even as a girl, I'd anticipated his approval. And when I say "anticipated," I mean pretty much ached for a sign that I'd done okay in some regard, that he didn't consider me an embarrassment or a failure. I don't expect he liked being saddled with a child when he was a still a child himself, but I imagined a peace that would fall over me, light and airy, if he said he wasn't sorry I was around.

My father, by the time of this accident, which occurred when he was forty-eight and I was thirty-two, was a wealthy man. He'd climbed right up a 1970s corporate ladder; along the way, he'd shipped himself off to get a degree at Harvard. After we were grown, my mother divorced him, and he married a well-to-do socialite, started palling about with the influential, such as there were in our little state. The few times he invited me to go along to, say, a bank board meeting or a political function—there I was, all young and thin, dressed up with my long blonde hair pinned on my head—he introduced me to others by saying his wife hadn't been able to come and that he'd found me out on the street and asked me to be his date. My part was to look irritated at this. "Actually, I'm his daughter," I'd say while my dad stood by, grinning at people's awkward confusion. I looked too old to be his child, and yet I didn't appear—at least I don't think so—hooker-like enough for his story to make sense. I sometimes mentioned I had a bunch of daughters of my own. "Mike has grandchildren?" I remember one man asking. "All these years, I didn't even know he had kids."

With mid-life money, a fancy marriage, and new friendships, particularly one with a man named Skip, my father decided to reclaim a few youthful prospects. One of those was to be a rodeo cowboy. My father was, and continues to be, a wonder on a horse, a skill he'd honed as a boy. He and his father often ventured on weeks-long pack trips, deep enough in the Idaho wilderness that they saw not one other human being—days of riding in silence except for the squeak of saddles and the rustle of brush. That's my image of their journeys, anyway. Horse hooves sparking off loose rock as one man follows the other into a distant ravine. My father has a way of merely standing next to a horse that makes the creature behave, its ears pricked for the master's growled commands. Dad slides up on the saddle, one smooth movement, ticks the reins in his hand, and off they go.

In the spring of 1990, my father and Skip bought a huge tract of land along the Boise River. Fans of the novel, they called their new place Lonesome Dove, and they had a replica of the little town built—the Dry Bean Saloon, the Livery Emporium. In the center was a rodeo arena surrounded by shiny bleachers. Dad and Skip, who now often called each other Cap and Gus, invited riders from local colleges to hold competitions there, and they showed up to be part of the rodeos themselves. During the second one—fortuitous for my father, since the recently churned-up ground was not yet pounded hard as steel—my dad volunteered to act as flagger for a cutting competition. It was never explained to me why he rode a strange horse that day rather than one of his own. This horse wasn't used to the rider's gruff voice or his jabs, nor was my dad accustomed to a nervous horse. My father had wrapped the reins around his right wrist so that he could manage the flags, but what he hadn't counted on was the horse fidgeting under him, pulling and yanking. The horse half-collapsed onto his back legs just as my father was reaching forward to take the bridle and settle things down. At least this is the story I've managed to compile; my father has not recited an account of that day within my hearing. I doubt he's spoken his version to anyone. What I understand, though, is that their heads collided, man and horse, and that my father was knocked out, seeing stars, falling backward with those reins still tight around his arm, pulling the nine-hundred-pound horse over on top of him.

It happened that a paramedic driving home had, an hour or so earlier, noticed the rodeo and turned in to watch the action on the sawdust. He was the one up from his seat and hopping the fence by the time others had rolled the horse off its rider. The paramedic used CPR to get my father's heart restarted, and then Dad opened his eyes. "The truck keys are in my pocket" was all he said, and then he went back under.

When I entered the room up in the ICU—way up, the top floor of the hospital, with windows that overlooked the parched valley—my thought was that my father looked like a turkey stuffed for the oven.

His body was the pale hue of raw meat; he was swollen into a mound while tubes of various colors sprang from his skin and dripped into containers hanging from the rungs of the bed.

I stood over him that first afternoon, curious if he still had an eye under the glob of grape pudding between his nose and left ear. I thought about poking his puffed-out flesh, oddly soft, but I didn't. I wandered back into the dim hallway and met with the doctor, who stood scribbling notes on a chart. He seemed more gleeful than concerned about my father's condition, which I suppose was a relief. He told me that he planned to cart X-rays around to medical conventions so others could get a load of this case. "You know, when he came in," the doctor said conspiratorially, "he was bent in half the wrong way."

The difficulty for this surgeon, and for any medical facility in Idaho, was in deciding what to do next. When they'd opened him up stem to stern—and he has the riverine scar down his back to prove it—the team of surgeons found rubble, each of the twelve vertebrae of his thoracic curve and several of the lumbar vertebrae turned to dust. The surgeons mopped up the mess around the exposed spinal cord, repaired the damaged organs as they could, and sewed him together. This meant that our main job—my sisters, brothers, and me—was to make sure he didn't move, this man who rarely stopped moving. We mostly watched him sleep, if *sleep* is the right term for being that unplugged. Every fifteen minutes we'd hold the edges of the sheepskin under him, and we'd slide our father a quarter of an inch to prevent oozing pressure sores from breaking open on his backside. Other than regularly punching the morphine button, though we'd been strictly warned not to, we sat in chairs, watched bad TV, caught each other up, and we waited.

A week was what I felt I could spare: I had four children, classes, work. A marriage that, splintered as it was, had yet to finally break. A week should be enough to be certain he'd live. He might revive a bit; maybe a few words would come from him about his relief at having made it through. Even a couple of squeezes of the hand to let me know he was glad I was there. I settled in my chair, next to his bed, in case any of those things happened.

The third day of my vigil he began a kind of muttering that none of us could make sense of. I got up and bent close enough that his drug-laden breath was sticky on my face. I noticed gray grit in his hair from the fall, a bruised ear lobe. I leaned closer and realized that he believed he'd been tied to a tree, left there to die. "Just get it the hell over with," he said, "and hurry up about it." I stood and punched the button twice to flush him with what he'd soon start to call his feel-good juice. I didn't think about saying a few soothing words or rubbing his arm in comfort. I simply wanted to stop that unsettling talk. I hadn't been lingering near his bedside to hear anything like that.

The third afternoon is also when my grandfather arrived. I don't remember that Grandpa said anything to the rest of us in the room, although he must have. What the old man did was to pull a chair up to his son's bed. He didn't read or watch sports but simply sipped coffee and sat there, a man who objected mightily to the sitters of the world. He wore a buckskin vest that he'd had made by a Shoshone woman who lived near my grandfather's, and father's, hometown of Salmon. Hand-beaded red vines decorated the front panels, and she'd used cross sections of antler for the buttons. The next time I saw that vest was twenty-two years later—my father wore it on the day we spread Grandpa's ashes at our family hunting camp. On this day in the hospital, Grandpa crossed his legs, drank more coffee from a Styrofoam cup, and, now and again, reached over to pull a wire away from my father's face. He didn't appear particularly worried or sad, nor did he beg my father for a reaction to his presence or seem to expect much of anything. He was there, that was all, and I envied his calm, which I could not manage to find in myself.

On the sixth day, our grandfather, having been assured that his son would survive, packed up and returned to Salmon. I, too, felt eased off the life-death ledge, and, as much as I didn't want to miss a pronouncement, I needed a hot shower, a few glasses of wine, and a walk. While Cindy and I lounged in her backyard with gin instead of wine, she answered a phone call from our sister. "What happened?" I said when she hung up, and Cindy told me that our father had, in our absence, perked up, achieving his most lucid state yet. He'd opened his good eye, looked over the room, asked for water, and, though he'd been having trouble figuring out who was around him, he now recognized our sister, calling her by name. "I guess he started talking about all kinds of things," Cindy said, rubbing her face before she took another drink. "And, you're not going to believe this, but he told Becky that he loved her."

Love? This was not a word our father used. He'd not spoken it in my presence, anyway, not once, and I had known him the longest of the five of us. I remember a letter he wrote us one time when he was at Harvard—he'd gone there when I was thirteen—that was signed, "Love, Dad." We all stared at the paper back then, at the gushing that was not his way. But this? I was jealous, yes, but dread stirred in me as well. It felt too late and too strange to bring this word into our family, and I suddenly wanted my father to take it back. Cindy and I were quiet for a few seconds. "Are you sure?" I said. "Maybe she didn't hear him right?"

My sister shrugged and got up to check on the chicken in her oven. She stopped in the doorway and turned toward me. "You think this is going to change him," she said, "but it's not."

I didn't try to explain my muddled mind—I didn't tell her that by then the fear of him becoming a different man had become every bit as potent as the fear that he would stay who he'd always been.

I ended up being the only one in his room on my last night in Boise. I don't recall twisting my siblings' arms to give me this time, though I likely emanated the message that I ought to have a shot at his affection, wary as I was of that very thing now. Cindy lived in town, she'd have other chances, and Becky had gotten what she came for. Well, she'd gotten what I thought I'd come for, anyway: that Friday evening before my Saturday morning flight, I was no longer sure what I was after. I coaxed Dad to eat a few bites of Jell-O and scooted the sheepskin under his back. He asked about my children and my husband, and I mumbled a few words about the sour state of my marriage. He sipped water from a straw and I wiped up the dribbles on his chin, and then he opened his mouth as if he were going to offer advice. I pushed back in my chair, concerned he was about to insist on a plan for me that I wasn't ready to execute. He might tell me to go home, pack up and get out, and later call me chicken for not doing precisely what he'd said to.

Before he could get such words out, I hurried to find him a movie on TV, and, miraculously, I came upon an old John Wayne film that Dad could slide in and out of without losing track of a plot.

"You know what I'd like?" my father said then, distracted just enough from the topic of my doomed marriage. "A cup of hot chocolate. That sounds like about the best thing right now."

"I'll find you one," I said, thrilled by the unfraught nature of the request. I grabbed my purse and hurried down the hall. The nurse at the station thought there was a machine a few floors down. I found it and dumped in my quarters, and a thin stream of cloying brown liquid, piping hot, dribbled into a cup. I popped on a lid and headed back to my father's room, the drink burning my palm. I was determined to spill not a drop. A western movie with themes of conquest and heroism he delighted in, and now a treat he'd been yearning for: I beamed with the satisfaction of satisfying him, rushing to his bedside to reap my reward. And yet when I reached his door, I stopped, a twang of that dread—there it was again—keeping me from entering.

Here's what I couldn't let myself think of in that moment: how, in giving up on my marriage, I had hardened my heart toward my husband. I had begun to consider the man I'd married weak for his steady declarations of affection and silly for the tears that came up in his eyes during the most bitter of our arguments. I was afraid if the man in the hospital room did the same, if he expressed love or, God forbid, if he cried, he would be a stranger and no longer the man who could help get me out of the old life and into a new one.

I walked into the room after a few seconds to find my father asleep, the low drone of John Wayne's voice buzzing about the room. I put the hot chocolate on the table and settled into the chair that my grandfather had occupied earlier, pulling a blanket up to my chin in a mix of relief and disappointment that's been with me ever since.

If my father had been well and whole, I realize after these long decades, I would have eventually called him for his advice about ending my marriage. I would have followed whatever plan he concocted and funded, and then I would have resented the hell out of him for doing what I'd asked him to do: fix it for me. Instead, after a week of watching my father lie in bed without a backbone, I went home and found backbone myself. I packed up my kids and left—the unraveling of my marriage taking about a year, the same time period in which my father was flown to a hospital in Baltimore where a surgeon opened him up, front and back, to implant a twenty-inch rod that encases his spinal cord to this day. For nine months he wore a cast that started at his chest and went to his knees. Once he'd mended, my father cut the cast off with a hacksaw and threw it in the back pasture to disintegrate in the rain. And then he got on a horse and rode along his river during a dewy pink sunset fit for a John Wayne movie.

That night in the hospital room—and let's say that twelve hours passed between the time the others left and when Cindy arrived to take me to the airport—remains the longest stretch of time I have spent alone with my father. During those hours, I probably thought about nudging him awake again. Off his pins as he was, I might have shaken his blankets until he came around, and then I could have badgered him into a few reassuring platitudes, insisting that since Becky got the word I should get it, too. But it seemed, for the first time since the accident, that he had given in to rest. Even when a nurse jostled him around for the wee-hour readings of his vitals, he slept on. He had sunk into a place of healing, of—I like to think—trust that no one here would hurt him or frighten him, or turn their backs on a pain he could not admit to. Or is that me I'm talking about now? I can't decide. I stayed wrapped in my blanket, dozing now and then, but mostly watching his face soften, the bruise around his eye receding, rimmed with greens and browns. His reinflated lung accepting air. I watched and waited for morning, and though I didn't think so at the time, the hours passed as they should, with a familiar silence between us. The fantasy father I'd carted around since I was a child might have taken me out to lunch just because, or introduced me to others as his dear daughter, but that man would have neither the grit nor the ferocity to fight his way out from under a horse. And now it's time I live with a truth that's been obvious all along: that each of us gets only one father, and this man who'd survived the impossible is mine.

Dinty W. Moore

SON OF MR. GREEN JEANS: A MEDITATION ON MISSING FATHERS

Allen, Tim

Best known as the father on ABC's *Home Improvement* (1991–99), the popular comedian was born Timothy Allen Dick on June 13, 1953. When Allen was eleven years old, his father, Gerald Dick, was killed by a drunk driver while driving home from a University of Colorado football game.

Bees

"A man, after impregnating the woman, could drop dead," critic Camille Paglia suggested to Tim Allen in a 1995 *Esquire* interview. "That is how peripheral he is to the whole thing."

"I'm a drone," Allen responded. "Like those bees?"

"You are a drone," Paglia agreed. "That's exactly right."

Carp

After the female Japanese carp gives birth to hundreds of tiny babies, the father carp remains nearby. When he senses approaching danger, he will suck the helpless babies into his mouth, and hold them safely there until the coast is clear.

Divorce

University of Arizona psychologist Sanford Braver tells a disturbing story of a woman who felt threatened by her husband's close bond with their young son. The husband had a flexible work schedule, but the wife did not, so the boy spent the bulk of his time with the father.

The mother became so jealous of the tight father-son relationship that she eventually filed for divorce and successfully fought for sole custody. The result was that instead of being in the care of his father while the mother worked, the boy was now left in daycare.

Emperor Penguins

Once a male emperor penguin has completed the act of mating, he remains by the female's side for the next month to determine if he is indeed about to become a father. When he sees a single greenish-white egg emerge from his mate's egg pouch, he begins to sing.

Scientists have characterized his song as "ecstatic."

Father Knows Best

In 1949 Robert Young began *Father Knows Best* as a radio show. Young played Jim Anderson, an average father in an average family. The show later moved to television, where it was a substantial hit.

Young's successful life, however, concluded in a tragedy of alcohol and depression. In January 1991, at age eighty-three, he attempted suicide by running a hose from his car's exhaust pipe to the interior of the vehicle. The attempt failed because the battery was dead and the car wouldn't start.

Green Genes

In Dublin, Ireland, a team of geneticists has been conducting a study to determine the origins of the Irish people. By analyzing segments of DNA from residents across different parts of the Irish countryside, then comparing this DNA with corresponding DNA segments from people elsewhere in Europe, the investigators hope to determine the derivation of Ireland's true forefathers.

Hugh Beaumont

The actor who portrayed the benevolent father on the popular TV show *Leave It to Beaver* was a Methodist minister. Tony Dow, who played older brother Wally, reports that Beaumont didn't care much for television and actually hated kids.

"Hugh wanted out of the show after the second season," Dow told the *Toronto Sun*. "He thought he should be doing films and things."

Inheritance

My own Irish forefather was a newspaperman, owned a popular nightclub, ran for mayor, and smuggled rum in a speedboat during Prohibition. He smoked, drank, ate nothing but red meat, and died of a heart attack in 1938.

His one son—my father—was only a teenager when his father died. I never learned more than the barest details about my grandfather from my father, despite my persistent questions. Other relatives tell me that the relationship had been strained.

My father was a skinny, eager-to-please little boy, battered by allergies, and not the tough guy his father had apparently wanted. My dad lost his mother at age three and later developed a severe stuttering problem, perhaps as a result of his father's sharp disapproval. My father's adult vocabulary was outstanding, due to his need for alternate words when faltering over hard consonants like B or D.

The stuttering grew worse over the years, with one noteworthy exception: after downing a few shots of Canadian whiskey, my father could muster a stunning, honey-rich Irish baritone. His impromptu vocal performances became legend in local taverns, and by the time I entered the scene my father was spending every evening visiting the working class bars. Most nights he would stumble back drunk around midnight; some nights he was so drunk he would stumble through a neighbor's back door, thinking he was home.

Our phone would ring. "You'd better come get him."

As a boy I coped with this embarrassment by staying glued to the television—shows like *Father Knows Best* and *Leave It to Beaver* were my favorites. I desperately wanted someone like Hugh Beaumont to be my father, or maybe Robert Young.

Hugh Brannum, though, would have been my absolute first choice. Brannum played Mr. Green Jeans on *Captain Kangaroo,* and I remember him as kind, funny, and extremely reliable.

Jaws

My other hobby, besides watching other families on television, was an aquarium. I loved watching as my tropical fish drifted aimlessly through life, and I loved watching guppy mothers give birth. Unfortunately guppy fathers, if not moved to a separate tank, will often come along and eat their young.

Kitten

Kitten, the youngest daughter on *Father Knows Best,* was played by Lauren Chapin.

Lauren Chapin

Chapin's father, we later learned, molested her, and her mother was a severe alcoholic. After *Father Knows Best* ended in 1960, Chapin's life came apart. At sixteen, she married an auto mechanic. At eighteen, she became addicted to heroin and began working as a prostitute.

Masculinity

Wolf fathers spend the daylight hours away from the pack—hunting—but return every evening. The wolf cubs, five or six to a litter, will rush out of the den when they hear their father approaching and fling themselves at him, leaping up to his face. The father will back up a few feet and disgorge food for the cubs, in small, separate piles.

Natural Selection

When my wife, Renita, confessed to me her desire to have children, the very first words out of my mouth were "You must be crazy." Convinced that she had just proposed the worst idea imaginable, I stood from my chair, looked straight ahead, and literally marched out of the room.

This was not my best moment.

Ozzie

Oswald Nelson, at thirteen, was the youngest person ever to become an Eagle Scout. Oswald went on to become Ozzie Nelson, the father in *Ozzie and Harriet*. Though the show aired years before the advent of reality television, Harriet was indeed Ozzie's real wife, Ricky and David were his real sons, and eventually Ricky and David's wives were played by their actual spouses. The current requirements for Eagle Scout make it impossible for anyone to ever beat Ozzie's record.

Penguins, Again

The female emperor penguin "catches the egg with her wings before it touches the ice," Jeffrey Moussaieff Masson writes in his book *The Emperor's Embrace*. She then places the newly laid egg on her feet, to keep it from contact with the frozen ground.

At this point both penguins will sing in unison, staring down at the egg. Eventually the male penguin will use his beak to lift the egg onto the surface of his own feet, where it will remain until hatching.

Not only does the penguin father endure the inconvenience of walking around with an egg balanced on his feet for months on end, but he will also forgo food for the duration.

Quiz

1. What is Camille Paglia's view on the need for fathers?

2. Did Hugh Beaumont hate kids, and what was it he would rather have been doing than counseling the Beav?

3. Who played Mr. Green Jeans on *Captain Kangaroo?*

4. Who would you rather have as your father: Hugh Beaumont, Hugh Brannum, a wolf, or an emperor penguin?

Religion

In 1979 Lauren Chapin, the troubled actress who played Kitten, had a religious conversion. She credits her belief in Jesus with saving her life.

After *his* television career ended, Methodist minister Hugh Beaumont became a Christmas tree farmer.

Sputnik

On October 4, 1957, *Leave It to Beaver* first aired. On that same day, the Soviet Union launched Sputnik 1, the world's first artificial satellite. Sputnik 1 was about the size of a basketball, took roughly ninety-eight minutes to orbit the Earth, and is often credited with escalating the Cold War and launching the US-Soviet space race.

Years later, long after *Leave It to Beaver* ended its network run, a rumor persisted that Jerry Mathers, the actor who played Beaver, had died at the hands of the Soviet-backed communists in Vietnam. Actress Shelley Winters went so far as to announce it on the *Tonight Show*. But the rumor was false.

Toilets

Leave It to Beaver was the first television program to show a toilet.

Using Drugs

The presence of a supportive father is essential to helping children avoid drug problems, according to the National Center of Addiction and Substance Abuse at Columbia University. Lauren Chapin may be a prime example here.

Tim Allen would be one, too. Fourteen years after his father died at the hands of a drunk driver, Allen was arrested for dealing drugs and spent two years in prison.

I also fit this gloomy pattern. Though I have so far managed to avoid my father's relentless problems with alcohol, I wasted about a decade of my life hiding behind marijuana, speed, and various hallucinogens.

Vasectomies

I had a vasectomy in 1994.

Ward's Father

In an episode titled "Beaver's Freckles," we learn that Ward Cleaver had "a hittin' father," but little else is ever revealed about Ward's fictional family. Despite Wally's constant warning—"Boy, Beav, when Dad finds out, he's gonna clobber ya!"—Ward does not follow his own father's example and never hits his sons on the show. This is an example of xenogenesis.

Xenogenesis

(zen′ə jen′i sis), *n. Biol.* 1. the supposed generation of offspring completely and permanently different from the parent. 2. heterogenesis.

Believing in xenogenesis—though at the time I couldn't define it, spell it, *or* pronounce it—I changed my mind about having children about four years after I walked out on my wife's first suggestion of the idea.

Luckily this was five years before my vasectomy.

Y Chromosones

The Y chromosome of the father determines a child's gender, and it is unique in that its genetic code remains relatively unchanged as it passes from father to son. The DNA in other chromosomes is more likely to get mixed between generations, in a process called recombination. What this means, apparently, is that boys have a higher likelihood of directly inheriting their ancestral traits.

Once my wife convinced me to risk being a father—this took many years and considerable prodding—my Y chromosomes chose the easy way out: our only child is a daughter.

Maria, so far, has inherited many of what people say are the Moore family's better traits—humor, a facility with words, a stubborn determination.

It is yet to be seen what she will do with the negative ones.

Zappa

Similar to the persistent "Beaver died in Vietnam" rumor of the late 1960s, Internet discussion lists of the late 1990s were filled with assertions that the actor who played Mr. Green Jeans, Hugh "Lumpy" Brannum, was in fact the father of musician Frank Zappa.

Brannum, though, had only one son, and that son was neither Frank Zappa nor this author.

Too bad.

Neil Mathison

MEMORY AND HELIX: WHAT COMES TO US FROM THE PAST

MY FATHER LOST his childhood. He lost it in Nevada tumbleweed towns, in Union Pacific rail yards, in Oakland flyspeck boardinghouses, on San Francisco's Embarcadero and Powell Street and Fisherman's Wharf. My father lost his childhood because *his* father, my grandfather, took my father with him when he abandoned the rest of his family. In Detroit. The year was 1919. A black-and-white snapshot taken before they left shows my father with fair hair, pale skin, and an air of guarded watchfulness, as if he were used to being the smallest pup in the pack. He was five years old.

During our family vacations throughout the American West, my father looked for his childhood, much as Ahab looked for his whale. (I do not say this lightly.) What clues my father found often depressed him—and on occasion enraged him. I doubt that my father ever found what he'd lost.

Oliver Sacks writes that the human brain is more like a river than a recording machine. In his essay "Neurology and the Soul" (*New York Review of Books,* 22 November 1990) Sacks suggests that in the human mind "nothing is ever precisely repeated or reproduced" and that there is "a continual revision and reorganization of perception and memory, so that no two experiences (or their neural bases) are ever precisely the same."

"It's a poor sort of memory," the Queen of Hearts tells Alice in *Through the Looking-Glass,* "that only works backwards."

This is my memory: We are parked in a Nevada rail yard in 1958, my family on its way home from Mexico. Eisenhower is president. "Purple People Eater" is playing on the car radio. In four years, in 1962, Watson, Wilkins, and Crick will share a Nobel Prize for their 1953 discovery of DNA, but I'm unaware in 1958 that DNA exists, and I have no idea how anything passes from generation to generation—except that I carry a vague, almost biblical acceptance that my siblings and I have inherited certain family attributes: the sharp, narrow, middle-European nose of Grandfather Will; the athleticism of my mother's Uncle Carlton; the hot temper of my father's brother Frank. Otherwise, I'm an eleven-year-old cooped up in a sweltering Ford with my mother, my younger brothers Charlie and Duncan, and my baby sister Charlotte. The Ford is "mountain green," a color I remember as aquamarine. The camper-trailer hitched behind the Ford is named *Papagayo,* after a parrot my parents owned in Brazil, one that died from drinking too much Coca-Cola.

My father stands outside the Ford so close to the tracks that if he wanted he could touch the diesel engines—a quartet of yellow Union Pacifics coupled back to back. The engine headlamps peer west as if they've already probed the Sierra passes and tulle-laced deltas between the town of Sparks and the Pacific, but the rear lamps face east, back toward deserts and basins and mountain ranges and prairies. My father's past is twined on the double rails. For something like twenty minutes—an eternity, it seems to me—my father has stood like this, back to us, thumbs stuck in his seat pockets, his homemade back-flap ball cap tilted up on his head—his *kaffiyeh* he calls it. His left arm, the one he hangs from the car window, is red with sunburn. My father, standing in that dusty Nevada railroad yard, is forty-four years old.

"What's Dad doing?" we ask.

"Remembering," Mother answers.

The odor of cilantro and salsa and refried beans wafts from shacks slat-sided and huddled under sun-baked cottonwoods.

Duncan has to pee.

"Hold it," Mother advises. "Or go behind the trees."

Lime-green refrigerated reefers, red-slatted stock cars, piggyback flatcars with tractor-trailers crouched like beetles on their backs, oil tankers and grain-dusted hoppers—all stretch back so far we can barely make out the crimson caboose, so far away that we wonder whether it is part of the same train. The names painted on the cars sing of foreign places—Great Northern; B&O; Southern Pacific; Reading; Atchison, Topeka, & Santa Fe—the poetry of a continent, the lyrics of my father's lost youth.

Having tried so many times to recall what my father said of his childhood, to record the incidents that were its clues, to revisit in my mind the campgrounds and travel-trailer parks of our western odysseys, I'm no longer fully certain where the boundary lies. What was true? What was family legend? What memory stood alone? What was composite? If I know these incidents happened, or were said to have happened, I also know that memory serves both the present and the past, modified over time to justify prejudices, to define identities, to conceal what is too hurtful to bear.

My grandfather may or may not have been mentally ill, although he definitely spent the last years of his life in an asylum; my father may or may not have inherited my grandfather's mental instabilities. Perhaps what my father inherited, what would always haunt him, were just memories: indelible to his life, truth to him, fluid over time, perhaps unrecognizable to others, but, at least, remembered.

But what else do we inherit?

There are the invisible, unrecallable tendencies, aptitudes, proclivities, and liabilities that have come to us through our genes. Are we quick of foot or quick to anger? Do we tend toward heaviness or optimism or anxiety? How does the double helix manifest itself in our lives—as an ally, an enemy, or a tyrant?

On the fiftieth anniversary of the discovery of the structure of DNA, Natalie Angier wrote in the *New York Times* that "with all the breathless talk of human DNA as a grand epic written in three billion runes, the scientists complain that an essential point is forgotten: DNA, on its own, does nothing. It can't make eyes blue, livers bilious or brains bulging." She goes on to say that DNA

> holds bare-bones information—suggestions, really—for the construction of the proteins of which all life forms are built, but that's it. DNA can't read those instructions, it can't divide, it can't keep itself clean or sit up properly—proteins that surround it do all those tasks. Stripped of context within the body's cells, those haggling florid ecosystems of tens of thousands of proteinaceous fauna, DNA is helpless, speechless—DOA.

My wife, Susan, majored in microbiology in college. Her faith is science, her catechism DNA. Before our son John was born, Susan decided to research our genetic histories. Her father's father was a mystery, unknown to her and even to her father. A genetic dead end. Elsewhere, however, Susan found the usual markers: high blood pressure in her family's women; heart disease in my family's men; male baldness, blue eyes, and left-handedness in both families; no autism or diabetes in either.

When she asked about my father's father, I had no answers. He died in an asylum, I said, right after I was born.

"Asylum?" Susan asked. "What kind of asylum?"

"An insane asylum."

"In what way," she asked, "was your grandfather insane?"

I didn't know.

I can't remember the exact date of this conversation, nor can I recall the exact words we exchanged or even if the conversation was a single one. But I am certain that afterward Susan questioned me with incredulity, even anxiety.

"How could you," she said, "*not* want to know?"

Her father, I pointed out, hadn't known anything about *his* father. Wasn't he managing perfectly well?

But thereafter Susan watched me. She watched my father, too. Every storm of temper, tick of depression, flash of joy. Susan watched for a marker, a sign, a trace of whatever it was that had doomed my grandfather.

Once Susan suggested I write for his death certificate, but I refused. I didn't want Grandfather's death certificate. I rejected predestination—via God, history, or Susan's DNA studies. My catechism was anti-predestination.

Certain mathematical and geometrical relationships suggest more order in the universe than we might expect: the number *pi* in geometry, the *e* of exponential decay, light speeding at its invariable 186,000 miles per second. The universe converges on fundamental forms—and the helix, it seems to me, is one such form. Who hasn't marveled at a vine twining a pole? Who hasn't felt the energy latent in a spring or in the turn of a screw? Who hasn't noticed the curved fold of the external ear or wondered at the spiral shell of the common snail?

If you draw a straight line on flat paper, connecting two points, and you roll the paper into a cylinder, the line—as long as the points are not directly one above the other in the vertical plane—will describe a helix. (Because of this fact, and because a straight line is the shortest path between two points, squirrels chasing each other up tree trunks follow helical paths.) Unlike a circle or a cone or a cylinder, a helix looks as if it's in motion even when it's standing still: it appears to advance around its axis like a corkscrew, to unleash its hidden energy like a watch spring. Helixes are right-handed or left-handed. If a helix is vertical and the front strands move from the lower left to the upper right, the helix is right-handed. If you turn it upside down, it is still right-handed, the property of handedness (chirality) being independent of perspective. Most screws are right-handed, meaning turning the screw clockwise causes the screw to move away from you. Pairs of horns usually appear with one horn in each chirality, except for a species of an Arctic whale, the narwhal, one of whose two teeth forms a long, thin, spiraled horn, not unlike that of a unicorn—but in the narwhal both teeth spiral left-handed. The A and B forms of DNA—the long polymer molecules of heredity—are right-handed, as is the alpha helix, a basic structure of proteins. The rare Z form of DNA is left-handed. (The left-handedness of the Z form is thought to enable specific Z-DNA binding proteins, also left-handed, to recognize it.) If a DNA helix coils in the direction of its chirality, then the bond between the paired molecules is strengthened, but if it coils in the opposite direction—its natural state—the bond is weakened, the helix poised to unzip and release its miracle of recombinant life.

"The lives of men . . . and the world," Sir Thomas Browne wrote in *Religio Medici* (1643), one of the earliest English-language references to a helix, "run not upon a helix that still enlargeth, but on a Circle."

But I wonder: did Sir T. get it wrong?

When I was a boy, my father rarely spoke of his father. What I knew of Grandfather was that he had been a tool and die maker in Detroit and that he might have become a millionaire—or so my father said, given that the automobile industry in Detroit in 1919 was like the software industry in Seattle at the turn of the twenty-first century. Instead, Grandfather fled west with my father and my Aunt Harriet, then nine years old; in so doing, Grandfather abandoned my pregnant Grandmother Charlotte, two other daughters, and another son. Grandfather worked a railroad roundhouse in Omaha for a few months and then moved farther west to another roundhouse in Ogden. Eventually he sent Harriet back—a young girl being, Father explained, too difficult for Grandfather to care for. Father and Grandfather ended up in San Francisco. I don't know why Grandfather left Grandmother, why he took the children he took, nor even which of these facts are truly facts—when my father was older and wanted to discuss his childhood, I made no time to listen.

Now he's gone. Now I can't ask. Now I'm ready to listen.

The week my father died—it was February 1997—Mother asked me to write out his eulogy, one she dictated while I sat across from her, both of us as bleak as the drizzle that darkened my study window. She spoke of Father's journey west in the 1920s, of his living in railroad hotels and broken-down boardinghouses, of the prostitutes who shared the hotels and who cared for him while Grandfather was at work. She told me how he hitched rides on Powell Street cable cars and sold newspapers on the Embarcadero. If much of Father's tale was by then familiar to me, the fullness of its arc I learned that morning.

The first time Mother saw Father, she said, was shortly after he'd returned to his family, now living in New Kensington, Pennsylvania, an aluminum-company town northeast of Pittsburgh. He was riding a bicycle in front of my mother's house.

"Who," my Grandmother Catherine had asked, "is that beautiful boy?"

Three times a week he passed the house, always alone, always on his bike, always on his way to visit Grandfather. What asylum was it? Dixmont, named for Dorothea Dix? Or Mayview? Or Torrance? Which asylum was only a young boy's bicycle ride away?

The afternoon we wrote the eulogy I asked what illness it was that had confined Grandfather to an asylum in 1925, when, after he reunited with his family in Pennsylvania, Grandmother Mathison incarcerated him. Mother shrugged. Months later, she told me she thought he might have had syphilis. Her statement shocked me. Even now I don't trust it, thinking her supposition originated in her need to hold her father-in-law accountable for his fate. I choose not to trust it. But from Father I learned only that Grandfather was "sick in the head" and that Father was certain Grandfather loved him.

My father's hands were large and warm. In the car he would reach back behind the seat until we children placed our hands in his and he gently closed his fingers over ours and told us he loved us. There was no particular stimulus for this ritual; it might occur anytime. I do the same thing now with my own son.

But where did Father learn it?

Years of research, according to the National Institute of Mental Health website, have demonstrated links between genetics and a most-wanted list of mental illnesses: schizophrenia, bipolar disorder, autism, early onset depression, anxiety disorders, even attention-deficit hyperactivity. Genes are the prime suspects, but if sometimes a specific gene is culpable, more often the perpetrators are a combination acting in concert with each other or with nongenetic factors. This multiplicity of suspects complicates the task of gene sleuthing, requiring large sample sizes and sophisticated technologies to pinpoint which genes, among the many expressed in the human brain, are truly guilty, as well as requiring researchers to determine which brain components each gene codes for, and how each affects behavior. Some evidence, however, is incontrovertible: the risk of schizophrenia is 1 percent in the general population but rises to 17 percent if one parent has schizophrenia and to 46 percent if both have it. Classic studies in closed communities—Laplanders in Sweden, the Amish in Pennsylvania—were the first to show this connection, not because the Lapps or Amish have a higher incidence of mental illness, but because their excellent genealogical records and uniform communities make tracking easier.

The Amish have an expression for aberrant mental behaviors: "*Siss im Blut,*" they say. "It's in the blood."

The winter my father died, I unearthed a 3 × 5 photo among the guidebooks and Michelin maps and *Popular Science* clippings he loved to collect. He'd filled a room with such stuff, box after box of folders—dusty, askew, and mildewed, each labeled in his blocky engineer's printing: TURKEY, PALEONTOLOGY, MISCELLANEOUS, BARGING BRITAIN, THE BIG BANG, SIX WAYS TO EXTEND THE LIFE OF YOUR OUTBOARD MOTOR. Father called the place his "library." Mother called it his "dump." The room had always troubled Mother. When she asked me to help clean it out—"to get things in order," as she put it—I resented her haste. Father had been gone only a few weeks. Later I realized she must have seen the room like an unmade bed. She needed to change the sheets, tuck in the corners, and straighten the quilt to ensure that her dreams would be different than his. Mother would not live in Father's past.

The photo I discovered in MISCELLANEOUS is of my father's siblings and his mother: a studio portrait, sepia-tinted, as was the fashion in the 1920s. The three older girls—Janet, Harriet, Molly—wear dark dresses with lacy white collars and stagy, adolescent smiles. They stand next to Frank, my father's brother, whose lips are twisted in a sad, sardonic grin, his eyes hooded, his eyebrows heavy. (Frank resembles my grandfather, my mother says. I have only one snapshot of Grandfather and none of an adult Uncle Frank, so I can't tell if Mother's observation is true.) Seated in front of them is Grandmother, short, rapier-thin, with rimless glasses, her hair pulled back. She wears a black dress in a satiny fabric that gleams like anthracite under the photographer's lamp. In her lap is the baby Charlotte, born after Grandfather abandoned his family.

In the lower-left corner, inscribed in my grandmother's angular, schoolteacher's handwriting, is this statement: *You have a family.* My grandmother mailed hundreds of these photos to the elementary school principals in every railroad town from Pittsburgh to San Francisco. *I'm looking for my son,* she wrote. *If you know of him, please give him this picture.* She also enclosed a snapshot of my father; that photo is lost.

I remember seeing my grandmother only twice—the last time when she was dying. From Seattle we drove three thousand miles to be with her. I remember the coal-smoke heaviness of Pennsylvania's Allegheny River valley, the unsettling palette of flaming October foliage so unlike our cool green Seattle conifers. I remember Grandmother's house, one story, with its porch seeming as wide as the bridge of an ocean liner. There was a coal scuttle and a laundry chute that dropped into the basement, the chute an unaccountable luxury to my eight-year-old mind, although Grandmother forbade us to play anywhere near it.

My father showed us the room he'd occupied as a boy—how he'd papered the walls with maps of the forty-eight states, the seven continents, Brazil and Argentina. The maps were still there. Ball-headed pins were stuck in all the railroad towns where he and Grandfather had lived, but also in London, Paris, Rio de Janeiro, and Buenos Aires.

My brothers and I paid little attention to Grandmother, distracted by cousins we'd never met, by the unfamiliar smell of my aunts' cigarettes, by a tide of adult interactions flooding from a history unknown to us. Grandmother sat in a rocker, wrapped in wool sweaters and with a shawl over her legs. She was surprisingly small, even to me, even then. Mostly she listened without talking, a thin smile on her lips, although all my aunts and my uncle and my father fell silent if she spoke a single word. Grandmother was dying from stomach cancer, and her doctor had ordered her to drink beer to keep up her strength. My father bought her a six-pack of expensive German pilsner.

Father showed us the apple trees he'd planted—now full-grown; the houses that had been on his newspaper route; the high school he attended; the snapshots of his dog Mugs. But in all our time in Grandmother's house, we never saw nor heard a trace of Grandfather: not a photograph, not an anecdote, not a single utterance of his name.

Susan and I have one child, a teenage son embarked on his final passage to adulthood. His name is John Gordon—the first name from my father's first, a contraction of the Hebrew *Yehohanan* ("the Lord is Gracious"), and the middle name from mine but also from the last name of the British general, Charles "Chinese" Gordon, who put down the Taiping Rebellion in China and then perished in 1884 during the Battle of Khartoum. The general was a distant relative by way of our Gordon-clan ancestry. In these names there is a weight from the past, one more weight John bears along with that of his parents' expectations: that he will get good grades, attend college, and stay fit, healthy, happy, and alert to the world. He has the fair complexion and blue eyes of his mother, my sturdy broad-shouldered build, and a disposition far sweeter than either Susan's or mine. We have often wondered where John's geniality comes from, believing that everything about him is inherited from us or is the consequence of our parenting, both for good and ill.

My three siblings all have more than one child. We amuse them by holding ourselves so accountable for John's traits.

Why, they ask, *can't you see the individual in the individual?*

Once again I'm remembering 1958, in Nevada, after Sparks. We climb gravel switchbacks into the Sierra Nevada Mountains. Dust rises behind the station wagon and trailer like smoke from a wildfire. The track shrinks to double ruts where gullies have washed out the roadbed. There are no guardrails. Below us, the mountain drops two thousand feet. We've climbed from rabbit-bush flats up through chaparral-covered foothills, finally reaching groves of spear-straight pines, whose bark is mottled orange and brown. I watch Father in the rearview mirror. Aviator sunglasses mask his eyes. He grins as he wrestles each turn.

Mother braces herself against the dashboard. "This is why," she murmurs, "the sign said no trailers."

Father answers. "They mean big trailers."

"What if the road is blocked?"

"We'll turn around."

"There's no room to turn around."

"Then we'll back down."

"Ten miles? You'd back ten miles?"

In this fashion they've argued since my father ignored the No Trailers sign ten miles back. But the argument echoes one that preceded it, when my father announced his intention to detour through San Francisco. Mother responded with alarm. She cited his promise to visit Crater Lake, the possibility of car problems, her desire for us kids to "settle in" before school started.

"A week's plenty of time to settle in," my father insists. "I want the kids to see where I lived."

"They aren't old enough to appreciate it."

"You lived in San Francisco?" I ask.

"You bet," my father answers. "*With my dad.*"

A revelation. Grandfather is a cipher. Usually silence conceals him.

"We need more time," Mother says.

"I get two goddamned weeks a year. It's all the time I've got."

Even as a child, or because I was a child, I sense the shadow over their words.

Mother sinks into silence, staring out the window at the pine-groved peaks as we climb higher into the Sierra Nevada.

Father worshiped Grandmother. He incorporated her into his pantheon of deities along with Wernher von Braun and Sir Ernest Shackleton and Rudyard Kipling. (*Do you like Kipling?* Mother asks. *Don't know,* Father replies, *I never kipled.*)

As he grew older, too, Father often told the story of how Grandmother found him in a San Francisco flophouse, persuaded the school principal and the San Francisco Police to send him (and Grandfather) home, protected him from a brother and older sisters who were less than happy at his prodigal return and more than ready to correct his half-feral behavior. Against the backdrop of the Great Depression, Grandmother sent all her children to college, taught autistic students at half-pay, met the mortgage payments. Heroic.

I can't imagine this time in color. I see it bathed in black-and-white, a grainy WPA photograph, until Pearl Harbor Day when everything explodes into Technicolor. When the war began, Father found work as an aeronautical engineer in Baltimore. He bought a sailboat. He courted Mother. After V-J Day he married her. They moved to Brazil. How much farther away could Father go?

Mother is guarded about Grandmother. *She was a good mother-in-law,* Mother says, *but she hated to be embraced.*

Father referred to Grandmother's students as *little idiots,* a term that for him was medical rather than pejorative, although remembering it now I realize the words sound harsh. If we called each other (or anyone else) idiots, he was certain to correct us: such comments were unkind, he would warn, to those who *really* are idiots. But when he described his mother's pupils in this way, I think he also distanced himself, as if to emphasize that their disability was one he and his sons and daughter didn't share. He warned us never to forget mental illness was a disease, like polio or chicken pox. But was he teaching us or reassuring himself?

We enter San Francisco over the Bay Bridge and the city is bone white under the sunlight, so white it hurts our eyes. What year is it? Which trip? 1952? 1958? My father conducts a manic guided tour of a vanished 1920s metropolis, punctuated by rapid-fire commentary, interspersed with silences when he can't find an elementary school he attended or a hotel he lived in. We drive. We park. We walk. We ride cable cars and streetcars. We visit a museum in Golden Gate Park where, my father tells us, he first learned about dinosaurs. He insists we view a diorama of a Stone Age village where hunters are butchering a mastodon. We wander through the Palace of Fine Arts. Our feet hurt.

"I'm hungry," my brother says.

"Pleased to meet you," my father replies. "I'm Dad."

When we complain of the cold—we're in shorts and T-shirts—he tells us, "The coldest winter I ever spent was summer in San Francisco." We trudge after him. Mother insists the children really *must* have lunch, and we end up eating soggy fries at a Fisherman's Wharf stand. It's late afternoon, and we huddle against Mother trying to keep warm. Seagulls swoop and dive over our heads. Father leans on the pier railing, his eyes fixed on Alcatraz Island, on the whitecapped bay, on the fog spreading like fungus under the Golden Gate Bridge. His morose interludes are longer. His silence distances us.

"Tonight we'll camp in the redwoods," Mother says, "below the oldest trees in the world."

"How old?" my brother Charlie asks.

Mother answers, "As old as Jesus."

In 1997, when my son John was in the first grade, he and I booked passage on Amtrak's Coast Starlight route from Seattle through the Bay Area to Los Angeles. I had misgivings prior to the trip—not only that I might be bored by a long train ride but also that seeing San Francisco Bay might tip me into melancholy. The Bay Area had been darkened for me by divorce in the 1970s, and more recently by an unhappy departure from a high-tech job. The past threatened to be a stain that seeped through and blackened the present.

Our sleeper compartment was a tiny cube with a fold-up table and fold-down bunk. Two seats faced each other across a table covered by a starched linen cloth. A vase of red and white carnations sat in the center of the table and managed to stay upright no matter how much the train wobbled down the rails.

John was liberated. I allowed him the run of the train. He was off in a flash of six-year-old enthusiasm, and he soon found the video-game car. I'd brought along a number of books to read as well as my laptop computer, but it turned out I could barely pry myself away from the window. We were traveling through America's backyard: warehouses, rotting fish-house piers, encampments of the homeless, auto auctions, trailer parks, concertina wire, abandoned lots, pool tables under screened-in porches, barbecues, children's swing sets, doghouses, cars rusting on wooden blocks.

In Salem, halfway through Oregon, a tour of retirees boarded the train. The women were blue-haired, talkative, and vigilant, the men wistful and shrunken under ball caps embroidered with the logos of golf courses and fishing clubs. I joined the retirees for a parlor-car wine tasting. The Willamette Valley rolled by, greener than all the clover in Ireland. Then, after Eugene, the rail line bore east, climbing beside the Willamette River's Middle Fork and on through Westin and Oakridge and McCredie Springs until we crossed the Willamette Pass into eastern Oregon, where the Coast Starlight resumed its southward track. Snow began to fall.

We sat in the dining car, John and I—trout amandine for me, macaroni and cheese for him. The snow streaked by in thin, white, horizontal lines. Later, I slept through Klamath Falls and Dunsmuir and Redding, waking beside the Sacramento River running high and fast and thick with spring melt. Red-winged blackbirds flashed crimson and black over drainage ditches and green glassy sloughs. At Suisun Bay mothballed navy ships lay at anchor, gray silhouettes in the morning sun.

I needn't have worried about my memories. The Bay Area morning was so sun-bright and silver, so filled with the high color of April, that it could have lightened the blackest of black memories. Across the bay, clouds rose over the peninsula. The old navy dirigible hangars in Mountain View loomed like megasized caterpillars. The Coast Starlight rattled across mudflats and tidal grasses, and past empty buildings abandoned in the marsh. Rain was falling in Cupertino, translucent veils curtaining down from the sky. Here in the mudflats, white egrets and brown sandpipers and green mallard ducks and other seabirds in tuxedo-black plumage paddled among the sloughs and canals. A Ferro-cement sloop hid in the tall grass—a bright blue awning sheltering its cockpit.

A retiree in careful tweeds and wire-rimmed glasses gazed out at the bay. "Is that Camp Campbell?" he asked. "The Japs surrendered only two days after we shipped out from Campbell. We were scheduled to invade Japan."

"Did you turn back?" I asked.

"Damn straight!" the tweedy man replied. "We were glad for the bomb."

A couple held hands across the parlor car table. They wore neat, rectangular badges: AAA TOUR–COAST STARLIGHT.

"We took our honeymoon on a train just like this," the woman confides, lowering her eyes, a twenty-year-old once again.

Like me, she was traveling—not just in present time but in memory time as well—accompanied by the triumphs and pitfalls and passions that underpinned our individual pasts.

Flaws in memory are the quicksand to faithful recollection. In a profile in *Wired* magazine, Oliver Sacks reports that an anecdote in his autobiographical book *Uncle Tungsten: Memories of a Chemical Boyhood* turned out not to be true. During the London Blitz two bombs fell near Sacks's childhood house. In his memory, Sacks saw both bombs and vividly believed that he was present for both, even though the second had actually fallen while he was away at boarding school—a fact brought to his attention by his brother after the book's publication. Sacks's brain had played a trick, the second memory actually being the result of a detailed letter from his brother. "In that [first bomb] memory," Sacks recalls, "I can *feel* myself into the body of that little boy. And in the second memory it's as if I'm seeing a brilliantly illuminated scene from a film: I cannot locate myself anywhere in the scene."

Does recollection act with less power when untrue, or does its power derive from the intensity with which we believe it to be true?

This is my memory: We're crossing the Golden Gate Bridge. Is it 1952 or 1958 or 1966? Is it one memory or several? Father slams the car from lane to lane, stomping the accelerator, pounding the brakes, hammering the horn. We kids cower in our seats.

"Dear," Mother says. "Please."

Mother's pleadings only make Father drive more violently. He engages the other drivers in a contest where they don't know they're opponents, where he can have no conceivable victory. He races to squeeze out merging traffic, following the car ahead of us with only inches to spare. He drives on the shoulder to pass vehicles that slow him from wherever it is that he races to or from. His fury exceeds anything we've seen.

"The children," Mother says. "Think of the children."

Before us, on Highway 101, a river of taillights glitters like a trail of blood. A pickup squeezes into a gap in front of us. Father pumps the brakes, presses the horn in a prolonged blare. The pickup driver, a denim-clad man in a Stetson hat, hurls a beer can through his open window. The can clatters down the side of our station wagon. My father accelerates. We smash into the truck's rear bumper.

"Stop it!" Mother screams. "Stop it!"

The pickup driver swivels his head, his face contorted in anger—but also fear. Our station wagon surges forward. We crash into the truck again. Our heads snap forward. I'm certain all my life is changed—nothing will remain the same; everything is at risk. I don't know who I am or why I'm here or why my family has suddenly become like strangers to me. My sister (or is it my brother, or is it me?) bursts into a wet wail.

"I'll jump!" Mother shoves the car door open. Wind scatters candy wrappers and baseball cards and comic books. "So help me God, I'll jump! You'll never see me again."

The truck zigzags onto the shoulder, then skews away from the edge like a jackrabbit trying to outrun a ravening coyote. My father, who has been hunched over the wheel and grappling with it like a wrestler, straightens. Slowly he eases the station wagon onto the shoulder. We stop by a guardrail. Beyond the rail the hill falls away through stubby oak and waist-high golden grass, falls away to Tiburon and Sausalito, falls down to white, diorama-sized houses clustered on a blue cove. The car shudders in the blast of passing trucks. My father swings the door open, steps out, and begins to run. He runs thirty feet and then vaults over a guardrail. I watch him dodge down the hill like the antelopes we have so often seen in the Nevada desert.

"I'll never," my mother sobs, "never visit this lousy city again. Never!"

Father has dropped out of sight.

"Oh damn!" Mother says. She pulls a handful of Kleenex from the glove box. "Stay put, kids." She slides from the car, steps gingerly over the rail. I watch her traipse down through the grass until she too is no longer visible. I open the door and step to the guardrail. Our parents are sitting together no more than fifty feet below us, on a flat shelf of grass underneath a twisted oak. My father's head lies on my mother's lap and his body is shaking. Mother strokes his hair with one hand. She pats his back with the other.

"Why is Daddy crying?"

"I don't know."

But one day I'll guess he's crying for what he hasn't found: a family left behind, a mother lost, a father incarcerated. He hasn't found his childhood: not in the railroad yards, not in the dusty playgrounds, not where the Union Pacific meets the bay. He has yet to appreciate that it's my brothers and my sister and our mother and me—*we're* his family now—and that his past—the childhood he lost like the long freight train in Sparks—is far, far behind him, a weight he'll always pull but that no longer predestines where he'll go.

And what did I discover?

A father's fallibility, of course. I would always watch him for a sign, a marker, an echo, wary of the moment when his past might overcome him. After all these years, the question remains: was it his memories or his genes that took him to the brink in San Francisco?

As the years have gone by, I have also discovered that although Father's childhood was his and not mine, something of it passed to me anyway. It still arbitrates in my life, sometimes shapes my course, drives me toward one end and away from others. Am I too overprotective of my son John, when it might be better to allow him more free air? Are there times when I fail to hold my peace, when it would be better not to speak?

And John? Just as Susan watches me, I watch him for a sign, a marker, an echo—for a hint as to how his future will be shaped. By his memories. Or by mine. By the helical strands—I can almost see them, glittering like strings of white pearls in our blood—that tie my son to me and me to my father and both of us to all of our ancestors known and unknown.

Siss im Blut, the Amish say. "It's in the blood."

Gina Frangello

THE LION AND THE MOUSE: NOTES ON LOVE, MORTALITY, AND HALLUCINATIONS FOR MY FATHER'S NINETIETH BIRTHDAY

"DON'T CRY FOR me when I'm gone," my father recently told my mother. "I'm ready."

My mother relays me this at my upstairs apartment. She and my father have lived downstairs from us since 1999, but my father no longer comes to visit because he can't manage the stairs. If we want to see him, we go down there, which doesn't sound complicated, though it sometimes is. My life moves at the speed of light, and I often go days without seeing my dad. When we do visit, he's usually listening to the television turned so loud that nobody can hear anyone else speak. His TV is so blaring, in fact, that although my husband and I sleep on the third floor, when we go to bed we can hear the thumping voices of my father's crime dramas vibrating through our floorboards, mattress, pillows. Sometimes my mother makes him put the TV on mute when we come over, but since my father is essentially deaf, he doesn't hear us when we speak anyway.

This is hilarious to my daughters, who are eleven and not yet afraid of their own decay. "Hi, Papa!" one of them shouts at the top of her lungs to the other, and then the other hollers back in an old man voice, "Why don't they ever say hi to me?"

At one point, my dad would have been the first one laughing at this joke. When my mother's mother was getting old and someone would ask her if she wanted a glass of wine, she would jump up in alarm and shout, "Lion? What lion?" My father did imitations of her for years. He used to chide her, too, for never eating anything but sweets. Her pantry was jammed full of Little Debbie snack cakes, her freezer full of popsicles. He thought it particularly batshit that she wasn't just addicted to sugar, she was addicted to cheap, *crappy* forms of sugar. At one time, my father would travel to New York for authentic cheesecake—even in my teens he was known to hunt for the best apple pie all over the state of Michigan, just because. He knew which bakery in Chicago made the freshest doughnuts, and drove across the city for a particularly fine custard cake. "If I ever get like that," he would say of my old nana chowing on her pre-wrapped brownies and freezer-burned, neon-colored popsicles, "just shoot me."

Now, a big day out for my father is a trip a mile away to the Entenmann's warehouse, where he can stock up on enough processed coffee cakes and doughnuts covered in waxy chocolate that an avalanche falls out of his freezer when you open it. He buys whichever ice cream is on sale. If my husband and I go shopping for him and buy an ice cream he deems too expensive, he has a fit.

"Just shoot me," he would tell us.

But it's never that simple, is it? You can't snap your fingers that way. Sometimes, you live to turn into your mother-in-law. You remain trapped inside your body, unable to walk, unable to hear, taste buds faded, increasingly incontinent, napping during the day and awake all night, in chronic pain. Waiting.

Lion? What lion? Indeed.

I've come to think of this past summer as a season of death. An old friend of mine from grad school, blithely handsome and the youngest member of my first writing group, died swiftly and painfully of cancer that had been misdiagnosed for years as a blood-clotting disorder. Less than a week after his passing, one of my best friends, Kathy, was diagnosed completely out of the blue with Stage III-C ovarian cancer, which had spread to her stomach and colon linings as well as her entire lymphatic system. Even my husband's longtime family dog, who'd never left his mother's side as she wasted away from cancer and liver failure last year, was—as though part of a sick plot twist—essentially roasted to death in an Indiana heat wave when accidentally left inside a car. Amid all this, I was reading the manuscript of my friend Emily Rapp's luminous memoir (just sold to Penguin), about her son's diagnosis with Tay-Sachs disease. It was hard reading—not just because of the raw grief Emily so passionately captures and interrogates, but in part, too, because I found myself so floored by the potential horror of watching one's child die that I began to undermine other things happening around me. How could I call it "tragic" for forty-something adults—people who had traveled, worked, fallen in love—to be diagnosed with cancer when there were *babies* trapped inside their own bodies waiting for death? How could I dry heave on my bedroom floor over an elderly dog, or even fear losing my own dad—someone lucky enough to have already lived for nearly a century?

What is the continuum of grief?

One of my close confidantes, the writer Rob Roberge, would quote Baldwin to me at a time like this. He would say that suffering "may be the only equality we have," and that all pain is real and not easily quantified or measured. Emily herself, when we have e-mailed about all this, wrote me a beautiful treatise on the importance of friendships, and how the culture often undermines them as trivial, making an impassioned case for my right to love, value, and grieve my friends. And on one hand, these things are true—of course they are. Who would want to live in a world where they weren't?

On the other hand, emotions, even strong ones, are not equal at all. I don't mean this in a "privileged liberal guilt" kind of way—i.e., *I could be starving in Kenya or a victim of genocide, so how dare I complain?*—even if those things may be partially true. I mean it, rather, in a literal *I would push my father under the bus for my children* sort of way. I mean it in the *If something were to happen to my kids, the first and most appealing thing I can think of would be to take several hand-*

fuls of pills and disappear forever, so that I would not have to live in that kind of pain way. I'm not saying I would do it. There would still be my husband, my parents, my friends to consider. I *hope* I wouldn't do it. But it would definitely be on the menu. When I think of my father's impending death, I feel sad—I feel, even, afraid—but I do not think of killing myself.

What does it mean to love by degree? What does this say, too, about my place in my own children's love-chain? Is *this* the cycle of life, then? To be prepared to be thrown under the bus, if necessary, by those you value most in the world?

My oldest friend, Alicia, sometimes tells me that if she had to live inside my spinning brain for half an hour, she would have an aneurysm. At moments like this, I suspect she may be right.

Lately, my father sees mice. In addition to being on a dozen strong medications, he's also got macular degeneration, which can cause him to hallucinate spots. For several months, he claimed to see mice scampering across the floor, or to have glimpsed their droppings in corners. My husband would investigate these claims, but could never find a trace of the phantoms my father had seen. My mother began leaving little pieces of Entenmann's cake in the areas where my father claimed the mice had been, to see if any crumbs were missing, but all this resulted in was scraps of cake littered around my parents' (already-not-winning-any-awards-for-cleanliness) apartment. We even went so far as to call in my cousin Biff, who used to be a rat exterminator for the city of Chicago and now runs his own pest-control business, and Biff confirmed that there were no traces of mice in my parents' apartment, or even in our basement.

Still, my father reported on the mice's activities almost daily. They came out mostly, it seemed, when he slept. In addition to sometimes seeing them, he also—at night—heard them making their little mice sounds, and sometimes felt them scampering over his body in the dark.

He began to sleep with the lights on.

Soon, he moved out of his bed entirely. My parents have had separate bedrooms since I was five, but he proceeded to move into my mother's bed, driving her out to the living room couch. One day, when sitting on the toilet, my father called to my mother. He was sticking his foot out in the air and pointing at it.

"Look at that!" he hollered. "My big toenail was definitely longer yesterday. That damn mouse must have been nibbling on it in my sleep!"

My mother then calmly informed him that if he did not recant the completely deranged thing he had just said, she was going to take him to the psychiatric ward immediately.

Upon which, my father sheepishly admitted that perhaps the mice had not given him a pedicure after all.

After that, my mother called their longtime physician and got a prescription for an antipsychotic medication, and my father moved back into his bedroom.

I suppose I should clarify here that my father was never exactly a normal guy. He's been institutionalized before. Twice. He's been on antidepressants since I was about twenty, after sobbing at our kitchen table for a couple of days straight to the point that—although I may be misremembering some details because I later fictionalized this in a novel—he wet his pants, unable to get to the bathroom, and my cousin Biff, who then lived next door to us, had to come and forcibly put him in the car. Before I was born, my father went through a period in which he was convinced burglars would break into our apartment, so he stopped sleeping with my mother and took up a vigil on the couch. He became addicted to Valium and ended up hearing voices that told him to kill my mother and himself—*that* time, he checked himself into the hospital, no assistance required. While institutionalized, he begged my mother to leave him, but she wouldn't, even though her hair was falling out in chunks from worry and her doctor had to give her B-12 shots.

Despite his Paxil, my dad has grown increasingly high-strung these past twenty years. He keeps a stockpile of food under his bed (mainly baked beans—I guess our family will be having a very gassy quarantine should it become necessary to live on my father's rations in some futuristic emergency). He keeps decorative cookie jars on every flat surface of his bedroom, though none of the jars contain actual cookies. He spends his mornings reading *Star* and *People* magazines, even though in my youth he used to be a fan of Mike Royko and Bob Greene. Now he would be able to tell you every detail of Paris Hilton's latest sex scandal or Lindsay Lohan's rehabs and weight losses . . . except that he can't actually remember the details because he's on so much Norco. He usually reads these magazines aloud to himself, repeating most of the words multiple times (*Lindsay Lohan and and Lohan and Paris Paris Paris Hilton are no longer longer Linday Lohan and Paris Hilton are no longer speaking to speaking to one speaking to Lindsay Lohan and Paris Hilton are no longer speaking to one another*) at the kitchen table, giving my parents' apartment a distinctly *One Flew Over the Cuckoo's Nest* vibe. If he watches old home movies of my children, and one of them happens to be jumping or running in the film, he yells out warnings to the television set, afraid they will bust their heads open on the corner of the coffee table, or poke out an eye, even though in fact they are sitting right next to him—the movie having been filmed six years ago—eyes intact.

Shortly after being prescribed his antipsychotic, my mother woke one night to a loud noise. My father, who had dutifully resumed his place in his own bedroom, was writhing around on the bed sobbing. When she asked what was wrong, he told her, "We're all going to die." At further prodding he said, "The kids are going to get old and die too, and we'll all be dead already—the kids are going to die, what's the point of anything?"

My mother got his walker and brought him to the kitchen table and made him some warm milk and talked him down. In the morning, she called the doctor again. It seemed that my mother had made a mistake: when the doctor prescribed the new medication, my mother thought my father was to take it in lieu of his Paxil. "No," the doctor explained. He has known my parents since I was in high school. "John is never, ever going off the Paxil. He's on Paxil for life. This is to be given in addition."

My father had been off his Paxil for exactly two days.

How do you measure a life's worth? In laughter? In orgasms? In money? In how well-loved someone is? In how often they have been photographed? In children borne or raised? In the number of continents on which they have made love? In number of books published? In latest versions of iPads and iPhones? In jazz albums filling a giant trunk in the basement? In years?

We are all specks of dust against the specter of Time. Is ninety years so different from forty in the scheme of things? We are all the walking dead of history.

When I was in sixth grade, our teacher, a failed actor named Paul Tomasello, showed us the movie *On Borrowed Time,* in which an old man chases Death up a tree. Mr. Tomasello had gone to school with my father—the same school I attended as a girl. He chain-smoked in the classroom. School lore had it that Mr. Tomasello had been diagnosed with lung cancer years prior and given a few weeks to live, but in fact he lived to attend my wedding. He outlived all but one of my father's seven brothers, two of whom died as children in the flu epidemic and the rest of whom died of various heart and alcohol-related ailments such as rupturing an esophagus open while binge drinking. My father dreams almost every night of his brothers. My mother and I rarely figure in his dreams. In his dreams, his brothers are still young, his brother Ted playing the sax; his brother Joe, a mildly powerful bookie; his brother Frank on the front porch smiling and waving. In one dream, my father is forcibly taken away on a wagon across a barren white landscape.

"I never took my father out to dinner," my dad tells my mother, his voice thick with regret. "He worked himself to the bone for us and I never bought him a meal."

My paternal grandfather died before I was even born. "You were a young man," my mother assuages. "You had your own life. You didn't know he would die young. You thought you had time."

Mr. Tomasello is dead by now, too, of course.

We are on borrowed time with my father, I think daily. But of course, whose time *isn't* borrowed? My life moves on at the speed of light: adopting and having kids, teaching, editing, writing, cooking dinner, playing chauffeur to play dates and lessons, helping with homework, packing lunches, attending readings, planning continents on which to make love. How many trips down the stairs will I regret not having made?

Last month, my five-year-old son, Giovanni, asked to see the house I lived in when I was little.

"Be careful," my father told us on the way out the door. "You don't want him to get shot."

It seemed a strange thing to say in reference to the neighborhood where he chose to raise *me,* despite my mother's perpetual urgings that they leave.

I put Giovanni in the car, and we proceeded to drive four miles almost exactly due south on Western Avenue. We passed the church where I used to be an altar girl. We passed the funeral home where everyone I had ever met prior to the age of fourteen held their family wakes—where someday people will gather to pay last respects to my father. We passed my first elementary school, Holy Rosary, which is now a vacant lot overrun with weeds. We passed the Head Start program I attended when I was younger than my son, and the now-shuttered corner candy store where you could go to play Pac-Man or buy drugs. We pulled onto my old street, which is narrow and one-way, flanked on the other side by the elementary school my father dropped out of in eighth grade to work at a factory and from which I graduated: the first in many steps of running as fast and far as I could to flee my roots. Four scant miles, and yet this is nowhere my son would likely ever be. There at the west end of the street is where my cousin was murdered—shot in gang violence—seven years ago. I pulled into the school playground, where all the teachers park, and Giovanni and I got out of the car. We walked to the playground fence, surveying my old building: a brick two-flat with an awning that used to be green but now just appears a canopy of dirt and rust.

"Papa was born in that house," I tell Giovanni. "He lived there until he was almost eighty, and then he moved in with us. I lived there until I was eighteen, when I went away to college."

Giovanni stood silently at the fence. When I was ten and my father was in the hospital with a bleeding ulcer, on the verge of death, as was often the case in my girlhood, my mother would come to this fence every day during recess to give me an update on his condition. She and I would hold hands through the fence, even though this was the last possible thing a new transfer student should be doing at a rough, urban public school, and my mother must have realized that as well as I did. She and I were apparently complicit in my social ruin. One day, however, she did not materialize at the fence. I deduced that my father must have died and she was still at the hospital. I ran screaming from the playground across the street to the concrete steps that did not seem nearly as short or ramshackle to me then as they do now. I pounded on the door yelling, "Daddy! Daddy!" even though there was no possibility that my father was home. Mr. Tomasello, who was not yet my teacher, saw me and came across the street to fetch me. Although he was a frail man with a long white beard—the sort about whom rumors of terminal cancer circulated—and I was a pudgy child, he carried me back across the street, where I was taken to the school office so someone could reach my mother.

Now Giovanni touched the fence, staring at the little brick house. The air was cold and the sky a dingy gray: the color palette I remember most vividly from my youth, since my father had convinced all the neighbors that their tree roots were getting into our sewerage system, so they all ripped up their trees and cemented over their tiny lawns. That my father could have convinced an entire block full of people to do this seems preposterous to me, but indicative of his status in the neighborhood as a patriarch and a man of wisdom. One of my most vivid memories from my youth is of my father outside with his hose, spraying down the sidewalk in front of our house until it glistened like a bone.

Memories collided in my head like a movie montage gone wrong. A boy I grew up with was shot and killed on a bench in 1989, maybe twenty feet from where Gio and I now stood. But there, just across the playground, was where my cousin Laura and I would take her boom box and listen to Melissa Manchester's "Don't Cry Out Loud" while lying on our backs looking at the few visible stars, playing the song over and over again until it became the template for both of our lives. I held Giovanni's hand. He looked up at me. The moment seemed ripe for poignancy.

"This place looks really old," he said finally. "It looks like zombies attacked it."

How do you measure a life's worth? On December 14, 2011, my father will be ninety years old. He never thought he would live to see his fortieth birthday. When I was born, he said he hoped to live to see me graduate from elementary school. Now it is possible that he will live to see my daughters graduate. When he was a boy, Italian girls still didn't go out without chaperones. I would say that this was before people were shot and killed in our old neighborhood, but that wouldn't be true exactly. People were just shot and killed under different circumstances. The neighborhood has a long history of crime, just as it has a long history of family. What *is* true is that my father raised me there oblivious—or volitionally blind—to the neighborhood's shortcomings and conscious only of its strengths. When I went away to college, he cried. I had betrayed the family, in a way. I wouldn't stay put. I would not learn what he was trying to teach me. He believed I didn't understand about loyalty. I believed that too. I believed loyalty was cheap. I wanted to be Sabina from *The Unbearable Lightness of Being*. I wanted a life based on betrayals and escapes, and for a time, I created some sexy facsimile of that, although

I felt it unraveling in my fingers even as I clutched at it ferociously. In the end, despite years in Madison, London, New Hampshire, New Mexico, or Amsterdam, I ended up back in Chicago with my parents living downstairs from me, just as my grandmothers—first my father's, then my mother's—resided in our house when I was a girl. In the end, the only thing I was truly capable of betraying was my own fantasy of myself as someone else, someone other than my father's loyal daughter, who would throw him under the bus for my babies just as he would have thrown his parents under the bus for me. The night his mother died was Christmas Eve, 1980, and within hours of her death my father resumed our holiday festivities—though he was my grandmother's baby, the one with whom she had lived after all her other sons left home, he did not take the time to mourn alone because he didn't want to spoil my Christmas. I have taken my father out to dinner plenty of times, but someday when he is gone I will nurse my regrets as he nurses his about his own father: *The things I could have done, the more I could have given.*

"Sometimes I see things that aren't there," I tell my father when I am in my late twenties. "Figures walking into rooms and things like that."

"Oh, sure," my father says. "That happens to everyone."

"Sometimes when I'm lying in bed, I hear someone calling my name."

"That's normal," my father confirms. "That happens to me all the time."

We are the lion in the house, my father and I, waiting to pounce. On anyone who threatens the family—but first and foremost, on ourselves.

Once upon a time, my father was a hero. He was trained to drive a tank in World War II, but his ulcer and bad back got him sent home before he could be deployed overseas. Instead, his heroism took place on quieter grounds. Years ago, while hanging out at his men's club shooting craps with his friends, a young girl, maybe nineteen or twenty, entered the club. She claimed to want a few dollars for the bus, but it is clear to me now, from an adult lens, that this probably wasn't what she really thought to achieve, walking into a crowded men's club full of ex-cons and soliciting money, then failing to leave when all the men began suggesting to her the things she might do to earn it. They were laughing, saying the things men say, and the girl was maybe laughing with them, the way some young girls have to in order to survive. Amid this my father stood up, took out twenty dollars and handed it to the girl. "You need to leave now, honey," he told her, and walked her to the door.

Another time, many years later, my father was having some coffee in the little eating area of Target, when some scruffy teenagers came in. He saw them go to the counter, where one scraped together just enough change to buy a tiny personal pizza, and they all sat around a table while the one who had purchased the pizza ate. The way the others stared intently at the pizza was something my father recognized. Although he always managed to keep his own head above water, he had seen hunger in his life, and it was something he understood. He went to the counter and said quietly, "Give those kids whatever they want to eat, and I'll pay for it." The counter girl went up to the teens and told them they could have what they wanted, and they all ran up and ordered food excitedly. My father sat, drinking his coffee, while they devoured their food. He did not speak to them or tell them that he was the one who had paid for their meal. He waited until after they had been gone for a while before he himself left. "I didn't want them to think I was a masher," he told my mother, laughing himself off.

He would never relay these stories to me himself. It would seem to him like bragging.

My cousin Biff and his brother, my cousin Laura and her sister, my friend Alicia. The litany of young people who have looked to my father as a stable force in their lives, a father figure, is considerable. Even now, when we take him to a family wedding, men from the old neighborhood—middle-aged themselves now—jump up to help him to his seat, to get him a drink, to hover around him talking about old times, to hold open doors.

My mother and I have tried to suggest having a party for his ninetieth, where all the many people who love him could gather, but he won't hear of it. "Oh, Jesus Christ," he says. The trappings of a party—having to maneuver around with his walker, possibly falling down as he often does, or not making it to the bathroom in time—have been added to the long list of things that make him anxious. His world shrinks, month by month, day by day. Recently he realized that although he can still read, he can no longer recite the alphabet or remember the order of the letters. Only Lindsay Lohan and Paris Hilton, on the pages of his morning *Star,* remain as some reminder of wider terrain. Recently, I was on the nominating committee for the Chicago Literary Hall of Fame and nominated my father's longtime hero, Mike Royko, for inclusion. Although Royko was selected, there was no possibility of my father attending the awards ceremony with me. Those days have passed. When I told him about Royko's induction, I had to shout and repeat myself several times to get my point across, upon which he simply said, "That's nice, honey."

He is on a journey across the white barren land, inside himself, from us. We stand on the periphery and watch him ride away.

What is love? Is it possible to love by degree? If a love is not the greatest of all loves, is it love at all? Is a life lived to ninety more "full" than one lived to fifty? What if the life lived to ninety was consumed by anxieties, by illnesses, by complexes and regrets? Where does quality intersect with quantity? But what defines quality anyway? Is existence itself "quality" enough?

Sometimes I wonder if I am grieving because I know I will soon lose my father, or if I am grieving for the facets of life my father has already lost.

"Kill me if I get that way," I tell my husband and my surrogate brother Tom, after watching my mother-in-law die slowly, unable to speak, vomiting on herself if she tried to sit up, her flesh an empty sack loose around her bones. After listening to my father scream at a god in whom he does not even believe, begging for death, that Christmas he broke his hip and my husband, mother, and I had to change his diapers while the antibiotics ravaged him with explosive diarrhea. "I'll make sure I have enough pills in the house," I promise. "Do it quickly."

They look at me patiently. They know I seek to escape the indignity of Death just as I once escaped my old neighborhood. They know I grew up with the mistaken impression that cleverness could exempt me from anything. But I read Emily's memoir; I go to chemo with my friend Kathy; our phone rings in the middle of the night because my father has fallen again on his way to the bathroom, and the truth is that *nobody* is exempt. We are all the walking dead of history. This goddamn place looks like zombies attacked it.

It is a day in late 2011. My father's oldest friend in the world, Mario, whom he has known since they were three years old, has had his leg amputated and has been convalescing at home. My father has avoided going to see him because he can't stand the thought of Mario without a leg, and it is easy to avoid things when you are almost ninety, disabled, incontinent, and seeing nonexistent mice on the floor. But now Mario's sister has died and my father has to attend the wake. My mother, who did not know how to drive until she was seventy and learned only when my father's feet failed him on the brakes and he ran his car into a pole to avoid hitting pedestrians, drives to the funeral parlor. At the door, my father sees Mario in his wheelchair. Other men rush to get a chair for my father and place it beside Mario. They sit: two old men who used to play in front of the house we were all raised in, when they were younger than my son. They talk: the two of them with legs that are missing like dead brothers or that no longer work. In the contradictory movie montage of my mind, I have no access to the specifics of their dialogue, but somehow I know there is laughter. I know they call each other

"Baby" like Frank Sinatra, as they always have. They are historical relics from a day of covered bridges downtown and chaperones for young Italian girls. Through some accident of mistaken identity or grace, they are still alive.

That same day, in another area of Chicago, Giovanni has his first kiss. In the coat room of his classroom, like generations of boys before him, he asks a pretty blonde girl he has known since preschool, "So, do you want a kiss?" and she says, "Sure," so he leans in for the kill. When I ask him if he kissed her on her cheek or her lips, he shrugs at me and drawls evasively, "Oh, I don't know . . ." Since beginning kindergarten in September, he has already had four fiancées. As my father and his friend Mario sit in the dim fluorescent light of the funeral parlor foyer, my son gets ready for bed, excitedly reading aloud from the *Magic Treehouse* series. We "snug" together in the darkness, and he twirls a strand of my hair around his finger absently as he makes the jerky breaths the precipitate sleep.

His life is contained in this moment. In the moment of his first kiss. In the moment of sleepy breath and Mommy hair. In the moment of his brain's voracious recognition of symbols on a page: letters that form words that form language that form story. My father's life exists within the single frame of laughter with his childhood friend, as they commemorate yet another death—"doomed," as Faulkner wrote, to be the ones "who live." *Now.* Buddhists tell us to live in the moment, but the moment already contains us, whether we want it to or not. "When I find myself laughing at something now," my friend Kathy tells me in the tenth week of her chemo, "I feel conscious of it more, and I'm grateful." She did not *choose* this gratitude. In an instant, she would trade it back for her old, blithe ways. But it is coming for us all: the recognition of the miraculous ordinary. We ignore it as long as we can, until we can't anymore. We flash brief and bright against the sky just once, just a hundred, just a million tiny times. Beautiful, singular, vibrant; full of love and pain. Then we are out.

Matthew Ferrence

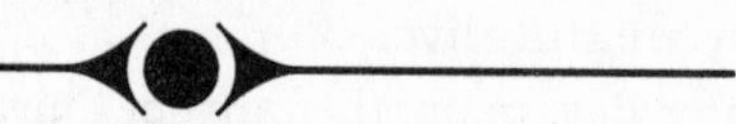

THE SLASHING

TWO DEER EMERGED out of the thick upper woods of my parents' farm, a place my father and brother called the Slashing. For two weeks, I had waited for this moment. Since the cold opening morning of deer season—always the Monday after Thanksgiving in Pennsylvania—I had climbed into one of three tree stands my father and brother had built from scrap lumber and pallets. For six years Greg had been hunting with our father, and in the winter of 1987 my time had come. When the two deer appeared, the numb of cold and waiting disappeared instantly in a thrum of adrenaline.

I raised my rifle, a .32 Special my father had handpicked from his collection because of its low kick and decent stopping power. I remember laying my cheek to the stock, trying to fix the muzzle's bead in the fork of the rear sight, but unable to keep the barrel from vibrating across the clearing in front of me. I aimed for the dark spot behind one of the deer's front shoulders, or tried to. I looked for the hollow my father had taught me would lead to a quick kill, the bullet driving through the lungs, heart, through meat and bone. But I never found the spot, nor even picked either of the deer as my target. Instead, the gun seemed to go off on its own, long before I'd settled my heartbeat, or thought to hold my breath, or do more than point the gun in the general direction of the deer.

One fell immediately, a sack of dead venison. Later, we discovered a neat hole through the spine, just below the head: a lucky shot.

In the quiet that followed the echo of the gun's blast, I watched the smaller deer stand confused, staring toward the fallen doe. I hadn't yet considered the kinship, doe and fawn, or that the younger animal was now alone in the Slashing, likely doomed as well, easy prey for a coyote, a bobcat, even a loose dog. In the days after the shot, my father kidded me about my choice of deer, about taking the tougher meat over the tender animal, a joke I sometimes even initiated. But in the silence that followed the shot, in the silence before my father's deep, proud voice asked if I'd gotten one, I started to wonder about luck, and choices, and connection. As I watched the confused fawn, hardly old enough to have lost its spots, I foolishly gave thanks that I hadn't hit the young animal. I thought the shot had been lucky on two accounts: that it had hit anything at all and that it hadn't found fresh flesh.

Fifteen years later, my father and I stood on the top of a mountain and stared out across a different open field, the flatlands of northern Sonora. I lived then in southern Arizona with my wife, who had agreed to relocate so I could follow the academic path I now think of as the family business. Professorships run in the family: my father in biology, my brother in chemistry. I had originally come to Arizona to follow suit. But on the day my father and I stood at the top of Montezuma Pass and looked out across the dry Mexican plains, I'd given up.

The Pass stands at the edge of Arizona, the last high point before the Huachuca Mountains descend into the desert, cross under a few strands of barbed wire, and become Mexico. As mountains go, it's an easy climb. A dirt road winds upward from the grasslands below, hugging the rock face of the pass. From there, the peak is only a ten-minute hike, a pleasant stroll along a steady grade.

My father and I walked it easily, in an awkward silence that he probably never noticed. I'd resigned a few weeks before, but had yet to tell him. As we walked, I worried, expecting disappointment and, likely, advice to reconsider. Advice came easily from my father, frequently as unwelcome as it was well-intentioned. Growing up, I'd recognized how the paths I desired weren't always the same as his, and his advice often grated, particularly when it sought to nudge me back to the course he knew. I took it poorly, if quietly, considering unsolicited guidance an imposition. I felt the pressure not to disappoint expectations half-existent and half-created by my own insecurities.

Somewhere near the top, where the trail opened to a wide knoll and where all of Mexico seemed to lie at the foot of the mountains, I explained what had happened: that I was now a writer, and a golfer. Wind blew, and the December sun felt warm against our faces. To our left, I spotted tiny Naco, where my home golf course appeared as a block of green.

My father said little. I knew he was disappointed, perhaps not in me but for me, not understanding why I'd so quickly abandoned what he knew to be a safe and comfortable life. Shock might have edited his response, pared it down to a side-by-side viewing of a brightly lit landscape. I worried about what we didn't share, that my decision to quit marked a heavy blow against us. As a child I'd always said I wanted to take over his office when he retired, a remark he repeated often and an idea I knew touched him deeply. We stood beside each other, each of us perhaps wondering where closeness resides when differences mount. So we avoided the topic I'd worried about, stowed it away in silent parts where we'd brood, in our ways, and never speak of my decision again.

The fawn lingered beside its fallen mother, then darted as it heard my father's voice call out to me. He appeared from the Slashing, his orange snowsuit glowing in the gray afternoon. Together, we dragged the deer into the open field that abutted the woods, where he showed me how to properly gut it. I used the knife, a young boy's honor, to hold the gleaming steel, to press it against hide and pierce the belly. He showed me what to remove, and told me what each glistening organ was—an impromptu anatomy lab—then left me to wait beside the steaming carcass while he fetched the tractor.

I don't know how long I waited. Likely half an hour, long enough for the afternoon to turn toward night. As I sat in the field, the setting sun blinked away. Twilight had set in by the time I heard the puttering motor of the tractor, and darkness gathered as my father and I heaved the deer into the wooden cart.

Climbing in beside the carcass marked a relief different from the shooting of the deer, which itself had been the culmination of a gathered force, the final act of a long-awaited moment. For six years, ever since my brother had killed his own first deer, then smiled giddily next to the dripping body hanging in the barn, I had wanted that moment for myself. I wanted to see myself in a picture like my brother's. I wanted to see myself posing beside a deer I'd brought down, wanted to see the smile plastered on my face. I wanted, also, a picture like the many I'd seen of my father—a deer in the trunk of his car or a deer dead beside him in the snow. Shooting a deer marked entrance into a fraternity of men, marked acceptance into a world my father tried always to sustain.

Now, in the cold woods, I had taken the deer I longed for. The relief I felt sitting next to its bloodied and emptied body came because I was glad to end the loneliness of my wait, came as I thankfully watched the darkened edges of the woods disappear behind me. My father pulled the throttle lever, roared the tractor.

I never liked being alone in the woods, even with a gun. I always felt uneasy and afraid, even when I knew my father sat nearby. Maybe I never quite understood his proximity, which always exacted a practiced illusion of solitude. I never knew where he was, always imagined him far away from me, alone under a canopy of branches. Truly, he never strayed far, always choosing a spot out of sight but within easy earshot. One high school summer on a family vacation, I took my saxophone to the boardwalk, to play by the waves with an open case and hopes of fortune. He disappeared, leaving me on my own, but I later learned he'd only walked far enough to allow me space. He sat in the dark on a nearby bench, listening to me play, partly to share my joy, and partly to guarantee my joy would not be threatened.

So there is some irony in the way I approached the woods my first hunting year, when I leaned against a tree with a shotgun held tightly in my hands, watching for squirrels, or when I perched in a tree stand on the edges of the Slashing, waiting for deer. For me, the gun became an object of protection, just in case my irrational childhood fears proved accurate. A wolf, a mad dog, a grizzly with a poor sense of geography. Against these, I hoped my gun would pass clear and final judgment. Yet I felt alone in the woods, inferior and out of my element, perhaps aware even then of the differences between my soul and my father's. I understood only the desire to be together with him, an emotion transferred to hunting, to shooting, to pulling the trigger and feeling pride well up. I understand now, of course, how little the pride related to hunting itself, and how much my father's own fears likely mirrored my own. Beyond all else, his fear was of separation, of being alone in the woods without his sons, of them being alone in the woods, afraid.

I came to golf on my own, linked to the game only by my maternal grandfather, who died before I was born. He was a golfer, even lived on a course, where he played quick holes after coming home from delivering mail. It was finding his old set of Wilson golf clubs in the basement that set my golfing life in motion.

In the backyard, I carved deep holes with these relics, at first missing the ball far more often than I hit it. And when I did manage contact, I mostly landed my shots in the bushes beside the barn, or in the pond, or in the bank of thick grass behind the pond. I rapidly spent my ammunition, those ancient balata balls with oddly shaped dimples, and I spent too much time on my hands and knees, inching carefully through the piercing branches of low-hanging pine trees.

One Christmas, my family presented to me a succession of wrapped balls, all formerly lost, a recovery effort my father had organized, and a presentation that left him breathless from laughter.

Hunting came with its own preparations: labor that earned us the right to shoulder rifles once the season opened. In the weeks before Thanksgiving, I would ride on the back of my father's tractor several times as we toted scrap lumber into the upper fields. A year of weather splintered the wood, as had the fists and boots of unknown locals, who waged war against my father's tree stands. In the summer, they tore them from the trees, leaving piles of broken wood in the Slashing. No doubt, such hunters resented my father's ownership of the land and, more, didn't like the competition for the antlers.

The abuse left work to be done, holes to patch, railings to repair. As the younger son, my duties were small and monotonous, the pulling of nails from old boards while my brother and father sawed and hammered. I gathered brush while my father trimmed shooting lanes in the clearing with his chainsaw and my brother lopped off saplings with a hand saw. We operated in a hierarchy of dangerous tools, and my place involved nothing sharper than a pry bar.

I recognize in myself a shared love of preparation, if not of labor: mapping golf courses, pacing yardages to sand traps and dogleg corners, drawing intricate course maps. Beside the Slashing, my father often climbed the tree stand I would use, looking across the clearing he'd opened in the woods, making sure he'd created the best conditions for me, to make sure nothing would get in the way if a deer appeared. He judged distances, too, like I do now on golf courses, setting in motion my understanding of preparation.

Now that he's turned in retirement to bigger animals, to moose and elk he hunts in distant states, my father has shifted his attention from tree stands to bullets. Before hunts, he bundles wet newspapers and riddles them with bullets of different weights, different powders, different tips. I spend quiet moments considering the merits of golf balls that spin more versus golf balls that fly farther, while he slowly winnows his choice of powder load. In the end, we both know the work makes it easier. I stand on practice greens, watching balls ricochet off the grass. He dons heavy orange ear protection and punches holes in his target. In the end, we do our work alone, each regarding the velocity of objects moving away.

I've always been impressed, even envious, that my father practices little as part of his hunting preparations. He rarely misses in the field, which comes in part through the careful selection of moment: he passes on shots most hunters gladly take, is unaffected by the fever that compels men to take wild risks in the hopes of killing an animal. I admire the familiar way he wields a gun, a comfort that has come through decades of use. Yet I've never known him to visit a gun range, nor known him to spend time shooting unless weighing bullet value or sighting in his rifles. I do not share this skill in golf. Rather, a few days away from the practice tee leaves my swing in shambles, and my shots soon resemble wounded fowl, fluttering obliquely to my intention, diving away into areas best left unvisited by score-conscious golfers. I've therefore learned to love the practice range, or at least to accept the dirty work of practice since it leads to better performance. I prune my swing as my father used to clear firing lanes, clipping away stray movements to make sure I'm ready when the shot appears.

I try to imagine, now, my time in the field, which has through the years become a dulled memory not easily recovered. I remember the darkness of the first day of my first buck season, of riding up the hill on the back of my father's tractor—willful noise he intended, partly, to irritate the anonymous hunters who had stolen his ladders. I remember standing in the tree stand with him that first day, growing colder and less interested as time wound on deerless. I remember looking out across the field from above, my father beside me, together watching silently.

I returned to the tree stand often through a fruitless buck season, then on into the consolation of doe season. My father's disappointment grew until, on the last day, he pressed into the Slashing to mount a drive. He moved through the undergrowth loudly to flush the deer, until he forced the doe and fawn out into the clearing. I imagine the leap he must have felt at the report of my rifle, and the brief catch in his throat before he shouted to me. I imagine him smiling when I replied, both of us giddy and victorious, neither realizing that the fallen doe marked the last time we would share a successful hunt, that I would soon skitter away toward other pursuits.

Not long after we climbed Montezuma Pass together, a tournament brought me to the driving range. My father joined me and sat in the afternoon sunshine while I pelted balls downrange. I struggled that day, mired in a slump, and a disappointingly high percentage of shots skittered away without integrity. I liked shots that emerged crisply, a brief entrapment of the ball against turf followed by a pinched release, a launch that came with an audible scouring of earth. My shots that day did not follow such a pattern, the unreliability of my swing yielding only weak, looping shots that fell wide of my targets.

Behind me, my father watched the shots sail away, the bad ones mostly to the right—a hacker's miss. Eventually, I found a groove of some kind and, buoyed by the better shots, showed off a little. I invited him to pick a target, trajectory, and curve, and I'd hit the corresponding shots. He called them out, suggesting I aim at the third telephone pole from the left, or the blue flag, curve it left, hit it low. I complied, and sometimes even mustered the right shot for the call, but mostly let out disgusted grunts as the golf balls refused to go where they were told. Golf has never mattered to my father, and my own failed command did nothing to suggest that it should. I intended this as my career, as an extension of myself into the world, and I couldn't pass muster. That my father didn't care about the poor shots should have been, perhaps, a comfort—that he cared for me regardless of what I could or could not do: coming with me to the range, even, had been an act of support. But I wanted to demonstrate mastery of myself there on the dusty range, to show I knew who I was and what I was doing, yet each errant shot traced an arc of incompetence and confusion, traced my own disappointment in the thin air.

My father watched as I aimed at the shopping mall far to my left, and the golf ball bent toward the empty lot far to my right. He considered this. The problem, he said, is the ball doesn't seem to be going where you want it. He offered the diagnosis flatly, with the measured tone of scholarly advice. This was, after all, the problem, obvious to even an untrained eye.

My father has never been a golfer. Once, he took up the game briefly, when I was still in high school, still struggling to find my game. The effort came from precisely the same place my early hunting days did: as a manifestation of desire. My father simply wanted to spend time with me, and with my brother, who had taken up the game a few years after me. He saw golf, no doubt, as a chance to get together as men, to reclaim the decayed hunting fraternity.

Things did not go well on the golf course, though neither did they go particularly badly. We played nine holes in a blend of joy and embarrassment. Two moments linger in our shared memories: one story that I retell with my father, and the other with my brother. My father and I discuss the last hole, where my brother launched a wicked line drive that sliced quickly away to the right. The ball whizzed three feet above the heads of a startled group of golfers while we watched in awe, sure someone would die. My brother and I reminisce about the hole before that, when my father disappeared into the underbrush. Time slowed there, while he searched for a ball Greg had launched into the thicket. For many minutes, we watched the woods for our father but saw nothing. We heard only his occasional baritone calling out a brand of golf ball. Top-Flite? Slazenger? Red Dot? At least a dozen times he shouted out names that did not correspond with the ball my brother had lost, and when he finally emerged, my father grinned widely at his windfall of golf balls. For him, the successful hunt in the woods rose above the game itself.

I recognized in myself this same gloried discovery, years later on a Maryland resort golf course that I played on quiet afternoons. A large lake bordered the left-hand side of the eighth hole, a collar of tall weeds separating the water from the fairway. Each time I played that hole, I walked through those weeds. Each time, I filled my pockets to brimming with lost balls, most in perfect condition. I supplied myself with enough ammunition to last the rest of that summer and most of the next.

I don't remember another golf outing with my father, and I don't think he ever even swung a club again after that day on the ragged nine-hole course. Instinctively, we both understood that the game would always remain as inscrutable to him as hunting does to me. And we both knew that pretending otherwise would be foolish. My grandfather's golf clubs returned to the basement, and my father and I never again walked together on the golf course, just as I never killed another deer. I hunted one more day, I think—the first morning of my second season—then gave up, cold and bored.

I have in recent years spent many days with my father-in-law on golf courses, in the process creating illogical but palpable sensations of betrayal. Often, my father-in-law has also invited me to join him in the field, explaining the pleasures of bird hunting with a dog. I always decline, and I know I'll never join him there, because to do so would be to insult my father's love. I don't enjoy hunting; I know this. And I know, too, that even as my father has accepted the many ways we aren't the same, he longs for things he imagined doing with his sons. I wonder if acceptance is enough, if my refusal to share the pleasures of the field is simply the willfulness of a son who, standing near his father, never feels grown up. At times I finger my old hunting license, which for nearly twenty years rested in the same spot in my parents' kitchen drawer and, now, hangs on the wall of my study. I've considered taking it in to the sporting goods store as proof of my training, paying my cash and bringing home a current license. I imagine, sometimes, calling my father up and setting a date to hunt small game. I wonder which shotgun he'd provide, probably something bigger than the old .410 I used in my brief hunting career, and I picture us walking together in sunlit fields among dried stalks of corn. I imagine my dog reclaiming her beagle nature, chasing a rabbit across our path. My father and I would both raise our guns, and he'd let me take the shot.

Jim Kennedy

END OF THE LINE

I WAS BORN in Baltimore on September 11, 1955. I am white, male, and a lapsed Irish Catholic. I love my family, immediate and extended, but keep my feelings too much of a secret. My father is gone. He lived a full life and left behind five children and a dozen grandchildren. One of my sons was snatched by the sea on a day when the water seemed calm. How things happen sometimes does not make sense.

I did all my growing up in Baltimore and then married Boston. For a living, as I used to tell my sons when they were very young, I crunch and juggle numbers. Then I would demonstrate this by writing giant numbers with a Magic Marker on several blank pieces of paper, crumpling each page and juggling them. I spend most of my free time writing, reading, and walking. The subway stop nearest my home is Forest Hills Station, the end of the Orange Line in Boston.

The Orange Line—at least, the portion from Back Bay to the southern terminus at Forest Hills—was reconstructed during the 1980s. I now commute every workday on the Orange Line. I know it well. I am intimate with the texture of the seats on the cars. I am familiar with the looks on the faces of the passengers when one more person insists on squeezing onto a packed train, when those standing—all strangers—have already used every cavity of space in order not to press closer together than they would if they had just joined together for a slow dance.

I once became so involved in conversation with someone whom I barely knew that neither of us noticed the train had stopped at Forest Hills, that more than the usual number of passengers had departed, that the train had lingered longer than it had at prior stations. Locked in our conversation, we did not even notice, after the doors had closed and for eight more stops afterward, that the train was then moving in the opposite direction.

But my stomach noticed the moment we reversed directions. I can no longer remember any of the words we spoke, but I remember very well the queasy feeling in my stomach, as if I had violated a law of nature by not getting off at the end of the line.

I remember, too, how my two younger boys, Thomas and Max, preferred to stand when they rode with me on the Orange Line. And I knew exactly why. They gravitated to that visceral feeling of imbalance, that stimulating inner tickle. Like kids spinning themselves dizzy, always laughing. They could feel so keenly the physical momentum that pushed them backward as the train sped forward and that thrust them forward as the train came to a stop. They could maintain their balance without holding onto anything. Thomas, as he did this, would cast a smile my way. He and his brother were surfing the Orange Line.

I was delighted by their delight, even as I hovered cautiously nearby, ready to put some part of myself—an arm, a leg, my whole body if necessary—between their heads and a metal pole or a hard seat, if either of them began to fall.

On March 17, 2005, I went in to work briefly. I met with two higher-ups about an important issue, and then I headed out of my office to Haymarket, the nearest Orange Line station. It was 10:30 a.m., and I was heading home to enjoy the rest of my Saint Patrick's holiday.

If I actually stood down on the tracks (not a good idea), the subway station platforms would be at my shoulder height. This was something I had never thought about before that day.

In Haymarket Station, you can see portions of one side of the station from the other side through openings in a partial wall that runs between the two sets of tracks. During my many waits in Haymarket Station, I had stared vacantly through these openings at people standing on the other side.

That morning, I looked through the opening and saw on the other side a large young man standing down on the tracks and desperately trying to pull himself up to the platform. A train would be coming through on those tracks any minute. I briefly considered jumping down and crossing over to the other side, but my eyes fixed on the live third rail and the terse warning sign above: a red lightning bolt. The thought of calling 911 on my cell phone or of running up to tell the station attendant flashed through my mind. Others would do those things. And all of that would be too slow.

I dashed up the stairs, ran across the station lobby, and then quick-stepped down the stairs on the other side. When I got there, a scrawny young man who did not understand English and a wisp of a young teenage girl, together, were attempting to pull the guy up. They were unable to lift him even an inch off the tracks. He was a very big, very large, very heavy guy. As they kept trying to pull him up, I lay down and stretched out over the platform's edge. With both my hands, I grabbed tightly onto the back of his blue jeans. I pulled upward for all I was worth. The three of us somehow managed to hoist him onto the platform.

The big guy looked Irish American, and he seemed inebriated. I assumed he had simply begun his Saint Patrick's Day celebrating very early this year, but he must have been high on some more serious intoxicant.

I had to use all my wits to keep him from falling back onto the tracks. He kept imagining a phantom train arriving. He kept moving forward to get onto this imagined train. Finally, I convinced him to sit down on a set of steps about ten feet back. To distract him, I told him bits of stories in rapid-fire succession.

But he kept looking past me to the tracks. He stood up, and I stood in his way and pointed to an advertisement on the wall and shouted, "Did you notice—?" He kept mumbling, "Here's the train."

At that point, I was prepared to tackle him if he headed toward his phantom train. I was sure I would not have the strength to pull him up if he fell again. Eventually, the police arrived in response to someone's 911 call and escorted him out of the station.

A few months later, I found myself sitting directly across from the same guy on an Orange Line train. I did not immediately recognize him. Sitting there, sober and quiet, he seemed like a different person. It took a minute for me to feel sure it was him. He did not recognize me. I did not expect him to. I thought he might remember the event. I tried to think up a conversation starter, something like, "A few months ago, you were down on the tracks at Haymarket," but I was sure such an attempt would be met with a blank stare. I sank back into my seat and waited for the train to make it to the end of the line.

At the end of the Orange Line is a cemetery, Forest Hills Cemetery. Eugene O'Neill is buried there. I have stood at his grave and pondered his long day's journey into night.

I feel at home in a cemetery. Cemeteries are usually devoid of vertical people, chatty people, people concerned with trivial matters. They are full of horizontal people, profoundly quiet people, many of whom lived long lives and now have plenty of time to digest the full meaning of a life that had a beginning, a middle, an end.

Well, not exactly, of course. But that is the feeling I experience as I wander randomly through Forest Hills Cemetery. Though I bear a superficial resemblance to the vertical people, I have so much more in common with the horizontals. Sometimes I walk among them for hours.

In 2008, I dreamed about my father for the first time in a long time. He died in 1993. The day before the dream, I had talked on the phone with my sister, and she described herself and Mom having trouble finding Dad's grave. The image of them wandering in the cemetery stirred my memories and surely stimulated my dream.

It was a happy dream, a happy version of my father, as if he were making a personal visit. He was fresh out of college—his handsomest, happiest, most alive and aware self. After college, he served in the navy on the aircraft carrier USS *Block Island,* which was torpedoed by a German sub, but he and nearly all his shipmates were rescued. After the service, almost by happenstance, he landed in the FBI, where he spent much of his career investigating bank robberies. He was a good father, a good husband, a good friend to many. In this dream, he said nothing. He simply showed himself to me, as if to say, "This is how to remember me," or, "This is who I am." The dream gave me a feeling of immense relief. It replaced the memory that had dominated my thoughts: my father, in his last years, physically shrinking away.

After the drowning in August 1995, the police began to search the ocean for my ten-year-old son's body. I was too distraught to be of much help. I have since written about every remembered moment Thomas and I spent together his last day, a day we joyfully spent together, until these last minutes:

The beach is no longer life-guarded and is relatively deserted. We are at an unusual stretch where the surf has carved a large, deep pocket into the beach, creating a surprisingly deep pool of water between the breakers and the tideline. It is an invitation to the kids, calmer on the surface than the stretches of beach to its left and right.

I stand at the water's edge, watching the kids closely. Max is finally going into the water a little bit rather than only digging in the sand or collecting shells. I decide it is better to be in the water with the kids. I go near the beach chairs to take off and toss my shirt. I speak briefly to my sister and then join the kids in the water.

I go in the water close to Max. I am there for only a moment when I hear Thomas and look over. He has been suddenly pulled off his feet and swept up in an undercurrent, his arms raised straight up as he lets out a yelp. I run as much as I can in the shallow water and then dive in and quickly swim up to him.

My sister makes sure Max and her son make it back to shore. They have been in water shallow enough to be outside the undercurrent.

I make it quickly out to Thomas and am holding him. I assume we will soon make our way back to the beach. Instead, together, we are losing control and being pulled out in the strong undercurrent, and the ocean floor is quickly beyond the reach of our feet. Just then, a series of harsh and high waves break on us with unusual frequency. I make an attempt to lift Thomas over these waves as they break, but this fails as the waves crest over his head. Exhaustion is now beginning to undermine my rescue efforts. Thomas is clinging hard to me; I can feel the fingers of one hand digging into my shoulder and those on his other hand tightly grasping the hair on my head. His weight is now on my shoulders. I cannot keep my head above the surface, and I breathe in water.

I experience the helpless feeling of heavily falling into empty space. We are drowning. Then, in one profoundly strong motion, I separate myself from Thomas's weight upon me by grasping him and throwing him off. It is a strong heave. He is facing me as he sails into the air. I see his look of bewildered surprise as briefly and as clearly as one sees lightning flash in the sky.

I soon see Thomas fifteen or twenty yards away and floating on the water's surface with his face turned down into the water. We are still being pulled out by the current. Because the waves are high and we are now far from shore, I can no longer see my sister and the kids on the beach. When I first spot Thomas face down in the water, I am paralyzed by exhaustion. Then I feel the return of energy. Because we are well beyond where the waves are breaking, I am able to swim out to Thomas and grab hold of him. He is unconscious.

The water is deep, and the only thing my instinct tells me to do is tug him in by the upper arm toward the shore; so I do, for a good distance. I am too much in shock to do any clear thinking. I am hoping Thomas can be revived once we reach shore; I am dreading that I am pulling in my dead son's body.

Then we reach where the waves are breaking. I look back and get a brief glance at a large wave just before it breaks on us. We are roiled by this powerful wave. My last grasp on his arm slides right off; my last attempt to grasp any of him is futile amid the underwater surge of the wave. I get tossed and turned under the water, and my back bounces hard against the ocean floor. I come back up, and Thomas is gone. He has been pulled into the underwater current and is not seen again that day.

I assumed an ocean burial. I took little interest in the search for the body and began instead, almost immediately, to search the ocean of my mind for what of Thomas's life was still in my possession and to commit that to paper, with the intent of sharing it with whoever would read it, as a poor substitute for the impact his life might have had on others.

The small police department had plenty of experience with drownings, apparently. Regarding the immediate grim task of recovering the body, they were familiar with the ocean's patterns. I was told that the bodies often disappeared for a few days but then washed ashore on Assateague Island, a few miles to the south, driven there by the near shore currents. They wanted to know what color of bathing suit Thomas was wearing. They thought that might help them spot the body from their helicopter.

I knew only one major fact about Assateague Island: Some unique breed of small horses—called ponies, I think, because of their size—lives there. The younger of my two sisters had described to me an experience that occurred years ago when she camped overnight on the island. She was having a dream, and in the dream, the thing that never happens in dreams happened: She died. She did not dream of herself almost dying and then wake up. She dreamed that she died. Imagine her surprise when she lifted her eyelids: She was alive, and one of these small island horses had its head stuck inside her open tent. Startled by her waking, the horse quickly galloped off down the beach.

Once, Thomas, a little boy then, was heading down our stairs, from the second to the first floor. I was in front of him. He was moving a little too fast and, halfway down, misplaced his next footstep. His forward momentum propelled him into a head-diving motion, but before his head hit the step, I was able to pivot and catch him upside down, my arms around his midsection.

My father, who was visiting and at that moment was just below us in the front hallway, witnessed it all. Just as I grabbed Thomas upside down in my arms, just inches from hitting his head on the steps, my father and I looked into each other's eyes and experienced the moment as one.

Joan Marcus

SURVIVAL STORIES

THE WAY MY mother told the tale, the tuna sandwich saved my father's life. She'd fixed it that morning—albacore and Bonbel cheese on Pepperidge Farm white bread—packed it in a brown bag and placed it in his briefcase. Then she'd driven him to the Catholic women's college where he taught art history. My father started feeling peckish on the way over. By the time they'd pulled up in front of the art building, he'd already unwrapped the sandwich and started eating it. Moving down the walkway toward the front door, he stopped to take a bite and heard a loud, long scraping noise, like a mess of slate shingles sliding off a roof. He froze in place, sandwich lifted to his mouth. A split second later, an enormous oak limb came crashing down not two feet from where he stood. "The *size* of that thing," my mother whispered over the phone to her friend Dorothy that evening. "One step more . . . " She shook her head, speechless with horror. "Don't tell *me* that sandwich didn't save him."

It was not my father's first close call. As a merchant marine officer in World War II, he'd sailed on the freighter *Scappa Flow* to the Gulf of Guinea to take on a load of manganese ore, then disembarked stateside and took his shore leave. He learned later that the ship sank on her next trip out, destroyed by torpedo. He'd narrowly escaped a run on a doomed liberty ship to Murmansk by contracting a stomach virus right before the ship set sail. He'd made a trip to West Africa in 1942 on the *Zarembo,* the only ship of seven in its company to make it back to port. And sailing in a convoy off the coast of Cuba, he'd seen a munitions freighter torpedoed three miles off his starboard side and blasted to bits.

Then in 1947, while working in a frozen foods warehouse, my father backed through the open doors of an empty elevator shaft and fell two stories. The metal loading cart he'd been dragging fell on top of him, crushing his hip. Nearly sixty years later, an older relative mentioned in an offhand way that my father should have died from that fall, and I realized with a dull jolt how true this was. The accident happened almost two decades before I was born. All my life I'd taken his survival as a matter of course, perhaps because *he* seemed to. "They always tell you to wear clean underpants in case you end up in the hospital," he'd joke. "But when the time comes, believe me, it's the last thing on your mind." His survival stories weren't frightening—they were amusing, a pleasant way to pass the evening. Dad would sit in his armchair stretching his lame leg in front of him—it was stiff and painful for decades after his fall. I'd lie on the floor making noncommittal scratches on my math homework and listening again to the story of torpedo survivors he'd pulled from the drink, men who'd been drifting for days without rations. It made sense to me that my father was the rescuer in this tale and not the victim. The fact of his safety was part of the natural order of things.

My mother had a different perspective. For mom, the world was full of invisible threats—leaking stovepipes and faulty wiring, things sure to cause misery somewhere down the road. I remember striking a forbidden match once, shaking it out fast, then waiting in trepidation as my mother entered the kitchen and paused to sniff the air. "You lit a match in here?" The question was sharp, edged with fear.

"What's that?" I was ready to deny it.

"A match. Please, Joanie, if you did it just tell me."

In an instant I understood that it wasn't my playing with fire that upset her—it was the odor. An unidentified smell in the kitchen was one of the marks of imminent disaster for my mother, along with a rattle in the car engine and a cough that lasted more than five days. A smell meant ruptured gas lines, invisible pockets of poison. It's a good thing she didn't know about carbon monoxide; the idea that some deadly gasses *can't* be smelled would probably have driven her mad. At least then she had her nose to give her fair warning.

"I lit the match," I admitted. "I was just, I don't know . . . "

"Good." She let her breath out and smiled at me. She didn't fuss or scold, just went about fixing dinner on a gas stove that, at least for the moment, did not appear to pose a threat.

The world was in a state of perpetual disintegration for my mother. Buildings settled and machines corroded, things came unglued and unhinged, or burst into flame. Nothing could be relied on. Small wonder, then, that when my father lost his teaching job in 1976 and had to return to sea, my mother worried that his ship would go down like a boulder in the middle of the Atlantic. Over the years my parents had come to see that falling oak limb as an omen. First the college was plagued by financial woes, then it closed its doors for good and Boston College purchased the pretty, suburban campus with its apple trees and woodland trails. My father didn't have a doctorate and finding full-time teaching work didn't look likely. His decision to return to the merchant marine when I was eleven made all of us miserable. My little brother and I dreaded the long, bleak months in his absence. Dad was anxious about adjusting to a new sleep schedule that included a midnight-to-4-AM deck watch. But mom saw a future marred by disaster on a massive scale. It wasn't inevitable, but it was possible. And if it was possible, it was worth fretting over.

As a child, I had the choice of adopting my mother's ideas about the risks of ocean travel or my father's. The decision seemed simple. Mom had always admitted that her anxiety was out of control. She made no secret of her many years of therapy or the vial of blue pills on her dresser. Other mothers let their children walk down the street to their friends' homes unsupervised. They didn't worry that a pedophile was lurking in the leaf-blown trolley underpass, or force their families on a tedious train ride to Florida because flying terrified them. I watched my mother pacing the hall of our apartment when my father's ship was overdue, watched her phone the shipping company and receive the inevitable response. The tanker was currently en route to the port of Alexandria—no saying when it would arrive. No, they could not tell her the exact location. No ma'am, there had been no reports of trouble. I stood beside her and heard the clerk's indifferent drawl. No one else seemed to take her fears seriously—why should I?

Anyway, it wasn't in my nature as a child to worry about large-scale disasters. Though I was already showing evidence of my own anxiety disorder in some nascent hypochondria, I still loved being tossed about by things larger than myself. I rode loop coasters and Tilt-A-Whirls and Screamin' Eagles with abandon, flew fearlessly, even enjoyed the turbulence. Nothing thrilled me more than an express trip sixty flights up to the top of the John Hancock tower. That surge in the core of me as the elevator flew skyward, then the vertigo rush of standing at the floor-to-ceiling windows with the whole world opening out beneath my feet. Ships were impressive in a similar way—their sheer size, the brave show they made docked at Castle Island pier. That one of those giants could go down in a gale at the end of the twentieth century seemed nothing shy of laughable.

The ship my father sailed most often was the *Marine Electric,* a World War II–era converted tanker that carried coal between Norfolk, Virginia, and Somerset, Massachusetts, for most of the year. In the summers they'd hose out the hold and fill it with grain, and the ship would head for the port of Haifa instead. My father preferred these trans-Atlantic grain runs. The weather was good, he could avoid coastal traffic, and he got to see Israel again and again—seven times in all. We weren't practicing Jews, didn't so much as celebrate Hanukkah, but my father felt a strong affinity for the place and took those grain runs every chance he got. In many ways it was the perfect assignment for him. He appreciated the familiarity of the old tanker with its primitive navigation system, and the captain was happy to have him, as he knew how to use a sextant and navigate by the stars, something many younger officers didn't. Work was scarce for merchant sailors in the early eighties; the union spread the jobs around by requiring a long break after every service period. But when his vacation was up, there was always work for my dad aboard the *Marine Electric*.

I can't remember where I was when I learned that the ship had capsized in a storm and sank thirty miles off the coast of Virginia. If my father had been on board, I'm sure I would remember perfectly. Moments of horror tend to seal themselves in our minds that way. I recall with sickening clarity the moment in the twelfth week of my first pregnancy when the midwife told me that she couldn't find my baby's heartbeat—her thin face, her cloud of dove-colored hair, the set of her mouth as she placed the stethoscope there and there and there. This, on the other hand, was just another day in mid-February. My father had left the *Marine Electric* in November and was safe at home. Of course I was shocked and deeply sympathetic—thirty-one men were drowned or frozen in the waters near Chincoteague, men my father knew well. But I didn't feel the horror viscerally, the way you do when your imagination is sparked and fear has its way with you.

It wasn't until my mother was diagnosed with amyotrophic lateral sclerosis the following spring that I started thinking about the *Marine Electric* disaster as a nightmare that could easily have been my own. Mom had been experiencing symptoms for close to a year—slurred speech and limited mobility in her left hand. When the diagnosis came, when we knew that she had five years to live at the most, I considered what our lives would have been like if dad had been aboard that ship in February. The tanker had capsized before they could engage the lifeboats, dumping the crew into thirty-nine-degree water. Only three people survived. One had clung to a life ring for two hours while the five men with him froze and drifted off one by one. There was no doubt in my mind that my father, a sixty-two-year-old diabetic with a hip replacement, would not have been among the survivors.

And then what? I was eighteen years old, a bookish kid in my first year of college five hundred miles from home. I imagined quitting school and coming back to bury my father and take care of my mother. In a few years she'd be gone. Then it would be me and my teenaged brother, alone, with a settlement from the shipping company and precious little else. I didn't torture myself with these thoughts very often. Each summer I'd come home to assist my mother, and it would occur to me suddenly—while helping her put on her stockings or blending up cooked chicken to feed through her gastric tube—how much worse things might have been. It was never a comforting thought. A religious person might have felt so—"the good Lord gives us no more to bear than we can handle," that sort of thing—but for me it was just spooky, a chill that ran through me at odd moments. I'd shiver and let it go.

My father went into semi-retirement when my mother was diagnosed. He'd take care of her for nine months, then ship out as soon as I came home in May. I didn't worry about his safety on these trips. I had enough to occupy me, what with mom's paralysis growing worse by the month. Back at school in the fall, I'd start worrying again. Not about my parents, not about ocean travel or anything like that. For whatever reason, because my mother was ill, or because I'd always been a tad obsessive about such things, I worried that my own body was failing me. I'd lie in bed mornings before my alarm went off and consider the cluster of vessels in the white of my right eye. The ophthalmologist had called it a nevus, a type of tumor, and though I was savvy enough to realize that not all tumors are malignant, I also knew that some become that way over time. The doctor had promised it would fade after adolescence, but here I was at nineteen with the damned thing as red as ever. If I concentrated, I could almost feel the vessels on the surface of my eye, a faint irritation, as though rogue cells were swelling and multiplying. I sensed the fear moving in me, the pain of it in my chest and arms, then that nauseating rush of panic. *Oh no,* I'd think, *it's here already. The nightmare I've been waiting for.*

It got worse after my mother died. At twenty-five I mistook a racing heart for cardiac arrest; at twenty-eight I thought I had stomach cancer. At thirty-three I convinced myself that I had Sjogren's syndrome, a rare auto-immune disease that attacks the exocrine glands, causing a host of unpleasant symptoms, from a raw, tingling tongue and flu-like pains (which I had) to burning eyes and rampant tooth decay (which I expected to have any day now). I forced myself to the doctor's, though the smell and the harsh light and the pictures of skin malignancies on the informational poster all made me sick to my stomach. Dr. Bruno pushed my tongue around with his wooden stick. "No thrush," he murmured. "No sores. That's a healthy tongue."

I braced myself and asked him about Sjogren's syndrome. He grinned despite himself, exchanged an amused glance with Dr. Nygen, the first-year resident who was shadowing him that day. Both men smiled at me indulgently.

"Sjogren's. This is a disease for old women. You know someone with Sjogren's syndrome?"

I shook my head. Truth is, I'd read about it on my own—picked up a copy of *Our Bodies, Ourselves* and thumbed through until I found a disease that matched a few of my symptoms. I hadn't meant to scare the living crap out of myself. I'd actually intended to reassure myself somehow, but it hadn't worked out that way.

"You're too young for Sjogren's. This is viral, what you're experiencing. Sometimes viruses hang around for a while. Just go home and give yourself some rest, lots of clear fluids . . . "

"And if it doesn't clear up?"

He shrugged. "Come back in a week."

This didn't reassure me one bit. For starters, I didn't believe that Sjogren's struck mainly older women. My book said it was most common in women ages thirty-five to sixty; I was just two years shy of the bottom limit. Bruno's insistence that my complaint was viral didn't convince me either. If he was so sure, why had he told me to come back in a week? Why was he sending me down to the lab for blood tests? Perhaps a harmless virus was the most likely explanation, but wasn't something much more worrisome also a possibility? Of course I wanted to believe Bruno, but I couldn't. I wanted definitive proof that I wasn't chronically ill, something no doctor could have given me.

Most medical practitioners are familiar with the aphorism "When you hear hoof beats behind you, don't expect to see a zebra." The most likely explanation for a set of symptoms is probably the correct one: hoof beats tend to mean horses, and a low-grade fever and tongue sensitivity in an otherwise healthy young woman probably indicates a mild virus that, for whatever reason—job stress, anxiety, the pressures of new motherhood—she just can't shake. It's wise to run blood tests to make sure that everything looks normal, but it also makes sense not to worry. Unfortunately, the concepts of "likelihood" and "remote possibility" didn't hold much meaning for me. Remote possibilities seemed likely, even inevitable. You heard about them every day. A friend has a baby with a nasty cold that turns out to be congestive heart failure. A relative's backache is caused not by muscle strain, but by a malignant tumor in the spine. If it happened to someone else, it could and would happen to me.

At the root of my anxiety lay the certainty that forces were conspiring behind the scenes to mar my life. If tragedy was to be avoided, these forces had to be imagined in frightening detail. Sure, the doctor says I'm perfectly fine, but what *isn't* he telling me? What will I find out in a week or a month? If I can live out the terror in my head, anticipate each detail, I'll have somehow protected myself. I know that doesn't make sense; magical thinking rarely does. I suppose I didn't want to be caught off guard. I still don't. I'm always on the lookout for marks of doom—not the smell of gas in the kitchen, but the purple smear of a bruise on my thigh. Jesus, look at you, I'll say to myself. Bruising like a pear from the smallest knock. They'll be discussing your case around the proverbial water cooler, your pals from work, those friends who haven't seen you in years. Did you hear about Joan? Got a little mark on her thigh, next thing you know she's hemorrhaging from her left ventricle. And she didn't catch it soon enough. She didn't catch it soon enough. What a shame. If only she'd known.

As of this writing, my father is eighty-seven years old. He's grown shorter and bonier with age, a slip of an old man with a smooth pate and a neat fringe of white hair. He sits in his armchair and tells me about the *Marine Electric*—things he'd never have said in my youth, back when that ship was his bread and butter. How the hatch covers wore so thin with rust the crew didn't dare walk on them. How in rough weather the sea would wash over the deck and down through rusted-out holes in the hatch, creating long pipes of rotten grain. There were men who refused to sail on that old tanker, especially in summer, out across the Atlantic where the coast guard couldn't save you if something went wrong.

"But you weren't worried," I say.

He shakes his head. "I was on my way to Israel," he explains. "When it's some place you love, you figure it'll be all right."

But it's more than that—I know it is. My father was not immune to worry. He worried about changing careers in middle life, and finding jobs when work was scarce. He worried about having money for retirement and for sending his kids to college. These fears must have obviated any concerns he had about the condition of the ship. A person can only worry about so many things at once. Anxiety takes energy—it can be downright exhausting. We pick and choose our fears as a matter of survival.

"And I didn't know about the *Poet*," he adds.

He's talking about the S.S. *Poet*, which vanished in 1980 on its way to Port Said, Egypt. Another World War II–era grain carrier, 13,000 tons of corn in its hold, thirty-four crewmembers on board. Like the *Marine Electric*, the *Poet* was well past its prime, a colossal rust heap that should have been scrapped years before. The life span of an ocean-going cargo vessel isn't long, twenty years or so, but few new American ships were built in the 1960s, and the old ones remained a big part of the industry. Instead of being retired, World War II carriers were sent off to foreign shipyards and "jumbo-ized," new midsections welded in between the old bow and stern. By the early eighties, ships like the *Poet* and the *Marine Electric* were positively ancient, pocked with rust and at risk for system failure as well. Even so, the coast guard, responding to a complex set of political and economic pressures, allowed them to pass inspection every time.

When an old ship sank, it was typically blamed on human error. Rarely, if ever, was the shipping company held responsible, and the coast guard was never really taken to task for rubber-stamping unseaworthy vessels. When the *Poet* went down, little effort was made to discover the real reason thirty-four men died. But the *Marine Electric* was a different story. The chief mate survived the wreck and was willing to testify to the poor condition of the ship. There were cracks in the deck that the crew had circled with spray paint so the inspection team wouldn't miss them. There were ninety-two separate rust holes in the hatches and deck plates, some of them patched with epoxy and duct tape. The hatches didn't even fit properly, having been returned after a dry-docking with improper gaskets and support struts. The chief mate himself had been forced to patch a hole in the hull with cement and a coffee can lid. Finally, the drains in the cargo hold didn't work because metal plates had been placed over them to prevent coal from clogging the pumps. If water got into the cargo hold, there was no way of getting it out.

The ship's permanent master knew about all of this, the coast guard knew, the shipping company knew. And still the ship was made to sail into a storm on February 11, 1983. She'd actually missed a dry-docking in January because they had to get that coal up to Massachusetts. This is what mattered most. Economic forces took precedent over the safety of working people, as they almost always do.

In the wake of the *Marine Electric* disaster, the coast guard finally reformed its inspection process and the old World War II–era ships were retired. Robert Frump, maritime reporter and investigative journalist for the *Philadelphia Inquirer,* detailed all of this thoroughly in a series of articles and, eventually, in a book-length account of the *Marine Electric* tragedy. The History Channel even devoted an episode of *Deep Sea Detectives* to the story. But of course no one was talking about this before 1983, back when my mother, with the high-pitched instincts of a woman suffering from a chronic emotional disorder, feared for my father's life. When a ship went down, it never made news the way airline disasters did, and my father never shared details of the tanker's condition with her. Was the sinking of the *Marine Electric* inevitable or a remote possibility? My mother couldn't have said for sure. She had only her fear to work with—that visceral, gut-level dread so familiar to me. It obliterates sleep and dulls the appetite, makes me jerk like a puppet at every loud sound. It's no way to live, wound up tight like that, a rubber band of a woman, waiting to snap.

But how should I tame my anxiety in a world where my mother was right after all? Where the grand, corporate conspiracy may indeed be fucking us over even as we sit here surfing channels and knocking back diet Cokes? Last year my husband's doctor, a young maverick who'd recently made the decision to leave his HMO and start his own preventative practice, advised Roger to stay away from soy, calling soy agri-business one of the greatest threats to American health today. "You won't hear many people talking about this," he added. "Archer Daniels Midland has a huge PR campaign going. You won't even hear this from most doctors." I'm starting to think that my mother would have fit in well in the twenty-first century. Had she lived, she'd have seen the day when educated people nurture a healthy skepticism about everything from cow's milk to non-stick frying pans, when it's wise to fear poison gas in the basement, when most of us refuse to let our children go anywhere unescorted. How do we define our discontent, what shall we name "disorder," in a world where the reference points keep changing? Am I neurotic or merely prudent? Am I sick or am I smart? Or am I both?

Those who are capable of negotiating risk without tumbling headlong into panic have always impressed me. I ask my father how he managed it, trip after trip across the Atlantic at the height of the war, in 1942, when merchant ships didn't even have naval escorts yet. The merchant marine lost a greater percentage of men in World War II than any branch of the military. Over sixteen hundred ships were damaged or sunk between 1940 and 1946, a third of those in '42 alone. Over nine thousand sailors lost their lives. "Weren't you scared?" I ask. "Didn't you feel you were going off to your death every time you shipped out?"

"I didn't really think about it," he shrugs. "I thought about what I'd do when I came home. It's like I was in some kind of fog."

Of course this makes sense. You'd have to generate a protective mist to keep yourself going day in and day out. Lately it seems as though half the people I know are on beta blockers or anti-depressants. If emotional health means consciously embracing that fog of ignorance, choosing for the moment *not* to think about dangers that may be devastatingly real after all, then it is the rare person of intelligence who performs that trick without some kind of assistance. What I wouldn't give for such an organized mind—to exercise doublethink lightly and willingly, without pills or good, strong drink. I've never been much of a substance user. But I'll have to try something—meds or biofeedback, herbal cleansing or insight meditation, the teachings of a wise and compassionate Buddha. Because worry didn't keep my mother alive, and not worrying hasn't killed my father. And maybe I could be happy that way, sailing to the Holy Land in my leaky tub.

My father told me something else. He was standing watch in the South Atlantic one day when he looked out over the side of the ship and saw something in the water. It was a bright, calm morning, slight waves of one or two feet lapping the prow. There, just off the port side, poking up through the surface like a tree in a flood, was the long, wooden mast of a torpedoed ship. I think of him there on deck, alone in that pocket of fog with his thoughts of home. All around him, silent markers of ruin are rising from the deep. He gives them a nod of respect, a little shiver of recognition. And then he sails on by.

Donna George Storey

THIRTEEN VIEWS OF GRIEF

I. Trapped

"How old are you?" the doctor asks.

My father pauses. For a long time. "One hundred and fifty-two."

He is sitting right beside me, on a hospital bed, but his voice sounds muted and hollow, as if floating up from a deep hole.

The doctor arches an eyebrow. "My, you do look well-preserved for your age." The expression on his face is not kind. You might even call it a sneer. "And who is the president of the United States?"

"Jimmy Carter," I shout, to myself. Maybe everything will be okay, if he gets this answer right.

My father pauses again. He seems to know he's failing the test. "George? George Washington?"

"Yes, well. That's enough for now," the doctor sniffs and motions us to the door.

"I can't tell you anything definite. We'll have to do more tests tomorrow." Alone with us, his bedside manner improves. When he looks at my older sister, his eyes definitely soften. But that is true of most men.

I stare down at the floor, at his brown shoes, his polyester slacks beneath the hem of his white doctor coat. I'm still shouting, inside my head: What kind of asshole gets his kicks out of making fun of a man with a brain tumor?

What he's just done is wrong and I know it, but I'm seventeen and he's a doctor, and my mother, who is a nurse and might have embarrassed him into good behavior, is still downstairs filling out the admission papers.

Before he got sick, my father had a way with words. But now, my mother explained, the growth in his brain is causing aphasia, which means his thoughts become twisted on their way to speech. The words he wants to say are trapped inside his head.

At that moment I know exactly how he feels.

II. Wired

There are no chairs in the rooms in intensive care, so I have to stand by the bed and look down at my father. The suture on his shaved skull looks like a zipper. His chest is dotted with round sensors, attached to wires that run to the beeping machines beside his bed. Since the tumor was removed, he's had several heart attacks. He keeps clawing at his chest. Years later, when I read Lauren Bacall's account of Humphrey Bogart's last days, she'll describe him doing exactly the same thing the night before he died, grabbing at his chest as if trying to pull himself free of his own body.

How did we get here? If I think back, I can piece it together. My father began acting strangely around Christmas, withdrawn, not himself. Then he decided to take a few weeks off of work for no real reason—just a break to do a few things around the house. Then he needed to go to the hospital for tests, but it might just be a virus or an abscess. Then they told me it was a tumor, but it could be benign. Then they admitted it was malignant, glioblastoma, the very worst kind, but he might live for a while, even a year, after the surgery and radiation.

Amazingly, I believed them at every step. Because I wanted to. But the day after Valentine's Day, the phone call comes. He is dead. There's no way to put a spin on that one.

That afternoon, after the crying, after my mother takes her sleeping pill, I'm sent to the grocery store to buy coffee and milk, boxes of cookies. We'll be having many visitors in the days to come.

"And how are you today?" the cashier beams.

I consider telling her my father just died this morning, but instead I smile. My lips move slowly, like a stick through clay. "Just fine," I say.

III. Receiving Line

I've seen a corpse laid out in a coffin once, my great-aunt Bertha, but she was ninety-two when she died. I was eight. I remember watching my aunts pat her blue-veined hands, a rosary woven through the waxen fingers. I wanted to try it, too, but was afraid.

My father wears a suit, a strange thing to lie down in. His chest seems to rise and fall, as if he were only sleeping, but if I blink, the motion stops.

Before the viewing officially begins, when it is just the family, I lean over the coffin and touch my lips to his. They are cold and hard. Like kissing a coffee table or the back of a chair. I'm not sure if I'm glad I've done this or not.

Many people come to pay their respects. Most are men in suits: my father's colleagues, the men he carpooled with to the city. My mother, my two sisters, and I stand in a line in our black dresses and shake hands with everyone. They've been through this before. My mother's first husband died in a car accident when my sisters were toddlers.

A man who looks like a younger Ted Kennedy introduces himself. I recognize the name from random stories about the car-pool buddies.

The man tells me he's heard a lot of wonderful things about me—my father was very proud. His voice is hushed and sorrowful, but I see something else in his eyes, that silvery flash of attraction, followed by a flush of guilt, ink blackening water.

This is the moment I remember best about that day.

IV. Ketchup

For a few months after the funeral, my father visits me in my dreams. He never speaks. He sits down at the dinner table—we're having fried cube steaks, peas, Pepperidge Farm rolls—and pours ketchup on his plate. We both like lots of ketchup with our cube steak. My head is bursting with questions. Ah, so you came back to life? What was it like to be dead? Or were they wrong about your dying? But even in the dream I know that to say one word is to make him disappear.

V. Haunting

I pretend I'm studying the display of mysteries at the end of the aisle, but really I'm watching them: A father and daughter deciding whether to buy a book.

The man is bald, like my father. Graying at the temples, like my father. Wears glasses, like my father. Has a beard and a round belly, not like my father.

But it isn't his looks that matter, it's the rhythm of his voice, the way he bends close to the girl.

On Saturdays, my father and I used to drive to the university bookstore, an hour away, and browse for hours. We would wander down into the aisles devoted to course books and imagine we were taking classes in Russian history or beginning Japanese.

And then at the end, we would decide which books to buy. He would limit himself to one, but I always managed to talk him into two or three for myself.

The girl is making her case now, why she needs this one and that one, too. The man nods—was there ever any doubt he would give in?—and they head toward me, books in their arms.

I pick up the closest paperback and leaf through it. I don't want them to catch me spying. Still, I take a deep breath as they pass, sucking in the wintry mineral spice of his trench coat, her Charlie perfume.

They walk by, smiling. I don't think they see me at all.

VI. Psych 101

We're sitting in my freshman dorm room, draped over the battered living-room chairs, when my friend informs me he knows why I'm promiscuous.

I feel my upper lip contract, as if I've eaten something spoiled. I don't bother to point out that I'm not really "promiscuous." I haven't even cracked double digits yet. In high school, the boys spurned smart girls. I'm merely making up for lost time. And still, I can't resist a response. "Oh, yeah, Mr. Psych Major, and why is that?"

"Because your father died."

I manage a "hmph" of dismissal. What would he know? He still has two parents, and the luxury of being annoyed with them. Most of my friends have two parents, or even four.

Later, when I'm alone, I let myself feel the sting of his words. My friend was wrong, wasn't he? I know well enough I'm not going to find any father replacements in the narrow, semen-and-Clorox-scented bunkbed of a college boy. What bothers me is that he, and they, might see me differently because I don't have a father. Damaged. Needy. Rudderless.

I thought I kept that part of me hidden from strangers.

VII. Cat Spirit

Abe-san squirms in her chair. She clearly has something she wants to say. That's fine with me. I loathe the usual lessons, stumbling through a binder of "true life" dialogues that my employer, Voice of Kyoto, forces on their English conversation clients.

"So, what's new?" I say.

She sighs. "Ah, very terrible happening. Last week my very dear cat became ill and—how do you say it?—*totsuzen naku natte shimatta.*"

"Suddenly died." Seeing her expression, I quickly amend it to "passed away" and add, "I'm so sorry."

"I am very sad. Very sad. But today, something very unusual happen. I put a dish of cat food, her favorite kind, at the family altar." Ms. Abe leans forward, a strange light in her eyes. "Later, some of it was missing. So, maybe I think, she has eaten it. Her spirit."

I know Abe-san is twenty-nine, unmarried, still lives with her parents. Her greatest excitement in life might well be coming to these half-hour English conversation lessons.

I am filled with envy.

She gets to experience grief the easy way. First a cat, then a grandfather perhaps, step-by-step, the way it's supposed to be. Not pushed into the deep end of the pool like I was. Five years later, and sometimes I still feel that frigid water.

But we have something in common, too. I know how she feels. Grief transcends cultures, creatures.

"Her spirit?" I say. "Yes. Yes, it might have been."

VIII. Festival of the Dead

Thanks to Dr. Uno, I can enjoy my first Daimonji Okuribi Festival in grand style from the roof of a hotel in the city center, far above the crush of the crowded streets. Every August, huge bonfires, in the shape of symbols for "great," "Supreme Buddhist Law," a boat and a torii gate are lit on the mountainsides around Kyoto to guide the dead back to the underworld after their annual summer visit to the land of the living. The Japanese seem closer to their dead. They wash their graves regularly, let them preside over the living from picture frames above the family altar, offer them sweets and fruit on holidays—or every day, in traditional households.

Sometimes, after a beer or two, Dr. Uno confesses I am like a daughter to him. He has two sons and always hoped for a little girl to spoil. No doubt it helps I have an opening in the father department. Spoil me he does, with boat luncheons on the Katsura River during cherry blossom time and evenings in three-hundred-year-old restaurants in Gion, the old pleasure quarter where geisha still trip through the streets. My father, with his Depression childhood of evictions and hunger, would never have dreamed of indulging in such luxuries.

But, of course, Dr. Uno is not my father.

The night of the bonfires, after Dr. Uno sends me home through the black velvet summer night in a pre-paid cab, I dream about my father again, for the first time in years.

I am walking along a highway winding through a forest of tall Japanese cedars. A car stops. It is an American car, driving on the right—or in Japan, wrong—side of the road. I climb into the passenger's side, then glance over and see a man's hand, the olive skin set off by the white cuff of a dress shirt, the crisp gray wool of a jacket sleeve. And I know suddenly it is my father. How strange it must be, I think, to sit up again, to grip a steering wheel. After lying still under the earth for so many years, his muscles must be so stiff and sore. I want to ask him if it hurts, but I know he can't speak. It was tiring enough for him to make his way here to this foreign land. Even in the dream I know he must still love me very much to come all this way to find me.

IX. At the Sushi Bar

Our shoulders are almost touching as we sit side by side on the low stools, watching the chefs slice octopus and tuna. We both order in Japanese—after all, we met in Japanese class—all the hardcore delicacies. Fried shrimp heads. Salmon roe with quail egg. Gelatinous orange sea urchin in seaweed cups.

"So, are both of your parents from Chicago, too?" I ask brightly. My engineer date is shy, and even on our third date, I still carry the conversation.

"Ah, well, my father passed away when I was fourteen."

"Oh, really? Mine, too. I'd just turned seventeen." My voice is still oddly cheerful. "How did he die?"

"A heart attack."

"Brain tumor followed by a heart attack," I chirp, as if we're comparing undergraduate majors or SAT scores.

My date nods. He is appropriately thoughtful and sad, not giddy and tactless, like me, but I sense he won't hold it against me. After all, he belongs to the Dead Fathers Club, too.

This is the moment I realize we have a future, my husband and I.

X. Oedipus Complex

My husband is just like my father in many ways. He is smart and kind-hearted. He treats me like a princess. In public he is quiet; at home he has a dry, biting wit. Sometimes he jokes about death and I double over with laughter.

In some ways they are not the same. My husband doesn't suffer from depression. He doesn't smoke two packs of cigarettes a day.

I thought I would never find a man who loved me as much as my father did, but I have.

If I think too much about it, it terrifies me.

XI. What My Mother Told Me

Occasionally, when I'm cleaning out my file cabinet, I glance through the folders of his papers. The death certificate, army discharge, a letter from his mother, who also died in her early fifties of heart problems, promising him his favorite homemade cream puffs when he came home on furlough in 1945.

The real jewels I keep are from my mother, told over a glass of wine, many years after his death.

She told me how they cried together in bed when they learned of his diagnosis, although in front of me he was always calm and brave.

She told me that my father was a still a virgin at thirty when they married, a good Catholic boy to the core. "You've never seen a man so happy," she said.

She told me that when they went to his thirtieth high school reunion and everyone stood up and listed all they'd done since graduation, the only thing he talked about as his life's accomplishment was me.

XII. Grandpa

The picture of my father I keep on my mantelpiece was taken ten years before I was born. He still has a lot of dark hair, a thin face, sensuous lips. He gazes thoughtfully off to the left, at something I will never see. He looks a lot like Humphrey Bogart.

I have two sons, eight and four. When they are concentrating on something—a Lego project, a puzzle—they both purse their lips in a *moue* they've inherited directly from my father, as if a part of him still lives.

My four-year-old has been asking me about death recently. He wants to know how old he'll be when he dies. (Very, very old, I hope.) He wants to know when I'm going to die. (Not for a long time, I hope.) He wants to be reminded where my mommy and daddy are. (Both dead now. They died before you were born.)

I show him a picture of his grandpa, the one who passed on his color-blindness to him so that peanut butter looks "green." My son gazes for a moment, politely, then turns away.

I'm disappointed. I wanted him to gaze for a long time, like I do.

Then I remember he is looking at a stranger, much as my great-grandparents in their nineteenth-century Sunday best are strangers to me. Someday, with the right stories, I hope I can bring my father back to life for him, but I'm afraid, too, that words might fail me again.

I put the picture back, in the corner with the other dead ancestors. I keep them separate from the latest portraits of the kids, as if death, like the flu, is catching.

XIII. Last Words

When I think about it, I have nothing to regret. The last words I said to my father, on the phone the night before his surgery, were "I love you."

We had a long talk that night, and oddly, he was perfectly lucid. Himself. He got the numbers right. There was no mention of George Washington. At the end he said, "Well, I'd better go now. I love you."

I said it, too. If I had the chance to do it over now, I'd say exactly the same thing.

But it would be different.

In the past twenty-five years, the meaning of each of those words has changed.

"I" am now a wife, a mother, a Japan scholar, a published writer.

"Love" is no longer something I take for granted, as I did then. I know, too, what a parent's love feels like, the heart-wrenching, life-twisting joy of it.

"You" is more complex, too, for he is no longer just an adjunct to me, but a man with his own dreams and fears—some the same as mine, perhaps—a man who confronted his death bravely, because of course, he knew that he was dying and that those were most likely the last words he would ever say to me.

I still mourn my chance to say these words with the new, richer meanings, which I could do if he were still alive.

Sometimes I say these words to him, to the air, anyway.

Sometimes I believe he hears them.

Thomas White

THE WISDOM OF SONS

Final Words

IN THE SPRING of 1994, as my father lay dying in the intensive care unit of a small hospital in Woonsocket, Rhode Island, my mother, brother, sister, and I were faced with the sort of decision families dread. My father was in a coma. A week earlier he had suffered cardiac arrest while having lunch with my mother, his wife of thirty-three years. They were eating cold-cut sandwiches, a platter between them of sliced tomatoes drizzled with olive oil, salt, oregano. It was his second cardiac arrest in six weeks. The first time he was also having lunch with my mother, a coincidence I have never made sense of except to conclude the obvious, that deep down inside he sought for his last moments on earth a simple meal with my mother. That first time, after my father slumped in his chair and struck his cheekbone on the edge of the table before collapsing to the floor, my mother called 911. Three local EMTs, all volunteers, burst into the house, cut open my father's shirt with a pair of scissors designed for this purpose—it is equipped with a flattened edge on the lower blade to protect the victim's skin—and with a thrust of current from a defibrillator restarted his heart in minutes. Several hours later he awoke in a hospital room. His short-term recall scattered, his voice croaky from intubation, he bore a purplish welt on the left side of his face that flooded blood into the white of his eye. His sternum ached. I was in graduate school in New York City and upon hearing the news had boarded the first train to Providence. I found a patch of skin on his arm that wasn't plugged with tubes or covered in bandages and placed my hand there. "Hi, Dad."

"Tom," he croaked. "Shouldn't you be at school?"

It was a trip I would make frequently in the coming months, there and back, to hospitals and rehabilitation centers in Boston and Rhode Island, and each train ride had a pall all its own, a different flavor of sadness—one rooted in self-pity, one in loneliness, another in loss—and the tears that streaked my cheeks bore a unique taste on my lips, sometimes sweet, sometimes so bitter I could choke, always the same the entire trip.

I told my father all I wanted was to be with him. "School can wait," I said.

Once stable he was transferred by ambulance to the Boston hospital where weeks earlier he had undergone surgery to replace two heart valves. This was a teaching hospital. Once or twice a day a group of impossibly young future doctors gathered round the bed with their white coats and clipboards and pens and stethoscopes dangling quaintly from their necks. Nothing much was ever said, neither by the senior cardiologist nor my father; certainly nothing was said among the young future doctors, who fought hard to never once glance at our family. Because they were usually such a confident bunch, I was surprised at the cardiologists' willingness to confess their perplexity about the cause of the cardiac arrest. We had expected an explanation so tangled in medical jargon it would be beyond our comprehension, but an explanation nonetheless, something we could repeat to friends and family. Maybe even a hook on which we could hang our hopes. The valves were operating perfectly, they said, and my father's heart was pumping blood into and out of its chambers with impeccable efficiency. Their work was done, and done well, they seemed to imply. After days of deliberation they decided to prescribe my father a medication that would regulate the electrical currents around his heart. These currents had most likely misfired, for one reason or another, causing his heart to stop. This new pill would prevent another cardiac event. I remain to this day so disgusted by this solution—after heart-valve replacement and subsequent cardiac arrest, a simple pill was supposed to address whatever had stricken my father—that I refuse to research this medication, its name, success rate, whether or not it is still prescribed, for fear the old, seething bitterness over its prescription will return.

While my father was transferred to a rehabilitation facility, I returned to New York City. Several weeks later came the call that, once again, he had had a cardiac arrest. Once again he had briefly died and been revived in the kitchen of my parents' house. He was in the same hospital in Woonsocket.

He would not wake this time. The staff neurologist, a dark, plump young man so kind and polite I wondered how he could embody the knowledge of the nervous system, its mysterious web floating up to the layers of the skin and, so doctors tell us, storing memory, along with his obvious compassion for the grief-stricken. He would pull back the sheet and tickle the soles of my father's feet. Pinch up his eyelids and shine a narrow light into the lifeless eyes. Like a lover he would run his fingernails backward along my father's forearms. Looking for what? His news was always the same: no change. Even so, we felt better. See you tomorrow, he would say, as sad, it seemed, as we, gathered around the bed.

Back at the house, the kitchen revealed what had happened. The table, an old oak piece needing three sets of hands to move, had been thrust aside, out from under the antique chandelier. Black boot marks striped the hardwood where the EMTs had pivoted like wrestlers around my father's limp body. Smaller than a napkin, a triangular shred of shirt, his blue-and-white-striped button-down, lay beneath the hutch. A few plates of fine china had toppled, unbroken, on the cabinet shelves. It must have been lightly bumped. They would revive my father with the defibrillator, prepare to transport him on the stretcher, and his heart would stop beating. They would revive him again and then, a few seconds later, his heart would stop.

They were trained; they wouldn't let him die, not on their watch. On the way to the hospital, my father arrested again and was once again revived as the ambulance careened, sirens howling, beneath the sprawling shade trees where I grew up.

But he was too far gone and we knew it. We sat in the comfort room down the hall. Fresh flowers and a Bible sat on a side table; inconspicuous pastels hung from the walls. Soft chairs. No matter where you sat, tissue boxes within reach. We reminded each other to drink lots of water. He was in that room, and we were in this room, for a week. Once he coded while we were there. Medical personnel rushed past us to his room. I peeked out from the comfort room and watched as they worked to bring him back. We waited silently for the news that he had died. He hadn't. Later, the neurologist convinced us there was no hope. The way he explained it, my father was as dead as you could be without being dead, though he put it much more gracefully, sprinkled as it was with the obscure medical jargon that we all found weirdly comforting.

My father's living will stated that he did not want to be kept alive by artificial means such as breathing or feeding tubes, which was how he was now kept alive. That and the occasional electrical currents when his heart stopped. Although we had to reckon with my father's wishes, we sought, as people will, a way to evade the decision to let him die. Searching, we found a hedged position: keep the tubes for now, but if his heart stops, let him go. My mother signed the form. The chance was slim that his heart would continue beating, so we said our goodbyes, one by one. Because I was the youngest, I went last. I sat on the bedside chair and held his hand. I could see his eyeballs roaming beneath the paper-thin lids. He wasn't quite drained of color, as we had described him for a week, more like translucent gray, as opaque as newly shed snakeskin. Not a human color. When I kissed his forehead my lips felt cold. I placed my cheek up against his, mouth beside his ear.

"I hate this," I whispered.

I no longer believed in suffering as an act of faith, as I once had.

My father, however, was a devoted believer in the benefits of suffering, from a shaving nick to emotional turmoil, and that to suffer in silence, without complaint or resentment, was a venerable, even glorious, expression of religious faith. To endure suffering was to please God, he'd told me more than once, but as far as I was concerned, if God ordered this sort of thing as a test of faith, then the hell with God.

In fact I was glad he was alive. I had a great opportunity, one that many people, after the fact, only wish they'd had. His was neither a slow nor a sudden death, but a more or less chosen one. I resisted the temptation to think about our lives together, knowing the flood of feeling would render me helpless. Strangely, I longed to crawl into his bed, so sterile with its stainless steel bars and built-in call buttons and tangle of tubes, beside him. Wanting this, I recalled a day years earlier when I had lain down next to him on a beach on Cape Cod. It was late afternoon, the perfectly round orange sun suspended above the dunes. Our whole family was there. We unfolded a great blanket and took our places, ostensibly to rest after an active day and absorb the sound of the waves, but soon we all fell asleep. Sometime later I woke moments before my father. His thin brown hair was whipped and tousled by the wind, resembling, I thought, the ragged grass that swayed high on the dunes. He rolled onto his back, folded his hands across his stomach, and gazed at the cloudless sky. We were in that giddy half-awake state, amazed at how easily we'd surrendered to the sounds of the sea and the steady breeze. I recall how content my father looked, now gazing at the sky, now closing his eyes as he listened to the laughter of his family above the waves. He was not an unhappy man, but he was a father of three adolescents then, diligent in his work and his home life, consumed, I now realize, with concerns about the welfare of his wife, his children, himself, and all our lives together, knowing the day would come when his children would leave home: he did not relish that day and he often told us so. He was stricken with his own brand of anxiety, maybe even a sort of dread. I grew up with the impression that all grown men scream out in their sleep, as my father did somewhere in the middle of every night. He would groan an awful undulation of sounds that never quite became words—think of a man under torture, or witnessing the torture of someone he loves. (He claimed to never remember what images induced this wailing; maybe they were simply too wretched to repeat.) His cries, loud enough to wake up the house, would cease only when my mother called out to him—her nightly bucket of cold water that brought him round. Most nights we all soon fell back to sleep, but sometimes I would hear my father make his way downstairs for a sip of milk and a snack, his calloused hand rasping the wooden rail. A glass on the counter and the rattle of utensils were the last sounds before I returned to sleep, snug in the comfort that my father, protector, was downstairs keeping watch. Perhaps I have inherited my father's disposition toward anxiety; certainly I have inherited his wakeful nights. And some nights, when I am trying to coax myself back to sleep, I imagine that my father is downstairs in my kitchen, hunched over his plate of crackers, where in my mind he stays until morning.

Sitting beside him in the hospital, with this urge to climb into his bed, I suppose I wanted all of us, but especially him, to return to that carefree state on the beach on Cape Cod. He'd slept that day, and woken, in peace, as we all did.

I felt a surge of urgency about this bedside visit. Knowing the condition of his heart, I didn't want him to die before I said goodbye. I knew my next words to him would be my last. The words that came to my lips that day came from nowhere. I neither considered them, nor, striving for eloquence, turned them over in my mind until I found the right combination. I wish I had said something poetic, something worthy of the moment. I simply said what I said, leaning into his ear in a whisper: "I'm sorry I gave you a hard time." I paused and waited for some sign that he absolved me of any guilt, any wrongdoing, and when none came I began to sob.

Finally I left the room without glancing back at my father. I walked down the hall to the comfort room with my face buried in my hands. I would never again see him alive.

For a long time I was ashamed, though not regretful, of what I had said. Ashamed because it needed to be said; ashamed because one final apology was what we had come to. Still, the words *I'm sorry* had lifted a weight from my conscience and delivered it to the place where confessions go to live out their days. In the years that followed, through the most difficult emotional times of my life, I felt lighter for having said it. But lately, especially since my son was born two years ago, the words have begun to intrude upon my thoughts, demanding, I suppose, to be reckoned with. Maybe they never actually went to the place where confessions go. Maybe my father never accepted them. In any case, I know that I must finally address the reason my last words to my father came in the form of an apology.

Hot Zones and Hinterlands

My mother was the vocal one, a micromanager of behavior. She engaged in a multitude of daily skirmishes in the hot zone while my father silently patrolled the hinterland of behavior's inflexible borders. In this, as in many things, they complemented one another. "We decided to raise you kids differently," my mother once confided to me. By this she meant with more resolve and with a greater notion of ultimate authority than the resolve and authority of other parents. They persevered in their inflexibility. *Strict* is an ambiguous term. It applies here in its most fundamental, unambiguous sense: if we look up the synonyms, they apply: *severe, firm, stern, harsh, exacting*. My parents were often congratulated for their children's good behavior, and for this they were grateful and, I would imagine, proud: a lot of hard work and conflict produced that behavior. But we knew they loved us more than they could ever say. They told us so and, more importantly, we felt it.

Sometimes it was with a heavy heart that they enforced their rules. My father once told me about a conversation he'd had with my grandfather, my mother's father. This was maybe a year or two before my father died. He asked my grandfather what he thought about the way in which my parents had disciplined us. "Was it ever too much?" my father asked him. They were sitting on the cool, shaded porch over breakfast. Faced with this question, my grandfather cried. This is what my father told me. My grandfather, speaking through tears, said, "Sometimes it seemed like too much, and it was hard to watch." My father, when he revealed this to me, was downcast, tears in his own eyes, perhaps plagued by second thoughts (as most parents are) about his approach to parenting. "I didn't expect him to cry" was all he said.

My brother and sister fared much better than I in my parents' system of rules and punishment. They understood the way things worked, recognized a boundary and backed away, while I wandered through childhood and adolescence in a state of perplexity about the validity of rules—a blueprint for transgression. I was born to break them, I often felt. Early in life I gained a reputation in our family as the one who inadvertently courted trouble. One of the classic stories occurs on Christmas Eve. I am five, marching through the dining room in my pajamas and slippers, my whole body a vibration of anticipation and excitement, rays of bright light, as it were, springing from my fingertips. I am awaiting a visit from Santa Claus. (Santa Claus, in this case, was a jovial, round-bellied neighbor who liked his whiskey and passed out gifts to neighborhood kids in exchange for tall gift-wrapped boxes with bottles inside, which the parents slipped to him as he made for his sleigh.) Marching stiff-kneed, a slipper flies off my foot, strikes the crystal chandelier above the dining room table, and jostles an almond-sized piece of crystal that falls and shatters a plate of the good china. The wedding-gift china. My livid mother sends me to my room. I will not see Santa Claus, not this year—next year. *Next year?* I have been anticipating this night for a lifetime already. A torturous thirty minutes later I hear Santa's laughter in the living room. The tear of gift-wrapping and my sister's shriek. *This isn't happening,* I tell myself. Then my father opens my door and I scamper past his wingtips, a caged raccoon freed in the wild. All was basically well, though the emotional swing left me spent and speechless in Santa's presence. The point is this: my brother or sister would never have performed the impossible: the stiff-kneed march, the inadvertent release of the slipper, the lone loose crystal, the perfect placement on the china. One in a million. All on Christmas Eve, moments before Santa arrives.

Not all of my parents' reprimands were due to inadvertent deeds. Years later I found a stack of greeting cards mixed in with the family pictures. By age ten I was beginning Mother's Day cards with the words *I know we haven't been getting along lately . . .* And later: *Although we have been arguing a lot lately . . .* When does *lately* become *always?* I was a steady customer of the genre of greeting cards that began with apologies. The guilt section at the local pharmacy. It's not that I wanted to make my mother so mad she screamed and whacked me with a yardstick or mixing spoon or, when I was older, hand across the face; rather, we simply struggled to find in each other that which neither of us could possibly offer—she needed an obedient son who maintained the appearance of good behavior, while I needed freedom from her heavy hand, the option to roam alone in my small world. Unfulfilled, we succumbed to conflict. As for my mother, anger was love's ugly cousin. She scolded with almost as much passion as she loved, though with less predictability.

You might think I fantasized about running away. Not once. Instead I fantasized about coming home. Often in my mind I was abducted, kidnapped by a group of men, and escaped only after years of captivity. Reminiscent of Marco Polo, I grew unrecognizable to the people who used to know me. Long stringy hair, a bruised and beaten face. I sprinted through the woods as the branches lashed like weapons fired until I reached the fabled doorstep. My mother, hunched with the burden of years of grief, stirred a steaming pot in the kitchen, the windows clouded all around her.

The abductors are vague; the place of my captivity is vague; my means of escape are vague; and yet, coming home is so clear I can smell the pasta cooking in the kitchen. So you see I very much loved my mother and father, and wanted to be a good son, and wanted them to love me. And I knew that they did love me.

A Vicious Silence

My father was a mostly silent authority. His clenched jaw would raise the hair on my arms. Being a father myself, I marvel at how he accomplished this, the ability to communicate so much without even looking at us, never mind speaking. When he did speak, his word was God's own.

When I turned fifteen or sixteen, however, there came a tipping point in our relationship. I ceased to respect his authority. As my adolescent wisdom accrued, I saw him for what he was: merely a man like other men. This insight, so common for boys of this age, leaves us bewildered and angry, but especially embarrassed, that our fathers no longer are, perhaps never were, the men who once surveyed the world from hallowed heights. I didn't directly challenge him so much as subvert the order he had imposed upon the household and, by extension, my life. Until now this order was the natural order, but no more. My mode of attack was more or less silence. I ignored him or mumbled responses to questions that I regarded as obtrusive or merely boring. If I spoke clearly it was to express sarcasm.

Whereas in childhood rules were broken inadvertently, now my transgressions were the product of determination. There were the usual offenses. If I was supposed to be home by 10 p.m., I strolled in at 10:30. When my father asked me to clean the dishes or rake the leaves, I said nothing.

"Did you hear me?" he would ask.

"Of course I heard you," I would say, certain to do quick and shoddy work on the dishes or leaves.

"You didn't thank me for raking the leaves," I would later say, the lawn sprinkled with leaves left behind after a quick once-over with the rake.

"Thank you," he would say sadly.

We could split logs in the backyard for two hours without saying a word to each other, the silence collecting in our throats like debris.

This continued until a deep rut of miscommunication formed from which neither of us could willfully emerge, and the rut, so toxic, became the relationship. From time to time he tried to haul the wagon, so to speak, onto level ground with jokes or kisses or kind words, but my indifference or feigned antipathy ensured that those wheels only spun deeper. His sense of humor was effortless—intelligent, wry, sprinkled with clever wordplay—and sometimes I was forced to purse my lips to prevent a smile, any intimation that he had provided the slightest bit of pleasure.

My father was not by nature a confrontational person. Faced with conflict as he was each day of his professional life as an attorney, he chose the modes of reason and logic and law, or natural law, in forging a path to resolution. And yet, resolving a conflict between two parties becomes something much more complicated when you, the expert in resolution, are one of the parties involved. None of the old tried-and-true tools were successful; the irony must have made his blood boil.

Although tensions rarely reached a breaking point, sometimes a breaking point was all that was left:

Even out of season, basketball was my obsession. The wooden backboard hung aslant from a dead tree beside the drive. The ball-struck rim thudded, not clanged, with the thump of the dead tree. I had measured out the free-throw line and would toe it for hours, the game always on the line. I passed to myself off the backboard and shot falling away. The crowd gathered in the trees, the nodding trees their applause. A gust of wind was the roar in response to something I had done that none thought possible. When a shot clanged and rolled off among the trees, my daydream dissolved into silence, but soon I was back on the court, ball in hand, and the crowd again filled in around me. My shooting arm never wearied. Dusk became night; the yellow streetlight down the street as dim through the web of trees as a distant star. One hundred was my number. One hundred lay-ups, one hundred free throws, one hundred bank shots from that divot in the tar. My parents were concerned about the time spent under that basket, but worse things could occupy a kid's time.

It is the summer before my senior year of high school. About 9:30

p.m. on a Sunday. Clutching the thick lapels of her terrycloth robe at her neck, my mother calls down through the screen door.

It's late, she says.

Be right in, I say.

Time disappears under the rim: it seems like seconds later when she calls down again.

Let's go, she says.

Coming, I say.

My shot has gone south. If I quit now, a restless night will ensue: My bedroom window looks down the drive where the basket hangs among the trees, and instead of sleep I will see the misses into the morning hours. I must finish with a flurry of swishes before I put the ball away and wash the driveway grime from my hands. I measure up sure shots, five-foot banks that I can nail with eyes closed, but time and again my elbow flies out and the ball rolls off my fingertips with an awkward spin and I watch that awful arc of the ball with a gathering dread. I begin to feel I'm shooting for the first time. The errant shots careen deeper into the woods. Back to basics: elbow forming an L, left hand guiding, knees bent, shoot with the legs. But shooting a basketball does not require thought—in fact it requires no thought, which is why I find the whole thing sort of transcendent and timeless to begin with.

Thomas, my mother calls, her voice high, on the edge of shrill. There is a point at which my mother goes from borderline shrill to full-blown hysteria. Sometimes she crosses that line without spending much time on shrill. Get in here, she yells.

Coming.

The words *game* or *play* do not express what I am doing in the driveway. Failing to make a succession of shots, the knot that has formed in my gut will not subside until I return to the court the next day, and this knot, which in retrospect I would call an unnamable dread or terror, will simply continue to constrict. Even if shots fall the following day, its toll will have been taken. The pressure to shoot well with my mother looming behind the screen crushes any chance of resolution this night. Still I try, rushing as if in a contest with the clock ticking.

Thomas, my father yells. Come here now.

Game over.

My father rarely intercedes in these kinds of squabbles, and when he does it is because my mother is out of her wits, and when my mother is out of her wits my father takes it upon himself to erect the boundary I dare not cross. I sink three lay-ups in quick succession and tell myself that that is enough to dissolve the knot. Later I will reassess this delusion and feel sick again. I dribble up to the house and set the ball on the stoop-side bench.

It is past 11 p.m. My father is also in his bathrobe. Standing in the family room are two slouching, hard-working people who desperately need sleep; nevertheless, I am troubled most of all by my failure to shoot well. I wash my hands at the kitchen sink.

Why didn't you come in when I asked you? my mother screams.

Here I am, I say, without looking up.

God almighty, she screams.

I dry my hands and walk past my parents as if making for bed. This is when my father lays his hands on me in anger: the first and only time. He grabs me by the throat, his thumbs pressing my windpipe, and pushes me against the family-room wall. I do not resist. In fact I have suddenly fallen so listless from shock that I stumble backward and knock my head against a door casing. My knees are jelly as he holds me upright by the throat. The thought flies through my mind that my father is a marine corps veteran of the Korean War and knows how to shoot a rifle, wield a weapon, attack to kill—facts of his life that are easy to forget when all my life I have witnessed his return from work in smart three-piece suits and silk ties and pressed shirts, which he soon discards to poke around the garden or play ping-pong. Here my mother attempts to intercede, and this is an image that will forever sadden me: her throwing her arms up between us and screaming stop, stop, eyes cast toward the floor because she cannot bear to see the attack. My father raises one hand, a cop stopping traffic.

Hon, he says calmly, I'm all right.

She backs away while he returns his fingers to my throat, pinching my inhalation.

Listen to me, he says. You do what your mother says. You come in when she tells you to come in, or your life will be more miserable than you can imagine. You hear me?

Yes, I whisper.

Goodnight, he says, releasing his grip. He heads for the stairs. As my mother follows, her gasps of exasperation rise in the stairwell.

I collapse onto the couch, hands trembling. In the sudden silence I realize it never occurred to me to raise my hands, to fight back. I stay on the couch for a long time, collecting the silence of the house, a tingly hum, inside my head.

The next morning I am hunched over the sports page at the kitchen counter. I know my father will be down soon and, uncertain how the previous night's clash will spill into morning, pretend to read. Hearing his steps descend the stairs, I transform into total stillness at the counter. I am an old patina-glazed statue that he might not notice.

Morning, he says, his wingtips clicking on the tile.

Morning, I mumble, attempting nonchalance.

He lifts his briefcase from the kitchen chair and heads for the garage. As he passes behind me, he places a hand on my shoulder with all the weight it naturally has and drops it down across my shoulder blade and the middle of my back as he moves away. The door to the garage opens, closes, and then the garage door rolls up, metal wheels clacking in the runners like a subway rail in miniature. As his car starts in the garage, the kitchen walls shudder. He is gone. Sitting at the counter, my heart is full of love as I gaze out the kitchen window at the backyard, the rock garden with its squat Japanese maple, the wire pen where we toss leaves and grass clippings, the woods beyond with its tangle of brush and the spindly limbs of all the dead trees, which instead of falling merely lean for years against the live ones, accepting their embraces.

A Lofty Ambition

The past hovers and wafts, a hazy shapeless thing. Out of this cloud certain memories assert themselves; they crystallize and assume the essence of a dream that has jarred us awake in the middle of the night, the details of which we must scribble down.

I don't "talk to" my father the way some people say they speak to the deceased. Instead my father flickers across the screen of my busy days, and the images I see, when I have a moment to ponder them, sometimes expand into memories. These memories tend to evolve around a singular core: love. Since the birth of my son, this love has intensified. Maybe it is more accurate to say that the litter of miscommunication and anger has decomposed into the past, while what was always love remains. The years of tension with my father lasted more or less from age fifteen to twenty-two, though there was never a day or moment when the door to that ugliness was shut forever. Not when he was alive. I tried to shut the door when he was on his deathbed, but to have truly shut the door would have given it an honor and a place—its own eternal room, you might say—that it did not deserve. It was all part of our unique relationship and could not be sequestered.

It would be tempting to file this under the "time heals all wounds" category of greeting-card sensibility. The resolution of the guilt I felt over the years, which has enabled me to see the past more clearly, does not fit inside a greeting-card paradigm precisely because it is not the product of something as passive as the mere passage of time, but of wisdom. I have lived long enough in an emotionally benighted state to savor this wisdom and to know that the pursuit of wisdom is the loftiest ambition in this life.

To Hell with Fear

A recurring dream. Standing before my son, I address him in Spanish, in the informal *tu* instead of the formal *usted*—nothing a father would think twice about calling his son. In the dream, my son takes this familiarity as an affront. He stares through me with bleached eyes. I recede from him, unable to speak. He punishes my insolence with those cold eyes until I awake.

We need not consult Jung.

Before my son was born, I feared that our relationship would consist of misunderstandings, hurt feelings, silent contempt: the low-lights of my life for a few years with my own father. This was the insidious pessimist in me, coolly reducing fatherhood to all the negatives I had ever known as a son. This pessimist lives on in the form of bone-chilling dreams. But I know with all the confidence that wisdom affords that a father-son relationship is much more than the rough times of a few years. And that during the rough times love stands its ground.

In a Ravine

I often notice my younger self in my son, and in myself I see traces of my father. Wit, a gesture, words of encouragement—I act or speak in a certain way and suddenly I am my father. This is a common sensation among parents.

In our home my father had a tendency to kiss me on the head as he walked by. This was post-adolescence, after I had grown too cool to kiss him on the cheek, during the years when our communication was at its lowest ebb. I might be sitting at the counter or the kitchen table, eating, reading, or doing homework, and my father would plant one on the top of my head. Silently he would continue past. Sometimes he would hold my head with two hands and kiss me hard—so hard I would have to laugh or pull away. Still he said nothing, merely walked on.

I had forgotten about this until one day I held my son's head between my hands while he was sitting on the floor over the pieces of a puzzle, and I kissed him hard. I was compelled to do this because I was overcome with love. It was all I could do.

It was all my father could do.

Pondering this, I was reminded of the deathbed words to my father. The apology. *I'm sorry I gave you a hard time.*

I was walking in a pine forest with my son, down in the bowl of a shallow ravine where muck and mud and decomposed needles settled in all but the driest summer months. We tried to hop from rock to rock to keep our shoes dry, though my son, being two, often trod in the squelchy, mosquito-infested mud. No matter. Bars of sunlight like leaning flagpoles angled down through the pine canopy onto the moist earth, leaving bright coins. My son walked among them, loving the slop. I stopped and watched him. Suddenly I knew that some enduring truth was about to percolate into my day. It was my father responding to my deathbed apology. *Save it. We loved each other. Now love your son.* I didn't hear the words, but I felt them, or something very much like them. It is impossible to describe the feeling this gave me, the impression of lightness in every sense of the word, without descending into melodrama or the hackneyed terms of Christian epiphany. I was old enough, and I had pondered all this long enough, to know it for what it was. Wisdom. The apology had become its own historical moment, one that I was able to inspect from an enlightened perspective. *We loved each other. Now kiss your son whenever you think of it, for the rest of your days, and maybe the essence behind this gesture will endure long after you are gone. Maybe it will save him some day.*

A few minutes later my son, yards ahead, toppled onto all fours in the muck. He stayed there, nose inches from the mud, uncertain whether to laugh or cry, until I slipped my hands under his armpits and plucked him to drier ground.

Robin Black

PLOT: VARIATIONS I, II, AND III (CHAPTERS ONE THROUGH TEN)

One

I.

I bought my family's burial plot in early April 2001.

II.

The students in my Advanced Fiction Writing course have continuing difficulty distinguishing between what—if anything—happens in a story and what—if anything—it means.

III.

I've been trying for more than five years to write something about the days right after my father died.

Two

I.

The plot is large enough for me, my husband, my two brothers, my sister-in-law, and my parents. When I bought it, I stopped at that number, recoiling at the thought of the next generation—my own children, niece, and nephew—ever buried there. Or anywhere. And anyway, I decided, by the time they're all old enough to die, death will almost certainly have been cured.

It's just about a mile from my house. My mother lives in Manhattan and my brothers north of Princeton, but we settled on a place here in Philadelphia for two reasons. First of all, it's beautiful—a Civil War–era cemetery filled with mature trees and marble monuments landscaped into hills. Some of the mausoleums are true works of art. The other reason we chose it is that when the decision came up, when it became pressing, I told my mother and my brothers that I would like to have Dad nearby—that I'm a cemetery visitor by nature and would find comfort in his proximity. That was about a month before he died.

II.

"On a sentence by sentence level," I write on one student story, "your work is really very fine. I found myself making very few line edits. And I have a vivid sense of the characters and the setting. You might want to check for areas where the descriptions could be tightened—you'll see I've marked a couple of those, but basically you should be very proud of the prose itself.

"I do have some questions, though, about the larger meaning of the piece. A lot happens, but it isn't clear to me what you want me to take away from having read this. I'm not insisting that Harvey go through any kind of earth-shattering epiphany here; that doesn't feel like what you're going for and, trust me, I don't think every story needs that kind of ending. But still, all these events you're recounting don't seem to add up to much—I don't have the feeling by the end that I understand something more or better than I did when I started reading—even just something about the story itself. That sounds a little harsh, I know, and I don't mean to be harsh—because, really, there's a lot here to be admired. One of my own teachers used to talk to me about the difference between a story and an anecdote. We can speak about this more when we meet, but I wonder if pondering that distinction a bit might be useful for you?"

III.
This week, I tell my mother it's useless trying to write about the whole *what the hell went on with me around Dad's death* thing. After more than five years, I'm done trying.

"Not everything that happens is a story," I say. "I should know that by now."

Three

I.
The first time I see my father's grave all sealed up, there isn't any stone, just a laminated piece of paper with his name, stuck on a small metal post. Otherwise, it's pretty much a patch of dirt. I'd thought I'd find it comforting to visit him, but I don't. I find it upsetting to think of him lying there, encased in his casket, and I don't stay very long.

II.
"One of the problems I think some of you may be having is that though you're presenting your work as fiction, you're possibly writing about things that have actually happened to you . . . ?"

I wait to see what percentage of them nod, who looks caught—as though I have just leveled a terrible accusation. Nobody so much as even blinks.

"Well, OK, let me just ask you all outright. How many of you would say that the stories you turned in this week were based pretty closely on true-life events?" It takes a few seconds, but most hands do go up.

"And that's fine," I say. The hands go down. "There's absolutely nothing wrong with using events from your own life. There's nothing *wrong* with writing anything at all. Some people would even argue that that's ideal—the whole 'write what you know' advice? You've all been told that at some point, I assume?" They nod, look relieved.

"The thing is, though, that there are some pretty common pitfalls to taking real-life events, especially ones in which you yourself played a role, and trying to, well, more or less regurgitate them undigested, as fiction."

III.

The problem with the whole project, I tell my mother, is that I did something terribly, terribly wrong.

"I fucked up. Even if I hurt mostly myself in the process, I still did something wrong. Or at least something most people consider to be wrong. It's impossible to write about Dad's death without seeming to be making excuses for myself. Forget even writing it, just when I tell people what happened, just in conversation, I can see them looking nervous. And then I start trying to explain myself. But it's useless. One possibility is that I'll cast it as fiction," I say. "I think I might be a more sympathetic character in third person."

Four

I.

Against all expectations, the plot remains unchanged. A full year after my father's death, there's still no grass. "He's refusing to be dead," I say. "He is literally refusing to push up the daisies. That's so like him. Why does he always have to be so difficult?"

I send my husband over. He inspects the dirt and comes home saying that Dad isn't being adequately watered; so I put a call into the cemetery and they assure me they'll get on it right away.

II.

I compile a checklist for my students.

> *Warning Signs That You May Not Have Adequate Narrative Distance from Your Story:*
>
> The central character is based on you.
> The central character is pretty much a victim, best described as "put upon."

There are other characters in the story who have no redeeming traits whatsoever.

The You character never does anything wrong . . .

III.

I take a stab at it in the form of a letter:

> Dear Dad, dead four years now,
>
> I think I may owe you an apology. I did something inexplicable on the night that you died . . .

But that's as far as I get.

Five

I.

The day before Thanksgiving 2003, my brother turns up at the kitchen door holding a pumpkin pie and two bottles of wine. He's been to the bakery, to the liquor store, and then to the cemetery on his way to my house.

"It's horrible," he says. "Absolutely barren. I honestly don't think I can go back. There are tire marks, frozen solid in the dirt. Otherwise, nothing has changed."

"No grass?" I ask. "Because I thought there might be a tiny bit in September. I don't understand about the tire marks. What kind of tire marks?"

"It looks like a lawn mower. Though of course, as we know, right there, there's no lawn." He shakes his head, finds the corkscrew in my drawer. "It's positively ghoulish," he says. "It's been more than two years now."

II.

I give my students the assignment of writing something in first person and then shifting it into third. "You can go full out omniscient,"

I say. "Or you can choose one character through whom to filter your narration. But don't just fiddle around with changing the pronouns. I want you to see what else might be revealed with a different point of view. Really think about the reasons an author might think a story is best told one way or another."

III.

So, this woman gets on a plane in Philadelphia. She's just downed two hefty Irish whiskeys in the British Airways Lounge. She looks like she's been crying and she reeks of alcohol. It's obvious to the flight attendants there's the potential for trouble. Not hijacker trouble—that isn't the alarm that this woman rings. More like pain-in-the-ass kind of trouble. Their best hope is that she'll pass out before too long . . .

Six

I.

At Christmas in New York, 2003, my brother reports that he's phoned the cemetery and received assurances that by spring there will be lush, emerald grass growing over Dad. "And I really do think they mean it this time. I had an e-mail and everything."

"It's just unbelievable," an aunt of mine says. "They were so accommodating at the funeral. Remember? Who could have imagined that it would take them years to get grass growing? You would think a cemetery would be able to do *that,* if nothing else."

My mother and brother look over at me. I say nothing. Just get up and walk away.

II.

"I think what I've really been trying to get across to you all, this semester, is emphatically *not* that there are rules that you need to follow. Believe me, I'm the last person in the world to try to get anyone to adhere to a bunch of rules. Really, what I'm suggesting is that there are conventions—and I'm not even suggesting that you follow them. God knows. Though obviously, in fiction, as in life, when you start messing with conventional expectations, you assume some risks."

III.

There were days, even years later, when Penelope couldn't imagine why she had gotten on that plane.

Seven

I.

On the third anniversary, I force myself to go. May 5, 2004.

The cemetery isn't even a five-minute drive from my home, but I've ended up visiting far less frequently than I'd thought I would. Partly, I know, it's because of the whole grass problem. I joke about it a lot, blame it on his personality, talk about how over-determined it feels that his *would* be the most problematic grave in the history of the world. Of course. After all, he was the world's most problematic man. But the fact is, it creeps me out.

The dirt on my father looks like a scar that can't be healed. Three years in, there are grass seeds sprinkled there, but no sign that they're ever taking root.

II.

"The plot can get in your way sometimes," I tell my class, "if you're sticking with actual facts. One thing I made myself do for a while was put up a solid wall between what I'll call autobiography—as opposed to fiction. The distinction is often a shaky one, I know, but I found that if I knew what had really happened, I was resistant to making changes in the story. It felt as though the *real* plot had to be the plot. And sometimes the real plot just wasn't making it. Sometimes the plot has to be changed in order to achieve the effect you want the story to have. So, for quite a while, I had this rule for myself: if it had really happened and I wanted to write about it, I would write an essay or write memoir and never try to fictionalize that stuff."

"What about now?" a student asks.

"Now? Honestly? Well. Now I'm not nearly as strict with myself."

III.

Lawrence reached the conclusion that it hadn't hit her yet—not really. She was behaving so very much like, well, like normal. Maybe she was in shock. Maybe it was because her father had been dying for so long. Maybe it was because it had been months now since any of them had been able to have a real conversation with him. Death by inches, really. Or maybe this was just the result of how difficult yet intense a relationship theirs had been. She had loved him, of course she had, but then he'd also hurt her very badly over the years. But wasn't that true of many fathers and daughters?

There was no getting around it. This was just bizarre. Being here, in France, on vacation. As though nothing unusual had taken place. As though she hadn't known that her father was dying when she stepped on that plane. The whole thing seemed more than odd to Lawrence. Why wasn't she showing some more emotion? And what exactly was his role in this journey supposed to be?

Eight

I.

The president of the cemetery sounds exactly as I imagined he would; like a mortician from a sitcom. Steady-voiced, quiet, even-toned, he calls me Miss Black. And though he offers me what he terms *apologies* for what has happened, his *apologies* are tinged with the message that this really isn't anybody's fault. What he's actually offering are regrets. It's a distinction I understand all too well.

They have tested the soil, he tells me, and have found nothing wrong. They have assigned a specific crew to water the "area." They *are* very sorry that this is happening, but most of all they are confused. He sounds entirely sincere.

The problem is that I've lost all patience.

"It's very simple," I say. "Grass by May, or we come and dig him up. It will have been fully four years by then. I think that's long enough to stare at dirt, don't you?"

And when he laughs—emits a jovial, doubting sound—I assure him that this isn't any joke.

II.

"How many of you think a story has to have a plot to be a story?"

All hands go up.

"Why?"

Now nobody's talking.

III.

It was obvious, watching her, listening to her words, that this pain would be with them for a very long time. She held the phone in front of her face, yelling into it as though it were a microphone, as though there were no point to listening, as though she knew better than to think anyone could say anything to help.

"What the fuck am I doing here in here in France? Can you tell me that, Mom? My fucking father just died and I'm standing here in some fucking inn in fucking France? What the fuck is going on? I can't believe I won't be at the funeral. How did you let me do this? How did anybody let me do this? Why didn't somebody stop me? You had to have known that it was wrong."

Lawrence put his hand on her back; she shook him off.

"I want to come home," she said, quietly, the phone now at her ear. "I just want to come home, Mom."

But, of course, it was too late.

Nine

I.

Since it's November when the cemetery president and I speak, there isn't much he can do for many months—and, impatient as I am, I understand. "Could you at least put some kind of covering on him for the winter? So I can visit him at Christmas without having to see that frozen dirt?"

The poinsettias are plastic, as is the pine, but it's definitely cheerier than what we're used to. I take a picture with my cell phone and send it as a message to the whole family, subject line: The Plot Thickens.

"Merry Christmas, Dad," I say. "I love you very much. I hope this helps."

II.

I've decided to take the fiction vs. autobiography problem head on. So I ask my students to write their autobiographies in no more than five hundred words. And suddenly, they're all gifted. I can't understand what's happened.

"I have to tell you guys, these little things were the strongest writing every single one of you has done all semester. Maybe we should try to figure out why."

They take a while before they speak.

"It helped that I knew what I was trying to get across."

"Trying to get across? What does that mean?"

"I was trying to convey more the point of my life than exactly what happened. There was just no way to fit in all the real events in five hundred words."

"Mine doesn't even really have a plot. I told my whole life story as a metaphor."

"It felt more natural. Like I already knew how to tell this story. After all, I didn't have to make anything up. I just had to tell the truth."

III.

Dear Dad, dead five years now,

I've never told you what happened to me on the day you were buried, but I've decided that I should.

Oddly enough, I was in France, with Richard. We were traveling through Normandy, on a trip that we had planned months earlier. And here's the thing. The thing is that I knew, when I got on that plane, that you were going to die while I was in flight. Mom had called me and told me while I was still in the airport that it was going to be that night, just a matter of hours. And I have no explanation to offer for why I boarded anyway. I just did. I have no idea why. There are excuses I could make. I was completely worn out from months and months of caring for you, of watching you disintegrate. I may just have been too tired, too upset, to be thinking clearly. Or I could tell you that I did it because I wanted to pretend you weren't actually going to die. But the truth is, it's a mystery to me. And then, by the time the day of your funeral rolled around, it was as though I woke up from some kind of trance. I realized that I wanted to be in New York with Mom and everyone else—desperately. I'd made a horrible mistake. But by then it was too late.

That morning, we got in our rental car in Honfleur and we drove toward the big American cemetery at Colleville-sur-Mer. This had always been our plan, our original itinerary—I just hadn't ever guessed that I'd be spending the day of your funeral studying the graves of other people. A lot of the stones had the year of your birth on them: 1915. It made sense that they would. And standing there, I thought hard about those men, your generation, and about all the decades you'd had that they never had. You'd talked so often about your relief at never having been called to the front. It was a strange fancy of mine, and I admit I was trying to justify being where I was, but I had this idea that maybe you had sent me to convey your gratitude—your grieving daughter, an offering to your dead contemporaries on the day of your own burial, my tears for you, watering their graves.

It sounds silly now. I suppose I was just trying to get some kind of deeper meaning out of what had taken place. I suppose I always will.

I wasn't the only person crying. There was an old woman in a wheelchair. Some men. There were also teenagers, on a class trip, whooping it up, shouting and flirting. We stayed about an hour.

Your funeral was at eleven, New York time, which was four p.m. for us. By sheer luck, it happened that we were booked that night in the only fancy hotel we had chosen for the whole trip. Just one night. The room had a mini-bar and a speaker phone. Back in New York, there was a cell phone set up on the lectern at the funeral home—this was the plan that Mom and the boys had devised, for me. Richard and I drank our way from one end of the mini-bar to the other and then we dialed the cell phone number. And listened in.

Our own phone sat on a very low table, and the sound wasn't good, so for your entire funeral, we were both on our knees, as if in prayer.

Ten

I.

There's never been a good explanation given, nobody knows why it happened, but by the fourth anniversary, there was grass; my father's plot had finally blended in with the landscape. I had some unexpected reactions to the sight. I guess I'd attached so many meanings to that barren, unhealed ground. At the sight of all those healthy blades, a part of me felt guilty—as though we'd killed him. Finally, this time. We'd finally convinced him to give up the fight.

And then, too, I have to admit, I'd half hoped he would need to be moved. I'd missed his burial. I could be there this time. I could see the casket I never saw. Watch my father lowered into the ground. Start all over again, with a different plot.

But that isn't happening, I know.

And anyway, everyone agrees that the visits will feel more normal now—less as though we are battling a curse.

II.

In class these days, we're talking a lot about revision. I tell them to be brave when making changes to their work. "Remember," I say, "none of this is carved in stone. Don't be too married to your original storyline. Don't assume you already know how it will turn out. Just because you wrote it one way doesn't mean that's the right way to go. And don't forget: just because it really happened that way doesn't mean that's the story you want to tell. In fiction, truth is no defense. One of the great luxuries of writing fiction is how malleable and impermanent it is. It isn't like life. You're allowed to play God. You're supposed to play God."

They nod, sit up straighter, try to look like they're ready for the role.

III.

Without a doubt, it's all feeling much better for her now. Covered, the ground seems less reproachful, and so she goes fairly often. Just to be sure the lawn is still growing. And also to visit him as she'd always thought she would, before all the trouble about the plot began. And she talks to him a little when she's there. She tells him she loves him. Of course. Sometimes she even cries a bit. She looks at his name, at the dates carved in stone. She looks especially hard at that final date.

But she never stays more than a few minutes. Because even though the ground's scar has wholly healed, that familiar sensation of guilt still sweeps through her heart, every time. So she always ends up telling him she's sorry, once again. "I'm so sorry, Dad," she says, and goes back home.

~~The End~~

It's ridiculous though—and she knows it.

Because, in reality, none of it had been her fault. By the time the family reached her, it was already too late. In rural France, no phones working properly, the trains on strike, her rented Fiat broken, how could she have made it? It was unimaginable. The funeral was in a matter of only hours before she even learned the news.

Nobody could possibly blame her. And, deep inside, she knows she shouldn't blame herself. And maybe someday, she thinks, she'll be able to visit the cemetery without being caught by these inexplicable feelings of shame. She hopes she will. She doesn't deserve to feel this bad. She believes that with all her heart.

The End

Richard McCann

THE CASE OF THE UNDONE NOVEL

SOMETIMES, BUT NOT OFTEN, he would work on his novel, my now long-dead father. Those evenings, he set up a wooden step stool in the living room of our small suburban ranch house and then placed his battered Underwood atop it, so he could watch his favorite TV shows as he typed—*Gunsmoke* and *Perry Mason*. I knew his novel was about his childhood growing up in a mining town in central Pennsylvania, between Johnstown and Altoona, and even though I never read it, at least not back then, when he was still alive, I knew from his having described it to my brother and me that he had included within it real things from his own life: how his family had been so poor when he was a child, for instance, that they'd sometimes had to eat for dinner only what they called "coffee soup," made from breaking up stale bread crusts into the black coffee leftover from breakfast. How he'd seen his first plane when it flew over a thicket where he was picking blackberries with his father, a railroad engineer who always called him "honeybunch." How when he was ten a pot of boiling laundry water had tipped over from his mother's woodstove and burned him so badly he was scarred all down his left side, from his rib cage to his ankle. Afterward, he was kept in bed for over a year, so long he'd had to learn how to walk again, he said.

As for the rest of his literary life: he admired the poems of Walt

Whitman, or so I learned long after his death, when I came across the love letters he'd written to my mother in the months following their first meeting, cribbing long passages from "Song of Myself" and "I Sing the Body Electric" and mixing into them his own descriptions of my mother's breasts and genitals. I know he loved Erle Stanley Gardner and occasionally boasted of having read over fifty of Gardner's Perry Mason novels, including *The Case of the Perjured Parrot, The Case of the Duplicate Daughter, The Case of the Lucky Legs, The Case of the Terrified Typist,* and *The Case of the Counterfeit Eye.*

I know that his novel was important to him, because whenever he inserted a new page into the typewriter, feeding the paper into the platen and turning the knob, that page was always accompanied by four sheets of carbon paper sandwiched between four sheets of delicate onionskin, so that he always made a total of five copies on which he then penciled his meticulous revisions. I know that in the late 1940s, a few years before I was born, he wrote a letter to my maternal grandmother, asking her for a loan sufficient to a year's pay, so he could leave the job he hated—in those years, until he reenlisted in the army, where he eventually achieved the rank of lieutenant colonel, he was a repo man for Commercial Credit. He felt he needed to work instead, he told my grandmother, on completing what he described in his letter as a "great American novel." My grandmother declined his request by return mail, writing that she would be glad to send as her gift instead a brand-new 1948 Dumont television—a "12-inch Teleset in a Meadowbrook console cabinet"—that cost $525, a sum equivalent to $4,919.25 today. It was on this television that he later watched *Gunsmoke* and *Perry Mason.*

The Case of the Dubious Dumont, he might have said.

Or perhaps he might have simply said, "Thank you," or perhaps even nothing at all. He loved watching TV as he sat in his red La-Z-Boy recliner, with me and my brother and our dog Mickey lying on the floor in a semicircle around him.

In any case, I do know that in the dozen or so years between writing to my grandmother for a loan and his sudden death at the age of fifty from fulminant liver failure, he wrote a total of thirty single-spaced pages.

I know this because I have one of the carbon copies of his manuscript right here on my desk beside me now. Across the top of the first page, he has typed in caps the words "A NOVEL," and below that, in a more modest rendering of both upper- and lowercase, he has typed "by Richard McCann."

Yes, I was the son who was named for him. I was the one who became a writer.

I was eleven when he died.

After that, I'm not sure what I felt toward him, if in fact I ever knew before.

The summer before his death, at our family fishing camp in Pennsylvania, I could see his disappointment at my squeamishness each time I asked him to bait my hook with the night crawlers I hated to touch. By then, he'd already begun telling me not to play so much with girls. Once, when he overheard me gossiping with a classmate on the telephone, he told me, "You don't need to be a Chatty Cathy."

I know I missed him after his death. Sometimes, for instance, I'd find myself suddenly standing in silence before the opened door of the hall closet, staring at his army uniform, which my mother kept stored there, enshrouded in a plastic dry cleaner's bag. But even though I could have never said it then, I also know that I sometimes felt relieved to be no longer subject to what I took to be his scrutiny. Over time, perhaps in guilt, as a response to my relief, or perhaps because I had somehow imagined without even knowing it that he had betrayed me by having died, I began to recall him only in fragments, as an accumulation of his tastes and habits. I remembered that he liked catsup sandwiches. I remembered how he looked standing in the middle of Pine Creek in his rubber waders, casting his line for brown trout. I remembered that, the opposite of my mother, he preferred Ford over Chevrolet.

Each Sunday for almost five years after my father's death, until my mother remarried, my mother, brother, and I drove to Arlington National Cemetery, where my father was buried on a hill just below the Tomb of the Unknown Soldier, to kneel before his headstone and recite a half-dozen Hail Marys and the Lord's Prayer. Afterward, we drove to the Hot Shoppes restaurant, where I always ordered the fruit cocktail for my appetizer, because I felt it to be a sophisticated choice, the kind I imagined myself making in the years to come, after I moved away and my life became my own.

I'm not sure how it happened, then, that I was the one to come into possession of my father's novel. I remember that I had it with me in my freshman dorm at college, in that rundown double room I shared with Mike Cregan, a sophomore who was somehow five years older than I and who talked about almost nothing but the German carnival sideshow he claimed to have visited the previous summer, at which he'd paid an extra five marks to see a blonde Fräulein getting fucked by a donkey. Mike once told me that he had two wishes: to marry a nice girl he could take home to Connecticut, and to revisit that carnival sideshow, although I don't know if meant to realize them in that order.

In retrospect, I suspect that I simply asked my mother for my father's novel. By my freshman year, I'd received in response to an aptitude test that I had sent in to the Famous Writers School what I believed to be an encouraging personal letter, given that it seemed to have been hand-signed by Bennett Cerf himself. By then, I'd started to tell people that I was a writer, even though I had written almost nothing except for a few haiku leftover from high school. It was then, I think, that I came upon the idea of completing my father's novel.

I'm not sure why or how I conceived of doing this. I do remember, however, announcing the plan to my mother, who granted me her approval and reminded me, as she often felt the need to do, that my father had really loved me. I remember that my plan seemed to me almost a *practical* decision, as if I'd figured out that if I were going to be a writer, I'd be smart to join the family business, where I'd already had a head start, although, in retrospect, it's clear that writing was not my family business and that my motives were murkier and more complex than I then knew. What was I doing? Was I attempting to negotiate between the actual grief that I must have felt after my father's death and the guilty conscience I had for having sometimes wished, when he was alive, that I could escape his baffled and critical gaze, as if I'd somehow contributed to his dying by not having been the sort of son he surely wanted? I knew he would not have appreciated the poster that I'd hung over my dorm room bed, a larger-than-life photo of Bette Davis in *All About Eve*. I knew he would have continued to worry about the kind of boy I seemed unable to stop myself from becoming, a boy whose anxious laughter was too sudden and too shrill, a boy who could not keep his hands still while he was talking. Was I planning to complete his novel as some kind of atonement? Was I hoping that by entering his words, I might somehow come to know him?

How could I have understood myself then? I was seventeen. Only six years had passed between my father's sudden death and my going off to college—a drop in the bucket, as they say, at least from my perspective now. I am sixty-one years old. I have now lived more than a decade longer than my father did.

Whatever my motives, here's what happened, at least as I now recall it: one night that fall semester, I sat at my battered dorm room desk, reading the novel's opening pages, a notepad and a pencil at the ready beneath my gooseneck study lamp, should I have wished to start writing. Mike sat opposite, on the edge of his bed, clipping his toenails.

There was a protagonist, Johnnie Kirwin, a good but mischievous boy, an eighth-grader, whom my father had clearly based on himself. There was a setting, Bishop, Pennsylvania, an almost exact facsimile of Patton, Pennsylvania, population 2,023, the coal mining town where my father had grown up, its shingled houses covered with coal soot, its empty lots piled with cast-off slag and smoldering boney. There was a scene of local miners parading on John Mitchell Day, honoring the president of the United Mine Workers Association, who had been orphaned at six and then sent down into the mines to work. There was a town tramp, Vera, who loitered, smoking a Fatima cigarette, almost nightly beneath the lighted marquee of the Majestic Theater. I took note when I got to the Majestic. Once, while visiting family in Patton, my father had taken my brother and me to the Majestic Theater to see Elvis in *Blue Hawaii*.

But pretty soon I felt bored, thumbing through pages. It was the same boredom that I'd felt as a child when my brother and I were sent to Patton for two weeks each summer to stay with our uncle Pete and aunt Martha. Each day, after they left for work, we wandered their old house, trying to figure what to make of it, with its coal cellar, its steep back staircase that led only to a closet, and its dark, curtained rooms with their heavy window shades pulled down and their walls lined with blue-hued Maxfield Parrish prints and old family photos and framed religious mottos—WHAT IS HOME WITHOUT A MOTHER, TO THY CROSS I CLING, LOOK UNTO ME. At night, after supper, Uncle Pete drove us to get ice creams at different Howard Johnson's along the Pennsylvania Turnpike, some more than fifty miles away.

Bored by the novel, I thought that maybe I needed to take a break from reading it. I put the pages back into the folder in which my father had kept them. I leaned back in my chair and smoked a few Viceroys. Then I looked through a jar of loose change until I found enough coins to go downstairs and buy a Coke and a Clark Bar. After I ate the Clark Bar, I went outside and sat on the stoop to drink the Coke.

By the time I went back upstairs, Mike had gone to bed and turned the lights out. He liked always to be the first in line at the cafeteria for breakfast. I don't remember what I did after that. Possibly, I made my way across the room through the dark to put my father's novel in a drawer and straighten up my desk. Possibly, I just went straight to bed.

But I do recall that I did not look at my father's novel again, not that night, not that year—and not for more than forty years. I think I gave it back to my mother. Later, I think, she gave it back to me. And then for a long time it became one of those things, a memento mori, that periodically rises from a cardboard box that one is either packing or unpacking for a move.

And then I came across his unfinished novel a year or two ago, while I was packing up my own papers—literary manuscripts, photographs, ephemera—to ship to the university library that now houses them. At the last minute, I packed the original of my father's novel among the works that I'd written. What else to do with it? I thought. I have no children.

After the special collections librarian assigned to the task had processed and catalogued everything—13.2 linear feet, in sixteen boxes—the director of libraries invited me to speak at the opening of what was now termed the Richard McCann Archive—my father's name as well as mine, I kept thinking, because by then there was no one left alive, except for my oldest brother, who remembered that that name had once belonged to my father before it ever belonged also to me.

For the day of the opening, the library arranged an exhibit of items from my papers in glass tabletop display cases around the lobby. In one, there were multiple drafts of the first story I'd ever published, along with a few family keepsakes that I'd described in stories, like my mother's silver brush and comb set and my great-grandmother's black mantilla. In another, on the far side of the lobby, there was a stack of yellowing pages bound together with a black banker's clip.

I went over to examine it. There it was: A NOVEL, by Richard McCann.

A woman was standing beside me, also peering into the case.

"Did you write that?" she asked. When I looked at her, I saw she was wearing the kind of matronly dress my mother used to call a "D.A.R. Bemberg sheer"—something stern yet flowery. She was holding a cocktail napkin into which she'd folded some cheese and crackers, part of the library's celebratory repast.

"No," I said. "My father did."

She looked back down into the display case.

I didn't know what else to say, though for a moment I wanted to tell her how my father had sometimes sat in the living room after dinner, pecking out an occasional paragraph on his Underwood while watching *Gunsmoke* and *Perry Mason*.

"Oh, I see," said the woman. "Your father was a writer, too."

Yes, I thought to say. Yes, my father was a writer, too.

But was that really true? After all, hadn't he really been just a hobbyist—no different from a Sunday painter, say, or a man seated at an upright piano, pounding out "Chopsticks"? That's how I'd come to describe him to myself over the years. Occasionally, I'd find myself telling some friend or other about my father's unpublished novel—his "great American novel," as he'd once described it—and the friend would invariably ask, "So, tell me—is it any good?"

"No," I'd say, "it isn't good." I'd go on to explain that it was sentimental, that he hadn't reached too far into his own material and hadn't imagined his characters—his mother and father, for instance—as distinctive or possessing complexity. Sometimes, I'd add that I could have shown him how to fix it—if he'd lived, that is.

Why did I feel the need to speak of him like this—to disparage what he loved and to repudiate whatever bond we had between us, no matter how great or small? Was I attempting to settle some old score, to triumph over his anxious disapproval of what he regarded as my girlishness? Was this my way of punishing him for his having died?

The woman walked away from the display case without an answer. When I closed my eyes, standing there, I could still picture my father in our old living room, seated before the typewriter, in his faded fishing shorts, white T-shirt, and cotton slippers. He always changed out of his army uniform the second he got home from work. He said he felt more like himself that way.

He is rolling a piece of blank white paper into the platen, backed with the four sheets of carbon paper between four sheets of onionskin. Once he has the paper straight along the page guide, he looks up for a bit at the Dumont in the corner—maybe it's *Wagon Train* this time, or maybe *Have Gun Will Travel.* When the commercial comes on, he looks back down at the typewriter keys and pecks out a word, which he then regards: Is that the right one? Is there one that's better? He is resuscitating what he recalls of the coal mining town where he grew up. I know that place. Sometimes he took my brother and me along with him on his car trips to visit relatives who'd stayed behind. Once, he drove us past a few sites of his childhood, which my brother and I regarded in silence: a culvert by the tracks, where he played after school with other boys; the McCrory's 5 & 10¢ Store, from which he was occasionally allowed to buy some necessity, like galoshes; the railroad yard where he first went to work at thirteen, sweeping out the locomotives.

Who is this man I now recall sitting at night in his small suburban living room, the picture window at his back, periodically pausing to light a Pall Mall or sip from his beer glass before returning to his work, setting down on paper what he needs most to remember from what will prove to be his not-long life? He types. He erases. He draws on his cigarette. He types. This man was my father. He was Pop.

I opened my eyes and, for a moment, when I looked back down into the display case, I felt a sharp and even almost extravagant pride for my father and his unfinished novel, as if somehow I'd just published it.

Yes, he was a writer, whether he succeeded or not.

At least that's how I felt that day, standing in the library.

It's not what I felt back when I was a freshman in college, when I decided to put my father's novel aside and return it to my mother.

As soon as I abandoned my father's novel, I hatched a new scheme for becoming a writer: I would write stories for *True Confessions* and *Real Story,* since I'd heard that confessions magazines were always looking for new talent and that they paid two cents a word. All of my stories were always told from the point of a view of a woman, of course, and they all followed the familiar formula: first sin, then suffer, then repent. I wrote "I Hitchhiked through Hell" and "I Can't Forgive My Sister." I wrote "My Husband Is a Bigamist" and "I Can't Walk Down the Aisle to the Altar." I sent each one out to a magazine as soon as I completed it. None was ever published.

Jerald Walker

THE MECHANICS OF BEING

A DECADE AFTER dropping out of high school I'd managed to arrive, like some survivor of a tragedy at sea, on the shores of a community college. My parents were thrilled when I phoned to say I was pursuing my childhood dream of being an architect. They were just as happy when I decided to be a sociologist instead. And after that a political scientist. Finally, a writer. "I'm going to write a novel based on my life," I said to my father one day. I was in an MFA program by then, starting my second year. I'd recently found some statistics that said there'd been a 60 percent chance I'd end up in jail; I had stories to prove just how close I'd come. But after writing the first draft, my tale of black teenaged delinquency seemed too cliché to me, told too often before. I decided to write about my father instead. He, like my mother, was blind.

My father lost his sight when he was twelve. Climbing the stairs to his Chicago brownstone, he somehow fell backward, hitting his head hard against the pavement and filling his cranium with blood. It would have been better had some of this blood seeped out, alerting him to seek medical attention, but when the area of impact did no more than swell a little and throb, he tended himself by applying two cubes of ice and eating six peanut butter cookies. He did not tell anyone about the injury. He also did not mention the two weeks of headaches that followed, the month of dizzy spells, or that the world was growing increasingly, terrifyingly dim.

His mother had died of cancer four years earlier. His alcoholic father was rarely around. So at home my father only had to conceal his condition from his grandmother, Mama Alice, who herself could barely see past her cataracts, and his three older brothers and sister, who had historically paid him little attention. His grades at school suffered, but his teachers believed him when he said his discovery of girls was the cause. He spent less and less time with his friends, gave up baseball altogether, and took to walking with the aid of a tree branch. In this way his weakening vision remained undetected for three months until, one morning at breakfast, things fell apart.

Mama Alice greeted him as he sat at the table. She was by the stove, he knew, from the location of her voice. As he listened to her approach, he averted his face. She put a plate in front of him and another to his right, where she always sat. She pulled a chair beneath her. He reached for his fork, accidentally knocking it off the table. When several seconds had passed and he'd made no move, Mama Alice reminded him that forks couldn't fly. He took a deep breath and reached down to his left, knowing that to find the utensil would be a stroke of good fortune, since he couldn't even see the floor. After a few seconds of sweeping his fingers against the cool hardwood, he sat back up. There was fear in Mama Alice's voice when she asked him what was wrong. There was fear in his when he confessed he couldn't see.

He confessed everything then, eager, like a serial killer at last confronted with evidence of his crime, to have the details of his awful secret revealed. And when pressed about why he hadn't said anything sooner, he mentioned his master plan: he would make his sight get better by ignoring, as much as possible, the fact that it was getting worse.

For gutting out his fading vision in silence, Mama Alice called him brave. His father called him a fool. His teachers called him a liar. His astonished friends and siblings called him Merlin. The doctors called him lucky. The damage was reversible, they said, because the clots that had formed on and now pressed against his occipital lobes could be removed. But they were wrong; those calcified pools of blood were in precarious locations and could not be excised without risking immediate paralysis or worse. The surgeons inserted a metal plate (my father never knew why) and later told Mama Alice that the clots would continue to grow, not only destroying the little sight he had left, but also killing him. They gave him one more year to live, but they were wrong again.

They were wrong, too, in not predicting the seizures. He'd have them the rest of his life, internal earthquakes that toppled his body and pitched it violently across the floor. I remember these scenes vividly: as a young child, I would cower with my siblings at a safe distance while my mother, her body clamped on top of my father's, tried to put medicine in his mouth without losing a finger or before he chewed off his tongue. My father was a big man in those days, bloated on fried food and Schlitz—one wrong move of his massive body would have caused my mother great harm—but she rode him expertly, desperately, a crocodile hunter on the back of her prey.

I expected one of those attacks to be fatal. But their damage would be done over five decades rather than all at once, slowly and insidiously eroding his brain, like water over stone. So we knew it wasn't Alzheimer's when he began forgetting the people and things that mattered and remembering the trivia of his youth. He knew it, too. That's why, at the age of fifty-five, he retired from teaching, moved with my mother to an apartment in the suburbs, and waited, like we all waited, for the rest of his mind to wash away. By the time I started teaching, when he was in his mid-sixties, he had forgotten us all.

According to the American Federation for the Blind, every seven minutes someone in this country will become blind or visually impaired. There are 1.3 million blind people in the United States. Less than half of the blind complete high school, and only 30 percent of working-aged blind adults are employed. For African Americans, who make up nearly 20 percent of this population, despite being only 12 percent of the population at large, the statistics are even bleaker.

There are no reliable statistics for the number of unemployed blind prior to the 1960s, but some estimates put it as high as 95 percent. Most parents of blind children then had low expectations, hoping only that they would find some more useful role to play in society than selling pencils on street corners or playing a harmonica in some subway station, accompanied by a bored though faithful basset hound. Usually the blind were simply kept at home.

Mama Alice expected to keep my father at home for just a year, but even that was one year too many. She was elderly, diabetic, arthritic, and still mourning for her daughter and other accumulated losses. Now she had to care for a blind boy who spent his days crying or, when his spirits lifted, smashing things in his room. His school had expelled him, his friends had fled, and his sister and brothers had not been moved by his handicap to develop an interest in his affairs. And so, on the second anniversary of his predicted death, Mama Alice packed up his things, kissed him good-bye, implored him to summon more bravery, and sent him to jail.

My father never told any of his children about this. I read about it in his chart at the Sight Saving School, in Jacksonville, Illinois, where he'd been transferred after fifteen months in juvenile detention, and where, in 1994, the same year he and my mother moved to the suburbs, I went to visit.

Thirteen years later the trip for me is a blur, punctuated now and then with random vivid images. I cannot see the face of the principal who greeted my wife and me, and I cannot visualize the office we were escorted to, but my father's chart is seared in my mind, a black three-ring binder with "Thomas Keller Walker" handwritten on the top right corner. Before I read it, the principal gave us a tour of the facilities. It was a twelve-acre complex that included basketball courts, a baseball diamond, swimming pool . . . and classrooms. We were taken to the library, which was a museum of sorts, where the history of blindness was laid out in pictures and graphs behind glass cases. We ate lunch in the cafeteria where my father had eaten lunch. We went to the dorm room where he'd slept. Outside, we walked on the track where, cane in hand, my father had learned to run again.

After the tour, the principal took us back to her office and left us alone with his chart. It contained his height, weight, vital signs, and a summary of his academic performance before he lost his sight, which I cannot recall, though my guess is that it was exceptional. I also cannot remember the progress reports during his two years there. What I do remember was a description of him as "traumatized." That seemed about right to me. He'd lost his mother, his sight . . . and his freedom. The only person who'd consistently showed him love had put him in prison. He was sixteen. I thought about my own life at sixteen, my delinquency and lack of purpose, and I suddenly felt as disappointed in myself as I know he must have been.

When we arrived back at our home in Iowa City, I typed up my notes from the trip. I decided not to call my father to ask about being put in juvenile detention; he'd had a reason for keeping it a secret, and I figured I should probably honor it.

In 1997 my parents moved again. My father was having difficulty with his balance and could not manage the stairs to their second-floor apartment. They bought a house in Dolton, a suburb in south Chicago; its primary appeal, besides being a single-level ranch, was its screened-in porch. For two summers they pretty much lived in there, crowding it with a swing set, a glider, a card table, on which sat an electric water fountain, and four reclining chairs. My father was in one of those chairs enjoying a refreshing breeze and the faint sound of gurgling water when he had a grand mal seizure, the worst in years. For two weeks he was in intensive care on a respirator. When he was finally able to breathe on his own, he was moved to a regular room, and a month later, when he could finally speak, he asked everyone, including my mother, his wife of forty-two years, who they were. While he languished in this state of oblivion, struggling to recall his life, I finished the first draft of my book, having him die peacefully in his sleep. Wishful thinking. Another massive seizure put him back in the ICU.

A month later he was transferred to an assisted living facility.

Speech therapists helped him talk again, and occupational therapists showed him how to move with a walker. But no one could fix his brain. His thoughts were in a thousand fragments, floating in his skull, I imagined, like the flakes of a shaken snow globe. His filter gone, my father, this intensely private man, from whom I'd had difficulty extracting just the basic facts of his life, was now a mental flasher. My mother called me on occasion to report what he'd revealed.

"Mama Alice arrested me," he announced to her one day.

"I drink too much," he said on another.

"That Lynne can sure fry some chicken," he mentioned as well. After my mother relayed this last comment, there was a long pause before she asked me, "You *do* know about Lynne, don't you?"

Lynne was the woman he'd left her for. That was in 1963, thirteen years after my parents had met at the Chicago Lighthouse for the Blind, an organization that, among other services, provides employment for the visually impaired. My father was there assembling clocks while home on summer break from the Sight Saving School, and my mother, blind from a childhood accident, had been hired to do the same. They were seventeen when they met, eighteen when they married and, at twenty-five, the parents of four children. My mother was pregnant with two more when my father moved out. That was all I knew, told to me one day by an older brother when I was in my mid-teens.

My parents had never discussed any of this with my siblings or me. My mother spoke openly about it now, though, and then she segued into talking about the man she'd dated during the two-year separation and about the son they'd had together. Her story I knew more about because when my twin and I were ten or so, her son, our half-brother, would come to our house to play with us. Occasionally he'd be accompanied by his father, a lanky blind man who chain-smoked and had a baritone voice that made me think of God. These attempts at civility lasted two summers before suddenly coming to an end. I never again saw my mother's son. And I never met my father's. I did not even know that he and Lynne had one, in fact, until three years ago, when one of my brothers mailed me a newspaper clipping from the *Chicago Sun Times* describing his murder. His girlfriend had stabbed him thirty-one times. In the margins, next to his picture, my brother had inscribed, "He looks just like *you!*" At first glance, I had thought it was.

I made no mention of my half-brothers in the novel, nor of my parents' separation, even though my mother, after speaking about this tumultuous period in their lives and of the resilient love that saw her and my father through it, suggested that I should. But at the time these details seemed peripheral to my point, too far astray from the topic at hand, not so much character development and depth, in my view, as dirty laundry. After chronicling how he'd lost his sight, I'd described how my father had navigated the sighted world: his learning to walk with a cane, his mastery of public transportation, how he'd earned his college degrees with the help of student and technological aides, his purchase of a seeing-eye dog. Chapter after chapter focused on the mechanics of blindness when I should have focused on the mechanics of being. I should have explored my father's life beyond his handicap, just as, when I set out to write my own story, I should have explored my life beyond the trials common to inner-city black males. The novels I had written said no more about the range of my father's experiences or mine, no more about the meanings we had shaped from the chaos of our lives, than the newspaper clipping had said about his murdered son's.

I realized this while at my father's funeral. He died in September 2005, fifty-six years after the surgeons predicted he would, succumbing not to the blood clots after all, but rather to pneumonia. My wife and I left our two toddlers with their grandmother and flew from Boston to Chicago to attend the service. We sat in the second pew, just behind my mother, whose shoulder I would reach forward to pat as we listened to the organist play my father's favorite hymns. A cousin of mine read scriptures, a family friend recited a number of poems, and then the pastor gave the eulogy, a thorough account of my father's accomplishments punctuated by the refrain: *and he did this while blind*. As I listened to him try to convince us that sightlessness was the core and sum of my father's existence, I understood that my novel had failed.

At some point during the eulogy, when I could no longer stand to listen, an incident I had long forgotten came to mind. I was probably thirteen years old, and my father, as he had so often before, asked me to take some of his clothes to the dry cleaners. Ordinarily this wasn't a big deal, but I had plans to join some friends at the park, so I whined and complained about being called into service. A mild argument ensued, which I lost, and a short while later I slumped out of the house with a paper bag full of his things. At the cleaners, I watched the clerk remove each article of clothing, my disinterest turning to horror as her hand, now frozen mid-air, dangled before us a pair of my father's boxers. The clerk, very pretty and not much older than me, smiled and said, "We don't clean *these*." I couldn't believe that my father had made such an unpardonable mistake, a blunder of the highest order, and the more I thought of it the more upset I became. Halfway home, swollen with anger and eager to release it, I started to run. When I arrived, out of breath, my hands clenched by my sides, my father wasn't in the living room, where I'd left him, but sitting on the porch. The second I barked, *"Daddy!"* he exploded in laughter, his large stomach quivering beneath his T-shirt, his ruddy face pitched toward the sky. I could not, despite my best effort, help but join him. I rose after the pastor finished his eulogy and told this story to the congregation. If I ever attempt to write another novel about my father, this is where it will begin.

Dan Beachy-Quick

PUZZLE AND MUSIC BOX

MY FATHER CALLED to say a gift was on its way. It was for my three-year-old daughter, but I'd be interested in it too. More than interested. This gift, he said, would "blow your mind." It would "knock your socks off." My father loves my daughter past bounds, loves her wildly, adoringly—a love that often finds expression in gifts. I've come to anticipate such gifts with a healthy amount of wariness. Each present is heartfelt, undoubtedly, but often they are things my wife and I would tend not to purchase ourselves: plaid dresses with white-lace collars that look as if they might be the uniforms to a pre-school prep-school, teddy bears larger than the child trying to hold them. The last such gift, sent a few months before, for no occasion other than kindness, was a porcelain music box within which a poem, printed in gold-gilt cursive, read: "I was never so blessed / as the day you were born." It was a gift meant to be precious. It had all the clues that speak to a child of its value: the milky white material with a heft to it, the brass filigree around its edge, air-brushed flowers on the lid, morning glories, maybe, but pinker, larger—orchids perhaps. The poem begins as a dedication, with a florid FOR emblazoned in gold on the inside cover, and where my daughter's name should next appear (the precious is always personal) was a small piece of paper on which my father had typed my daughter's name, Hana, in italicized Times New Roman. He taped her name in on a scrap of copier paper. Then the golden engraving began again.

When Hana turned the key in the box, the hidden metal cylinder began to spin and out came the song, in the tinny pinpricks of the medium's music, "You Are So Beautiful." When the box is shut the music stops, the poem is hidden. Sometimes I find Hana on her bed with the box open, listening to the music in strange reverie. She loves it; I, of course, have my questions.

I told Hana that Grandpa had sent a present that should arrive in a few days and she, being at the age where the idea of a "gift" or a "surprise" is the finest thing in the world, began her anticipatory questions. "Is it here, Daddy?" ad infinitum, until the package would actually arrive. Her excitement is contagious enough for me to feel excited; it's an enthusiasm I can't help but stoke with my own repeatedly uttered "Soon, it will be here soon." The best part of waiting for the gift to come is asking Hana what she thinks it might be. "An elephant." "A macaroni bowl without macaroni." Nothing else gives me such a sense of how astonishing desire is. Desire gives equal weight to things of radically different worth. Hana would cycle through the possibilities at every meal. "A teddy bear." "A piece of glass." "Crayons." "A cloud." Desire erases boundaries by easing through them. Desire is wonder in motion. Desire finds that reality's border is loosely guarded. Someone—"reason's viceroy"—is always asleep at his post. My three-year-old girl knows already what many poets would do well to learn: desire pushes through the limit of what is possible; it does not recognize it and retreat.

A cloud in a box would blow my mind, would knock my socks off. I hoped the gift was a cloud in a box. I was curious; I had my doubts.

My parents divorced when I was three years old—the age my daughter is now. I have very few memories of my parents together, my life before my parents' divorce. My father letting me sip the foam from his beer as I sat on the brown-shag steps that led from the kitchen down to the living room. His yellow car. A small, mean dog named Porsche. I fear I might be making these things up. My mother raised me by herself in Colorado. I had no siblings. I would spend my summers in Ithaca, New York, with my father and my grandparents, with whom he lived. My father taught courses like Business Management and Entrepreneurship, things that inspired little wonder in me. What did seem wonderful was spending the summer in the same house my father himself grew up in. We would sleep in the same bedroom, a bed on each side of the room. At the head of my bed the wall was papered in a wilderness scene: the woods at sunset, the color of the sky changing from orange to yellow as the sun set between the trees. There were deer in the woods whose ears were pricked up as if they were listening for a footstep; I would go to sleep thinking I was entering the woods, getting lost in the dark. I liked to pretend, every summer I arrived, that I couldn't remember how the house was put together, which room led to which, and would ask for a "tour." Reassembling the house was reassembling the kid—the kid I was in the summers, so different from who I was with my mother during the school year. The kid who wandered through the woods, who had adventures, who idolized the dad he hardly knew.

Becoming a father myself was an experience that didn't shatter my expectations so much as make me realize I had no expectations to shatter. I didn't know what it was to be a father because I grew up without one. The summers? Those were a different life. The sudden realization of that vacancy in me, that blank resource—that shattered me. Who should I be, who could I be, for this little girl who would need me? It was a question that tormented me in those earliest days when Hana, colicky and crying for hours, could not be comforted through those sleepless summer nights, when my wife and I would wake together to try to calm our baby, when I felt desperate, when I wanted to call someone, anyone, my father, and say, "What's the answer? What should I do?" But there was no answer.

Hana grew out of her colic at three months and began sleeping through the night. This wasn't a feat of parenting but of biology. I was happy, grimly happy, that we all survived. Things got easier—they're still getting easier. But moments still come when the same fear suddenly blurs the outline of my image of myself: this father I am who knows how to be a father. Then the man I picture in my head when I think of myself as my daughter's father disappears, and there is no image at all. Just some emptiness riddled by nameless feeling. And I find in myself the same sense as years ago when I held my bawling infant and asked not, "Who is this child?" but asked instead, "Who am I?"

Hana and I set the large, thin envelope between us on the floor the day the gift arrived. The envelope was sealed too tightly for Hana to open it, metal clasp and tape, so I tore it open and took out the contents. "What is it?" Hana asked, voice wonder filled, expectant, hopeful.

What I took out was a picture of myself. I'd seen the photo countless times hanging on the wall of my grandmother's house in Ithaca. I saw it every summer I went to be with my dad—a photo taken from one of the first of those summers. It is, undoubtedly, the best picture ever taken of me. I'm a little boy, maybe five or six. I'm walking on the stone path outside the house that goes past the bougainvillea bushes whose scent seems heavier than the blossoms. I'm not wearing a shirt. I've been in the sun and my shoulders are golden. I'm walking away from the camera and looking back over my shoulder, smiling. My hair is blond. My eyes look only like black smudges beneath my forehead. My mouth, too, is dark where it is open. This photo, more than any other memento of my childhood, defined that time for me. When I think of myself as a child, this is the image that comes to mind. For me, it was a photo of the summer happiness that could have been permanent.

"What is it, Daddy?"

"This is a picture of me when I was a little kid."

"Oh." I figured she wouldn't be interested for very long in the photo, but she kept holding it, looking at it, examining it with a minute attention I found slightly uncanny. I figured that it must have been strange for her to see me when I was more or less her own age.

Then she held the picture out to me and said, "Look, Daddy, Grandpa sent me a puzzle."

She was right. A thin line coursed throughout the photo, a jigsaw line that cut through the picture. I'd never spent enough time looking at it to notice. I just glanced at the picture behind its frame as I walked down the hall, the image whole in my mind, taking root in my memory, gaining definition there, gaining permanence. Now, holding the picture in my hands, my daughter sitting on the floor beside me, I could see that the image—this image of my own face so many years ago, this image that memory made whole—had cut into it the lines by which it could be taken apart. And that's what we did. I popped it out of its frame, and Hana and I, one by one, pushed the puzzle pieces out from the picture. It had never been disassembled before. A little point of cardboard held each piece to the whole, a little resistance to push through. I tried hard not to think about the process and mostly failed. Sitting on the floor, taking apart my childhood self, this picture of me that looked up at us as we dismantled it, piece by piece, with the daughter I was trying to raise so she couldn't be taken apart so. All the little pieces. We spread them on the floor. We found the circular edge and assembled it: skin tones to skin tones, and the impressionistic background of blurry grass and rocks and flowers. We continued to reassemble the photo. And when I had again a sunlit torso, and my right arm again jutted forward below my face—except I had no face, except my arm didn't yet attach to my shoulder—Hana stood up and left, the puzzle not half done.

I wanted to call her back. I wanted to say, "We're not done." I wanted to say, "You can't leave me like this!" but say it in a tone so she knew I was joking. But I wouldn't be joking. I knew I wouldn't be. So I said nothing at all. I felt like a child myself, sitting on the floor next to the undone puzzle. I felt like a child with a child of his own. Parenthood, for me, is inextricably caught in the paradox of being a father and a child at once—a child with a child, a father with a father.

A paradox is another form a puzzle takes, one that desire is powerless to solve. It is a condition and not a game. One just recognizes that puzzle in oneself, as oneself—or, at least, I do. Parenthood, unlike childhood, is a puzzle into which no pieces have yet been cut. I know it can be taken apart, but I don't know how to do it myself. And until it's taken apart, how do you know how to put it back together again? It is uncanny, unnerving. It feels almost like fate. In fate, the pieces never seem to fit—and then they do. I have a daughter. Her name is Hana. That's the first amazing, impossible piece.

I'd like to say when Hana left me and the puzzle incomplete that she returned with the music box in her hands. That's what I desired, that recognition of the moment, these gifts through which, uncomfortably, we recognize who we are. I desired it past reason, but it didn't happen. To hear that tinny music would be a form of kinship, a kind of understanding. But it isn't true. It didn't happen. She came back into the room to ask for something. A glass of water? There I was, still spread across the floor. I was looking for the dark smudges that were my eyes. And there was my daughter, calling my name. Not my name. Calling me Daddy. There was my daughter.

I was in pieces on the floor.

She was a name in a box.

CONTRIBUTORS

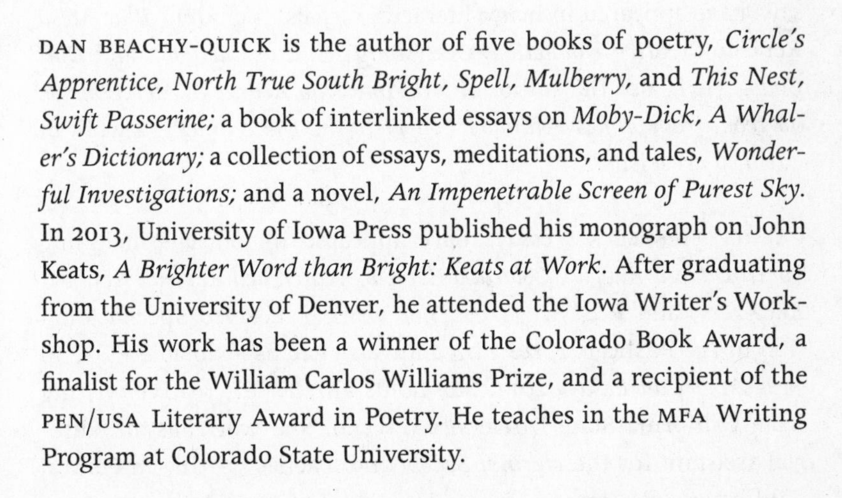

DAN BEACHY-QUICK is the author of five books of poetry, *Circle's Apprentice, North True South Bright, Spell, Mulberry,* and *This Nest, Swift Passerine;* a book of interlinked essays on *Moby-Dick, A Whaler's Dictionary;* a collection of essays, meditations, and tales, *Wonderful Investigations;* and a novel, *An Impenetrable Screen of Purest Sky.* In 2013, University of Iowa Press published his monograph on John Keats, *A Brighter Word than Bright: Keats at Work.* After graduating from the University of Denver, he attended the Iowa Writer's Workshop. His work has been a winner of the Colorado Book Award, a finalist for the William Carlos Williams Prize, and a recipient of the PEN/USA Literary Award in Poetry. He teaches in the MFA Writing Program at Colorado State University.

ROBIN BLACK is the author of the novel *Life Drawing* (2014) and the story collection *If I Loved You, I Would Tell You This* (2010), both from Random House, and both also published widely abroad. The essay that appears in this anthology was named as a Notable in *Best American Essays.* She lives in Philadelphia with her family, and is at work on her next novel and a collection of essays.

BILL CAPOSSERE's fiction and essays have appeared in *Colorado Review, Rosebud, Alaska Quarterly Review,* and other journals, as well as in the anthologies *In Short, Short Takes,* and *Imaginative Writing.* His first full-length play, *Galileo's,* was recently selected for a stage reading as part of GEVA Theatre's Regional Writer's Showcase and again for their New Plays Festival. His work has been recognized in the "Notable Essays" section of multiple *Best American Essays* and has received several Pushcart Prize nominations. He holds an MFA from Rainier Writing Workshop under Judith Kitchen and Stan Rubin. Capossere lives in Rochester, New York.

After a short stint in professional golf, MATTHEW FERRENCE now teaches creative writing and literature at Allegheny College. His essays have appeared in many literary journals, including *Blue Mesa Review, Creative Nonfiction, Gettysburg Review, CutBank,* and *Gulf Coast*. He is also the author of *All-American Redneck: Variations on an Icon, from James Fenimore Cooper to the Dixie Chicks,* a work of cultural criticism.

CAROLE FIRSTMAN's essays have appeared in journals including *South Dakota Review, Colorado Review, Watershed Review, Defunct, Knee-Jerk,* and *Reed Magazine*. Her writing received Special Mention in the Pushcart Prize 2014 and was cited as a Notable Essay in *Best American Essays 2013*. She holds an MFA in creative writing from California State University, Fresno. She works as an editorial assistant for the *Normal School* and teaches writing in Central California.

GINA FRANGELLO is the author of three books of fiction: *A Life in Men* (Algonquin, 2014), which has been a book club selection for *Nylon* magazine, *The Rumpus,* and *The Nervous Breakdown; Slut Lullabies* (Emergency Press, 2010), which was a *Foreword* magazine Best Book of the Year finalist; and *My Sister's Continent* (Chiasmus, 2006). She is the Sunday editor for *The Rumpus* and the fiction editor for *The Nervous Breakdown,* and is on faculty at UCR-Palm Desert's low-residency MFA program in Creative Writing. The longtime executive editor of *Other Voices* magazine and Other Voices Books, she now runs Other Voices Queretaro (www.othervoicesqueretaro.com), an international writing program in the Central Highlands of Mexico. She can be found at www.ginafrangello.com.

DEBRA GWARTNEY is the author of a memoir, *Live Through This,* a finalist for the National Book Critics Circle Award, and co-author of *Home Ground: Language for an American Landscape.* She teaches in the MFA Program at Pacific University, and lives in western Oregon.

JIM KENNEDY grew up in Baltimore and graduated from Johns Hopkins in 1978. He became a husband and father in Boston and works in Boston City Hall. In 2011, he received an MFA in creative writing from the Solstice Program. His work has appeared in *Prism International* and *Creative Nonfiction.*

Essays and stories by JOAN MARCUS appear in the *Sun, Fourth Genre,* the *Georgia Review,* the *Smart Set,* and elsewhere. She is a two-time recipient of the Constance Saltonstall grant for upstate New York writers and an assistant professor in the Department of Writing at Ithaca College.

NEIL MATHISON is an essayist and short story writer who has been a naval officer, a nuclear engineer, an expatriate businessman living in Hong Kong, a corporate vice-president, and a stay-at-home-dad. His essays and short stories have appeared in the *Ontario Review, Georgia Review, Southern Humanities Review, North American Review, North Dakota Quarterly, Agni, Under the Sun,* and elsewhere. His essay "Volcano: An A to Z" was recognized as a Notable Essay in *Best American Essays 2010.* A second essay, "Wooden Boat," was recognized as a Notable Essay in *Best American Essays 2013.* Neil's author's website link is www.neilmathison.net.

RICHARD McCANN is the author of *Mother of Sorrows,* a work of fiction, and *Ghost Letters,* a collection of poems. He is also the editor, with Michael Klein, of *Things Shaped in Passing: More 'Poets for Life' Writing from the AIDS Pandemic.* His work has appeared in such magazines as the *Atlantic, Ms., Esquire, Ploughshares,* the *Nation,* and *Tin House,* and in many anthologies, including *The O. Henry*

Prize Stories 2007 and *Best American Essays 2000*. McCann lives in Washington, DC, where he teaches at American University. He is also vice president of the PEN/Faulkner Foundation and a member of the Corporation of Yaddo.

DINTY W. MOORE is the author of *The Mindful Writer: Noble Truths of the Writing Life,* as well as the memoir *Between Panic & Desire,* winner of the Grub Street Nonfiction Book Prize in 2009. He edits *Brevity,* an online journal of flash nonfiction, and lives in Athens, Ohio, where he grows heirloom tomatoes and edible dandelions.

DONNA GEORGE STOREY has taught English in Japan and Japanese at Stanford and UC–Berkeley. Her stories and essays have appeared in *Prairie Schooner,* the *Gettysburg Review, Fourth Genre, Tampa Review, Wine Spectator,* and *Berkeley Fiction Review*. Her work has been translated into Italian and German and received special mention in Pushcart Prize Stories 2004. She is also the author of the novel *Amorous Woman* (Stonebridge Press) and translator of *Child of Darkness: Yôko and Other Stories,* by Furui Yoshikichi (University of Michigan Center for Japanese Studies).

DEBORAH THOMPSON is an associate professor of English at Colorado State University, where she helped develop the new master's degree in creative nonfiction. She has published numerous essays in literary criticism and nonfiction in venues such as the *Missouri Review, Fourth Genre, Creative Nonfiction, Passages North,* and *Briar Cliff*. Her piece "Mishti Kukur," which appeared in the *Iowa Review,* won a Pushcart Prize. Thompson belongs to the Slow Sand Writers Society, to whose members she is beyond grateful.

JERALD WALKER is the author of *Street Shadows: A Memoir of Race, Rebellion, and Redemption,* recipient of the 2011 PEN New England/ L.L. Winship Award for Nonfiction. His essays have appeared in numerous publications and have been widely anthologized, including three times in the *Best American Essays* series. His memoir *The Last Great Day* will be published next year. He is Chair of the Department of Writing, Literature and Publishing at Emerson College.

THOMAS WHITE was educated at the University of Rhode Island, Fordham University, and the University of Iowa Writers' Workshop. He has taught writing at colleges and universities in Connecticut and New Hampshire and comparative religion at Sacred Heart University's Department of Philosophy, Theology, and Religious Studies. His work has appeared in the *Journal, Colorado Review, Green Mountains Review,* and other journals, and has been nominated for a Pushcart Prize. One of his essays was awarded the Harpur Palate Prize for Creative Nonfiction. He lives with his family in New Hampshire.

BRENDAN WOLFE is a writer and editor living in Charlottesville, Virginia. His reviews and essays have appeared in *Colorado Review,* the *Morning News,* and *Virginia Quarterly Review.*

PERMISSIONS

"Man in the Moon," by Bill Capossere, from *Colorado Review,* volume 32, number 3. Copyright © 2005 by Bill Capossere. Reprinted by permission of the author.

"Liminal Scorpions," by Carole Firstman, from *Colorado Review,* volume 39, number 2. Copyright © 2012 by Carole Firstman. Reprinted by permission of the author.

"When the Future Was Plastic," by Deborah Thompson, from *Passages North,* issue 33. Copyright © 2012 by Deborah Thompson. Reprinted by permission of the author.

"Stories from the Lost Nation," by Brendan Wolfe, from *Colorado Review,* volume 36, number 2. Copyright © 2009 by Brendan Wolfe. Reprinted by permission of the author.

"When He Falls off a Horse," by Debra Gwartney, from the *Normal School,* volume 6, issue 1. Copyright © 2013 by Debra Gwartney. Reprinted by permission of the author.

"Son of Mr. Green Jeans: A Meditation on Missing Fathers," by Dinty W. Moore, from *Crazyhorse,* number 63 (Spring 2003). Copyright © 2003 by Dinty W. Moore. Reprinted by permission of the author.

"Memory and Helix: What Comes to Us from the Past," by Neil Mathison, from *Georgia Review,* volume 62, number 3. Copyright © 2008 by Neil Mathison. Reprinted by permission of the author.

"The Lion and the Mouse: Notes on Love, Mortality, and Hallucinations for My Father's Ninetieth Birthday," by Gina Frangello, from the *Nervous Breakdown,* November 28, 2011. Copyright © 2011 by Gina Frangello. Reprinted by permission of the author.

"The Slashing," by Matthew Ferrence, from *Gulf Coast,* volume 25, number 2. Copyright © 2013 by Matthew Ferrence. Reprinted by permission of the author.

"End of the Line," by Jim Kennedy, from *Creative Nonfiction,* issue 39 (Fall 2010). Copyright © 2010 by Jim Kennedy. Reprinted by permission of the author.

"Survival Stories," by Joan Marcus, from *Alaska Quarterly Review,* volume 26, number 3/4. Copyright © 2009 by Joan Marcus. Reprinted by permission of the author.

"Thirteen Views of Grief," by Donna George Storey, from *Tampa Review,* issue 35. Copyright © by Donna George Storey. Reprinted by permission of the author.

"The Wisdom of Sons," by Thomas White, from *Colorado Review,* volume 36, number 1. Copyright © 2009 by Thomas White. Reprinted by permission of the author.

"Plot: Variations I, II, and III," by Robin Black, from *Colorado Review,* volume 34, number 2. Copyright © 2007 by Robin Black. Reprinted by permission of the author.

ACKNOWLEDGMENTS

Thank you to the entire staff at the Center for Literary Publishing, especially Whitney Dean, Samantha Tucker Iacovetto, and Kaelyn Riley, who were instrumental in helping select these essays, and Andrew Mangan and Ben Findlay, who shouldered much of the proofreading. Thank you as well to Louann Reid, for giving me the resources and support to bring this anthology to fruition. I am also very grateful to my colleagues Steven Schwartz, John Calderazzo, and E. J. Levy, for their friendship and encouragement along the way. I am grateful as well to Bruce Ronda, for gently pushing me—perhaps unknowingly—to acknowledge my true stake in this. A special thank you goes to Hattie Fletcher, for so generously sharing her expertise and advice. And thank you to Arne G'Schwind, for cheering me on from start to finish.

Finally, thank you to the editors who first published these essays, for bringing them to my attention, and to the writers, for allowing me to feature them in this collection.

Typeset by the Center for Literary Publishing
at Colorado State University
in Apollo MT,
a typeface designed in 1964
by Adrian Frutiger.
Manufacturing by Courier Westford.
Cover design by Drew Nolte.